"Lee Griffith is a prophet among prophets, and his new book is the most brilliant reflection on Christianity and nonviolence to appear in the twenty-first century.... Griffith offers both a scorching critique of the virtues and practices of the so-called American Empire and a prayerful plea that disciples of Jesus will at last begin to conspire with the Spirit of God in a way that subverts violence, economic injustice, and divisions among humanity. But what sets this book apart from other anti-empire books is that it commends nothing less than Christian anarchy — a biblical vision long ignored or flatly dismissed by even progressive Christians. In this sense, *God Is Subversive* is arguably the most creative expression of Christian radicalism today."

— MICHAEL G. LONG
Elizabethtown College

God Is Subversive

TALKING PEACE IN A
TIME OF EMPIRE

Lee Griffith

WILLIAM B. EERDMANS PUBLISHING COMPANY
GRAND RAPIDS, MICHIGAN / CAMBRIDGE, U.K.

Published 2011 by
Wm. B. Eerdmans Publishing Co.
2140 Oak Industrial Drive N.E., Grand Rapids, Michigan 49505 /
P.O. Box 163, Cambridge CB3 9PU U.K.
www.eerdmans.com

Printed in the United States of America

17 16 15 14 13 12 11   7 6 5 4 3 2 1

Library of Congress Cataloging-in-Publication Data

Griffith, Lee, 1948-
God is subversive: talking peace in a time of empire / Lee Griffith.
p.   cm.
Includes bibliographical references and index.
ISBN 978-0-8028-6502-1 (cloth: alk. paper)
1. Christianity and justice.
2. Justice, Administration of — Biblical teaching.
3. Social justice — Religious aspects — Christianity.
4. Marginality, Social — Religious aspects — Christianity.
5. Peace — Religious aspects — Chrisitianity.   I. Title.

BR115.J8G75   2011
261.8'73 — dc22

2010045310

Unless otherwise noted, the Scripture quotations in this publication are from the New Revised Standard Version Bible, copyright © 1989 by the Division of Christian Education of the National Council of Churches of Christ in the U.S.A., and used by permission.

To students in the "Advocates for Peace"
group at Elizabethtown College,
and to the memory of my peacemaking friend,
Tom Kaufmann

Contents

Preface

As empires have come and gone (and gone is the ultimate fate of them all), the Bible portrays God as persistently taking the side of the occupied and exploited people at the periphery of the imperial enterprise — the slaves and the prisoners, the landless aliens and the homeless poor, the victims of violence and the objects of contempt. With no power at their disposal, these people at the margins placed their hope in God. With no earthly reason to expect that it would happen, they were freed from enslavement to Egypt, Assyria, Persia, Babylon, and Rome. They will be freed from captivity to America as well.

Is it fair to claim that we live in a time of empire? There is no denying that of late, all has not gone well with America's imperial aspirations. The "homeland" itself has suffered attack. Recent U.S. wars have not been won as decisively or as quickly as the rulers had promised. The capitalist foundations of the American Empire ("The business of America is business," said Coolidge) have been shaken by the very greed that once was touted as the impetus for prosperity. But every empire has its ups and downs. Even Rome was plagued by periods of financial slump, of battlefield losses, of incompetent rule, but the empire always bounced back — until it did not.

But is it fair to claim that we live in a time of empire when so many aspects of twenty-first-century American life seem to sparkle with liberal tolerance and benign intent? There are no stern-faced colonial taskmasters here. Repeatedly and smilingly, U.S. leaders assure the world that America intends only peace and freedom. At home, even ten years ago, who could have imagined that a woman would be in serious contention for the highest office in the land, or that a black man would be elected president, or that gay men and lesbians would be granted the right to marry in several states? Of course, no one said that empires could not present a benign visage or act in ways that passed for inclusiveness. If certain people from marginalized groups are welcomed into the ranks of the ruling elite, it would be credulous in the extreme to believe that thereby racism or sexism or gay-bashing have been brought to an end, let alone to believe that thereby the empire has lost its oppressive edge. In the Roman Empire, Goths and Visigoths were appointed to serve as generals and governors even as the wars against the "barbarians" persisted.[1]

What is the nature of empire? Empires are beings who respect no bonds or boundaries.[2] Empires need not have regard for laws, for treaties, for the druthers of enemies or friends. There were parts of the world that were unknown to Persia or to Rome, and I am certain that there are worlds that are unknown to America as well, but empires dominate the whole known world. Military dominance might be established through the primitive means of colonial occupation or through the more modern approach of deploying a network of military bases that spans the globe. Economic dominance might be established through the primitive means of simply extracting and stealing the resources of occupied lands or through the neocolonial approach of deploying World Banks and IMFs to impose capitalist regimes of privatization, austerity, and discipline on "underdeveloped" nations (but not on the biggest debtor of them all, which is the imperial state itself). With empires, resources flow from the margin to the center and power is accumulated at the top of a hierarchical pyramid. It is to the center and to the top that we must look to find the beating but hardened heart of empire.

With the biblical revelation of God, it is precisely the opposite. This is not a God of lofty perch but a God whose movement is ever downward to the point of incarnation. This is a God who moves toward the margin, who moves with the escapees who are leaving Pharaoh behind, who moves into the periphery of the very "least of these" (Matthew 25). Caesar Augustus claimed to be a god, and Constantine the Great claimed that empire and God were in alignment, but the biblical witness is subversive of all such claims.

---

1. Thomas S. Burns, *Barbarians within the Gates of Rome: A Study of Roman Military Policy and the Barbarians, ca. 375-425 A.D.* (Bloomington: Indiana University Press, 1994).

2. Beings? Oh yes, these are angels who have fallen to demonic depths, rebellious principalities and powers, creatures who have forgotten that they were created and who are therefore unconstrained by empathy for the lives of other creatures. Here and elsewhere, mythology offers a greater window onto the truth than can be offered by mere empirical data or staid political analyses. Resistance to empire must entail not just political activism, but prayers and exorcisms as well.

In the preface to his book on God and empire, John Dominic Crossan points to the revelatory nature of an exchange between Pilate and Jesus in John 18. Pilate had heard that some were calling Jesus "King of the Jews." Was Jesus making such a claim for himself? "Jesus answered, 'My kingdom is not from this world. If my kingdom were from this world, my followers would be fighting to keep me from being handed over to the Jews. But as it is, my kingdom is not from here'" (John 18:36).[3] Crossan notes that "the crucial difference — the only one mentioned — between the Kingdom of God and the Kingdom of Rome is Jesus's nonviolence and Pilate's violence."[4] The insistence of Jesus that his reign is not "from this world" is not some Gnostic suggestion that God's new reality is to be located in an ethereal realm that can be visited only when the material plane has been transcended through contemplation or death. No, this is a matter of real kingdom vying with real kingdom (a word which, for all its unfortunate male overtones, is simply the first-century equivalent of "state" or "regime" or "empire"). When John cites Jesus as saying that his kingdom is "not from here," it is because it is not from this world of fighting and violence that are the very foundations of the other kingdoms. It is not from this world in which glory and wealth are won at the expense of the lowly. It is not from this world of power, power, power. It is not from here.

Insofar as the difference between nonviolence and violence is a crucial difference between empire and the reign of God, then peacemaking is

3. Biblical references to "the Jews" have been vulnerable to the anti-Semitic misappropriations of later eras. In their provenance, however, the books of the New Testament were written by Jews, albeit adherents of the Jesus sect of Judaism. They were written about Jews and their interactions with a specific Jew, Jesus of Nazareth. This is not to deny that there were formidable theological differences among the various parties of Judaism, including Sadducees, Pharisees, followers of Jesus, and others. The intra-Jewish polemic among these assorted parties could become quite heated. There were political divisions as well. Some New Testament references to "the Jews" were directed against elite groups who were allied with the Roman occupiers rather than against the far larger group of Jewish peasants. See Richard J. Cassidy, *Society and Politics in the Acts of the Apostles* (Maryknoll, N.Y.: Orbis Books, 1987), pp. 48-49. In John 18:36, "the Jews" clearly refers to the powerbrokers allied with Rome. It would have been incoherent to suggest that the Jewish followers of the "King of the Jews" would resist handing him over to "the Jews" of whom they themselves were a part. The actual anti-Semitism that is unveiled in the narratives of trial and execution is that the King of the Jews would be killed on a Roman cross. For imperial Rome, crucifixion was the humiliating form of execution reserved for rebels and slaves, for marginalized people who were of no worth, for people like Jews.

4. John Dominic Crossan, *God and Empire: Jesus against Rome, Then and Now* (New York: HarperOne, 2008), p. 4.

not merely a political activity but a way of life, a spiritual practice, an affirmation of faith and a path of discipleship. All violent assaults serve merely to strengthen the empires of "this world." We can pray that the efforts of peacemakers, flawed and fallible though they be, might be of service to God's subversion of imperial rule.

*   *   *

All the chapters in this book were prepared as part of my work as "2007 Peace Fellow in Residence" at Elizabethtown College in Lancaster County, Pennsylvania. This annual, week-long residency is sponsored by the Elizabethtown College Alumni Peace Fellowship. When William Eerdmans, Jr., responded kindly and affirmatively to my question about whether these talks might be of interest to people beyond the Elizabethtown campus, my work for this book was already finished in large part. Since these chapters were prepared as lectures and less formal talks, the footnotes were added later, which explains why an occasional reference postdates the time of the residency. In a few instances, some talks were not delivered in full at Elizabethtown due to circumstances at the time. I liked those times when the questions and challenges of students drove me away from the written text. I liked it when the gathering of friends for "Old (Anti) War Stories" turned into a freewheeling swap of conviction and remembrance that defied any script. I liked it when the time on the radio became what I had hoped for, which was my interview of students more than their interview of me. The words in the radio chapter are mine, however, and students should not be blamed for them. The chapter is a conflation of what was actually said on the air and remarks I had prepared beforehand in case the material was needed.

I resist the practice, now common in scholarly circles, of authors referencing their own work in footnotes. I have not done that, but in this preface, allow me to be self-referential to the extent of acknowledging the revisiting of certain themes. The chapter on prison abolition is an updated summary of major themes from *The Fall of the Prison: Biblical Perspectives on Prison Abolition* (Grand Rapids: Eerdmans, 1993). In "Against Patriotism" and elsewhere, I have reiterated some of the perspectives first expressed in *The War on Terrorism and the Terror of God* (Grand Rapids: Eerdmans, 2002). So I confess to having ruts in my mind and to harping on certain motifs, but I hope that I have avoided quoting myself, let alone citing myself as expert on anything.

It is a happy task to remember in appreciation the many people who were kind and helpful during my visit to Elizabethtown. First among them is Jeremy Ebersole. As chairman of the Alumni Peace Fellowship residency committee, Jeremy started writing to me almost a year before the visit, gently nudging me into preparation and focus. While I was on campus, he was tireless. He was the one who made sure that I was where I was supposed to be on schedule, that I didn't skip meals, that I was comfortable, even to the point of making sure that there were no flags on display in my speaking venues. His suffering entailed sitting through all of my talks and never displaying the slightest hint of disinterest, even when he had heard the same talk in two or three different classrooms. Most important, in my year of getting to know him, I have learned that Jeremy Ebersole is a nonviolent man of profound and gentle faith. I hope that our friendship continues.

Thanks to the Elizabethtown College Alumni Peace Fellowship for appointing me to the residency, and to Nancy Neiman-Hoffman, who provided some of the founding inspiration and energy for both the residency and the Fellowship itself. Thanks to Karen Hodges and Charles Wilson for their service on the residency committee. While at Elizabethtown, I appreciated the opportunity to visit again with professors Ken Kreider, Bill Puffenberger, John Ranck, Jobie Riley, and Eugene Clemens. Gene hosted the "Old (Anti) War Stories" gathering, and my visit with him renewed memories of how helpful he had been when I was in college fumbling with nonviolence and with everything else in life. It was wonderful that my mentor from seminary days, Dale Brown, was in Elizabethtown during the residency, so my time there provided opportunity for several visits with him. Somehow, each visit with Dale is an inspiring refresher course in the radical nature of the gospel. Though the time with them was too brief, I was thankful to be in contact with Royal Snavely and Lucille Snowden, and on an earlier foray to Elizabethtown, with David Eller, Christine Bucher, Tom Dwyer, and Russell Eisenbise, who once bailed me out of jail. Thanks to the chairman of the Department of Religious Studies, Jeff Long, for sharing both lunch and some of his keen insights on Hinduism. Thanks to the friends who gathered to tell old stories and new: Judy Fasnacht, Larry Mahan, Steve Oliphant, Barry Palmer, Charlie Wilson, and others who shared stories of secret hiding places in dormitory walls.

So many people offered hospitality. Thank you Barry Friedly for the wonderful stay at Alumni House. Thanks to Pastor Greg Laszakovits and the members of the Elizabethtown Church of the Brethren for inviting me to share worship and reflections on Isaiah's word from God. Tracy Wenger Sadd welcomed me into her class on "Theological Questions." Bill

Ayres invited me into his first year seminar, and then at the largest assembly of my visit, he was brave enough to give me a kind introduction before I let loose with "Against Patriotism." Mike Long invited me into his classes on "Christian Social Ethics" and "The Social Ethics of Martin Luther King, Jr.," and then he was generous with time, spirit, and books during a visit to his office that I remember fondly. Jeff Bach and Don Kraybill welcomed me into the Young Center for Anabaptist and Pietist Studies. Don was the first to suggest that I should gather these talks into a form suitable for publication, and for that I am thankful.

Outside of Elizabethtown, I am grateful for the people who have encouraged my writing. A few years ago, out of the blue, Stanley Hauerwas called to say that he had bumped into one of my books. In several ensuing phone calls and letters, he goaded and instigated. "What are you writing next? Don't stop now." I'll bet that Hauerwas does that with a bunch of us lesser known writers, and along with his own large body of work, it is one of his contributions to encouraging theological discourse in our time. My mother, Julia Griffith, has done more than encourage my writing; over the years, she has met my failures and shortcomings with good humor and love. What is life without friends? I have been gifted with the best of them, including Brian Healy, Warren Drabek, and Mike Cinquanti. Even though he was in the midst of his own thesis work, Mike made sure that the cats and the woodstove were fed while I was hunched over with paper and pen. For that and more, I thank him.

The students, of course, were the sole reason for my visit to Elizabethtown, and so I save my final thanks for them. The students of Elizabethtown College combine the warm hospitality of Lancaster County with the intellectual rigor of an excellent school; they are always ready to listen, but never afraid to pose questions and challenges. Thanks to the students who made extra efforts to be helpful during my stay, especially Keanan Barbour-March, Jordan Bowman, Tony Dong, Carl Marrara, Sam Schlosser, Will Secrist, and Alyson Webb. I am thankful for the witness of the student group, Advocates for Peace. One of the highlights of my visit was on the final day when students from this group, Dale Brown, and I held a peace vigil in front of the local military recruitment office. It is there on the street that empire is renounced and friendships are forged.

1. *Bathing with Isaiah*

Grace and peace to all of you. Thank you for inviting me to join you this morning for worship of God and reflection on the word.

It has been over three decades since the last time I was inside this meetinghouse. I am sure some of the saints have gone on since then, but many of you are still here who will remember those days. I was a student across the street at the college, and it seemed like everybody was marching in front of the Elizabethtown Church of the Brethren. When you hosted a visit by a Russian Orthodox patriarch, an angry group of brothers and sisters led by the Reverend Carl MacIntyre gathered in front of your meetinghouse to warn the public that you were basically a bunch of communists. Although you were pleasant communists, MacIntyre said, that should not be allowed to obscure the fact that you were red to the core. Sitting across the street in my dormitory room, I was thinking, "Hmm, maybe that congregation is more interesting than I thought." In Acts 4, there is an admonition for the community of believers to hold *all* things in common — goods, resources, talents, burdens, joys, sorrows, hopes. It is what sociologists call "primitive Christian communism." Over the decades, I have visited dozens of worshipping communities with affiliations ranging from the Quakers to the Roman Catholics, and I must say, I have yet to encounter a congregation that would not benefit from a stronger dose of that primitive Christian communism.

And then there were other folks marching out front, too. Your meetinghouse served as the college chapel at the time, and there were students out front protesting compulsory chapel. They were saying that faith

---

Sermon on the text of Isaiah 1:10-18, Elizabethtown Church of the Brethren, November 4, 2007.

should not be a matter of compulsion, which is actually a good Anabaptist idea. So, members of your community would go out and join the protest.

And then there was the protest of the war in Vietnam. Gene Clemens would load us into his van and we would go protesting in Washington, D.C., and protesting in Harrisburg, and protesting downtown and on campus, and members of your community would be there. If I have visited dozens of congregations over the decades, I have been to hundreds of anti-war gatherings, and that is not a pretty feather in my cap, but rather it is an ugly stain on the soul of our nation to realize that, in our lifetimes, there has never been a day without war or preparation for war. There has never been a day of genuine peace. It ought to be dawning on the people of this nation that fighting for peace and freedom has not been working; today, we have less of both.

So, I hope that you are still protesting, and I hope that people are still getting mad at you. It can be a sign that you are doing something right.

Of course, there's anger and then there's *anger*. In today's text from Isaiah 1:10-18, the prophet is communicating the word of an angry God.[1] And who is the recipient of God's wrath? Who else? The chosen people. By the time of Isaiah in the eighth century before the common era, it was already abundantly clear that being chosen by God was not an unmixed

---

1. Why does the book of Isaiah have two introductions, first in 1:1 and then again in 2:1? Does chapter 1 contain the oracles of the prophet Isaiah, or is this the composition of a later redactor who inserted it (rather clumsily) as a preface to the text? It is far beyond the purview of a simple sermon to sift through scholarly opinion about where the "genuine Isaiah" is to be found in First Isaiah (chapters 1-39), let alone Second (40-55) or Third (56-66), or about whether the book can be divided into three sections, or about whether it is even possible to identify reliably any Isaianic core in the entire book. The greatest skepticism about being able to identify any authentic sayings of Isaiah is presented by Otto Kaiser, *Isaiah 1-12*, trans. John Bowden, Old Testament Library (Philadelphia: Westminster Press, 1983). For an overview of the debate about the division of Isaiah into three parts, as well as a proposal for the chronological subdivision of chapters 1-39, see Walter Brueggemann, *An Introduction to the Old Testament: The Canon and Christian Imagination* (Louisville: Westminster John Knox Press, 2003), pp. 159-75.

Regarding chapter 1, the chapter under consideration here, John Barton observes that one hypothesis that has gained wide acceptance (initially proposed by Georg Fohrer) views this first chapter as a carefully arranged digest of what is to come in chapters 2-39. This summary was clearly prefixed onto the book by one or more scribal redactors, but this does not negate the possibility that the chapter contains genuine sayings of the prophet. Indeed, the careful composition of a digest might entail a greater predisposition to draw on authentic oracles. Barton, *Isaiah 1-39*, Old Testament Guides (Sheffield, England: Sheffield Academic Press, 1995), pp. 25-26.

blessing. Isaiah confronts the people of Judah and Jerusalem with the reality that being the chosen people was not an honor bestowed but a commitment undertaken.

We know that God is angry because this text begins with a harsh rebuke as the prophet addresses the leaders and the people of Judah and Jerusalem: ". . . you rulers of Sodom! . . . you people of Gomorrah!" (1:10) That is harsh, no doubt, but there needs to be a note of caution about the content of that rebuke. It is because of our post-biblical obsessions that, whenever we hear the word "Sodom," we think of gay people, but that is not the biblical focus. Depending on who is doing the counting, there are between seven and ten texts in the whole Bible that make explicit or implicit reference to sexual contact between people of the same gender.[2] In contrast, there are literally hundreds of biblical texts casting aspersions on wealth and the wealthy, but rich folks are not rejected by the church; they're asked to build new Sunday school wings. In the Bible, the references to Sodom are clear, and they have nothing to do with sexual orientation. Among the many references that could be cited, in Deuteronomy 29, in Ezekiel 16, in Amos 4, and here in Isaiah 1, it is clear that "you rulers of Sodom, you people of Gomorrah" means "you kings of the slaughterhouse, you brokers of injustice."

If you are looking for a lower volume, if you are looking for modera-

---

2. It would be inaccurate to describe these as texts on "homosexuality" (a word that was not in use prior to the late nineteenth century) or "sexual orientation" (a thoroughly modern concept that is still debated between the social constructionists, who understand gay identity as contingent on historical and cultural developments, and the essentialists, who argue that, no matter the name that was used, there have been "gay" people as long as there have been people). The meaning of several of the relevant New Testament texts hinges on the translation given to the Greek word *arsenokoitai*, used by Paul in 1 Corinthians 6:9 and 1 Timothy 1:10. The word would have to refer to something that Paul was able to observe in his own setting, and therefore it is quite unlikely that the reference would have been to a mutually-consenting love relationship between two adults of the same gender. In an appendix on "Lexicography and Saint Paul," John Boswell argues that *arsenokoitai* referred to male prostitutes, specifically temple prostitutes. Boswell, *Christianity, Social Tolerance, and Homosexuality: Gay People in Western Europe from the Beginning of the Christian Era to the Fourteenth Century* (Chicago: University of Chicago Press, 1980), pp. 335-53. Robin Scroggs presents the contrary view that *arsenokoitai* may have referred to the sexual relationships that sometimes developed in ancient Greece between teachers and the boys who were their students. Scroggs, *The New Testament and Homosexuality* (Philadelphia: Fortress Press, 1983). For a helpful overview of biological, ethical, and biblical perspectives, see Pim Pronk, *Against Nature? Types of Moral Argumentation regarding Homosexuality*, trans. John Vriend (Grand Rapids: Eerdmans, 1993).

tion, do not look to the biblical prophets. Abraham Heschel wrote that the prophets are wild and maladjusted.[3] They are maladjusted to the routine suffering that society takes for granted. They are maladjusted to indifference and to the little acts of bloodshed that others regard as regrettable but necessary. The prophets are unreasonable fanatics who pronounce doom on an entire nation because a few widows have been driven from their homes. And then they turn cosmic with their pronouncements of doom.[4] Why do the mountains quake? Why do the fields lie barren? Because of bloodshed. It is the covenanted people, the chosen people, the beloved people who bear the brunt of prophetic wrath, but the prophets are not oblivious to the bloody ways of other nations. When Assyria is at the very height of its political and military power, Isaiah already sees the empire trampled underfoot (14:25). In the wild and unreasonable calculus of the prophet, the acquisition of power is a certain guarantee of ruin. *Et tu, America.*

Now, if we wanted to, we could probably write a treatise that would make the prophets sound quite reasonable. Of course, we would first have to discard some of their more outlandish theological claims, and we would have to tweak the shrillness out of their discourse, but once we have accomplished that, we might be able to dress them up as responsible citizens with progressive leanings. After all, who can doubt that militarism and all of the wars for oil are contributing to global warming, quaking mountains, and barren fields? But the prophets are not interested in being reasonable or in offering power point presentations. They *want* to be unreasonable and maladjusted in Gomorrah. The adage that "all we have to fear is fear itself" is wrong. In Gomorrah, what we have to fear is contentment. Do not fear becoming a malcontent. Fear becoming complacent.

In Isaiah, complacency is assailed by the anger of God. Of all people, the chosen people should know that this is a God of justice (in Hebrew, *mishpat,* Isaiah 1:17), but the people are not just. This is a God of righteousness (*tsedeq,* 1:21), but the people are not righteous. This is a God of mercy, compassion and steadfast love (*racham,* 14:1; *chesed,* 16:5), but the people are not compassionate. It is a harsh indictment, a literal indictment, which God is taking into the courtroom of the heavenly council: "Come now, let us argue it out . . ." (1:18). And God has already warned the people (1:11-14) that one defense ploy which will not work this time is religion. Through

3. Abraham J. Heschel, *The Prophets,* vol. 2 (New York: Harper Torchbooks, 1975), p. 188.
4. See Heschel, *The Prophets,* vol. 1 (New York: Harper Torchbooks, 1969), p. 4.

Isaiah, God says that all of this trampling around in these holy places on these holy days with these high, holy pretenses "my soul hates" (1:14). It is an interesting translation from the Hebrew, one that evokes odd questions that could be grist for other sermons: Does God hate? Is it religious people who God hates, or only their religion? Does God have a soul? *Is* God a soul? Let me try a different idiom for this verse, one that is earthy like the Bible itself: Tell the people, says God to Isaiah, that when it comes to their religion, I have a belly full of it. What did they intend with all of this religion? Did they think that some deity would find it pleasing, that some god might be manipulated by it? Were they trying to tickle the divine ego? Or were these gaudy displays aimed, not at gods, but at other mortals? God does not need religion. We need it. God has a belly full of it. Religion, which is a refined and elevated enterprise for people, produces only nausea for God.

When religion is all that people have to offer, God stops listening. After God has told the people to listen — hear, you rulers of Sodom, you people of Gomorrah — God decides to turn a deaf ear. "When you stretch out your hands, I will hide my eyes from you; even though you make many prayers, I will not listen . . ." (1:15). All this time, our anxieties have been misplaced. We have wondered if our prayers have not been heard because we lack refinement in proskynesis (head bowed, hands folded, eyes closed), or because we need to serve up a greater dose of schmoozing (O Lord and Master, your humble servant comes to you in prayer . . .), or because (truth be told, our greatest suspicion) the heavens are empty and there is no ear to hear or God to care. These are not the anxieties of Isaiah. Isaiah has seen the vision (1:1), has *seen* the word (2:1), and he is compelled to speak that word, but neither he nor God are compelled to listen. What would be the greater burden — to live without God or to live with a God who does not listen? The text does not tell us. Isaiah is not concerned with the burdens of religious people, but with the burden that this people's religion places on God (1:14). "I will not listen." God is not fighting fair. Why no listening? "I will not listen; your hands are full of blood" (1:15). It is not the heavens that are empty. It is not God who does not care. When the hands are full of blood, the emptiness is in the human spirit. ". . . your hands are full of blood. Wash yourselves; make yourselves clean . . ." (1:15-16).

To the modern ear, when this sudden concern for cleanliness pops up in the text, we get the impression that there might be something a little primitive going on here. With Isaiah's God telling people to go clean up, we seem to have entered the realm of cultic laws governing ritual purity, and those laws are based on ideas that are as old as the hills. Anthropologists tell us that, around the globe at the dawn of history, human spirituality entailed elaborate systems of taboo. If someone engaged in an activity that was polluting, that person needed to pass through a ritual of cleansing before he or she was allowed to rejoin the community.

Of course, taboo is not only a concern of a bygone age. I do not subscribe to notions that we modern folks are superior to our ancestors, as if the accident of being born at a later time equips us with an evolved, enlightened consciousness. Whenever I hear talk about how primitive something is, it sets me to looking for examples of it in our sophisticated, technological society, and I rarely have to look very long. If you think that we don't have any taboos today, I invite you to get a big American flag and take it with you to an American Legion gathering. You go in there, spread that flag out on a chair, and plop your fanny down on it, and you will be treated to a ritual cleansing that you won't soon forget.

The contemporary "taboo" is rarely called by that name. The idea of ritual purity and even the word "purity" have fallen out of favor in modern times. "Purity" smacks of something overly sanctimonious, a connotation that is also attached to the word "pietism." Dale Brown has helped my understanding and appreciation for pietism, not just as a word but as a movement of faithfulness.[5] The person who has been most helpful in providing a glimpse of the dynamics behind these cultic laws of ritual purity is the anthropologist Mary Douglas.[6] Douglas examined scores of cultures in which ritual purity seemed to become an obsession. These were cultures of proliferating rules — rules regarding what was clean and unclean in diet and garb and speech, rules listing the circumstances and dates that determined whether certain activities were prescribed or proscribed, rules measuring the space that needed to be maintained when in the proximity of certain people or objects that were held to be either sacred or polluted, rules detailing the meticulous processes of decontamination. What Douglas found in all of the communities that she studied was that these were communities on the edge, communities that were facing extreme threats to their very survival. The danger could come in one of two forms — either the threat of literal extermination, or the threat of being co-

5. Dale W. Brown, *Understanding Pietism*, rev. ed. (Nappanee, Ind.: Evangel Publishing House, 1996).

6. Mary Douglas, *Purity and Danger: An Analysis of Concepts of Pollution and Taboo* (New York: Praeger, 1966).

opted and absorbed into a dominating culture. The response of the threatened community is to try to save its very life by accentuating distinctiveness and creating boundaries enforced by cultic law and ritual purity.

After perusing the collections of laws in the Hebrew Bible, many Christian theologians have charged the Jews with love of legalism. Martin Luther juxtaposed Christian and Jewish faiths and found that the core distinction between the two was the good news of justification through grace versus a vain effort to win salvation through adherence to the law. Mary Douglas helps us to see that the law books are indicative, not of a love of legalism, but of an imminent threat to the existence of the Jewish community, a threat that Luther himself did not oppose.[7]

There is a broad consensus among biblical scholars that the cultic laws governing ritual purity that appear in Deuteronomy, Leviticus, Numbers, and elsewhere were collected by priestly writers during the period of the Babylonian exile.[8] With the northern kingdom of Israel disappeared, with Judah conquered to the south, with the best and brightest of Judah carried off to Babylonian captivity, what was left? These laws that strike us as peculiar, these strivings after purity, had nothing to do with a love of legalism. They had to do with a fading hope that this faith community would retain its identity, its distinctiveness, and its very life.

Now, when we take this understanding and apply it to the text from Isaiah 1, there's only one problem. Isaiah lived before the exile, before the period of the compilation and elaboration of the cultic laws. He was a prophet of the eighth century BCE, long before the Babylonians came onto the scene. That's not to say that Judah didn't have its problems. Assyria was making noises in the north, and some were proposing alliances with Egypt in the south, but none of that was new. Surviving as insignificant

---

7. Luther wrote that he could not hope to convert the Jews, since Jesus himself had been unable to do so. "But I can close their mouths so that there will be nothing for them to do but lie upon the ground." Luther, quoted by Paul Lawrence Rose, *Revolutionary Antisemitism in Germany from Kant to Wagner* (Princeton, N.J.: Princeton University Press, 1990), p. 6. If Luther's wish to have Jews "close their mouths" and "lie upon the ground" is less than a forthright endorsement of genocide, Rose notes that such intentional ambiguity is a persistent feature of anti-Semitic writing.

8. Daniel L. Smith, who draws on the work of Mary Douglas, notes that many of these laws date from earlier eras, perhaps as early as the pre-monarchic period, an era that also presented dangers for the community. Smith contends that the work of the priestly writers of the exile was less formulation than compilation and elaboration. Smith, *The Religion of the Landless: The Social Context of the Babylonian Exile* (Bloomington, Ind.: Meyer-Stone Books, 1989), p. 149.

countries at the crossroads of imperial armies meant that life was always insecure for Israel and Judah. But in Isaiah 1, God is not speaking to people who are threatened by destruction from without. They are threatened by destruction from within.[9] It was the same prophetic point that Jeremiah would make in quite treasonous fashion a century later. Let the enemy come in and take over (Jeremiah 21:8-10).[10] What could they possibly do to us that we aren't already doing to ourselves? Are they going to take away our freedom? Are they going to siphon off our wealth and use it for some military exploits? Are they going to make us lose our compassion? Are they going to make us forget about the poor? Are they going to make us abandon our faith and trade it in for some hate-filled religion? O Mr. Enemy, you have nothing to worry about. Your work is already done. We've done it to ourselves. So come on in, says Jeremiah. (Jeremiah, by the way, was not well-loved. And neither was Isaiah.)

So in Isaiah 1, the call to "wash yourselves; make yourselves clean" was not based in Levitical laws about ritual purity. This was before the period when those laws would be brought to prominence by exilic compilers and redactors. But in the whole experience of the Hebrew people and their relationship with God, it did not take cultic laws to tell them that there was something fundamentally impure about the shedding of human blood —

9. On Judah's political and military circumstances during the period of Isaiah's prophecies, see Gerhard von Rad, *The Message of the Prophets*, trans. D. M. G. Stalker (New York: Harper & Row, 1967), pp. 119-20. During Isaiah's lifetime, the two major threats to Jerusalem were sieges by an Ephraimite-Aramean coalition in 734 BCE and by Sennacherib in 701, dates that have rough correspondence to the chronological parameters of Isaiah's public prophesying. The onslaught of these foreign powers does not contradict Isaiah's view that Judah was facing destruction from within. The foreign forces were merely the unwitting instruments of God. B. Uffenheimer, "Isaiah's and Micah's Approaches to Policy and History," in *Politics and Theopolitics in the Bible and Postbiblical Literature*, ed. Henning Graf Reventlow, Yair Hoffman, and Benjamin Uffenheimer, Journal for the Study of the Old Testament Supplement Series 171 (Sheffield, England: Sheffield Academic Press, 1994), pp. 177-84.

10. Norman Gottwald points to the activities of two opposing parties in Judah during the period of 609-586 BCE. The party that favored forming an alliance with Egypt and organizing military opposition to the threat of Babylon included the ruling elites, the bureaucrats, the priests, and the court prophets like Hananiah (Jeremiah 28). The party that opposed military resistance to the Babylonians included prophets like Jeremiah, Uriah of Kiriath-jearim (Jeremiah 26:20-23), and Habakkuk (Habakkuk 1:6). This latter party maintained that nothing of importance was dependent on the continuation of prevailing power arrangements. Justice, peace, faithfulness to the covenant, the welfare of the people — none of it was reliant on the power brokers of temple or state. Gottwald, *The Hebrew Bible: A Socio-Literary Introduction* (Philadelphia: Fortress Press, 1987), pp. 402-4.

something that could not go uncleansed. The requirement that warriors undergo a rite of cleansing before being allowed to rejoin the community antedated the compilation of purity regulations (Numbers 19:16-20; 31:19). *But* Isaiah 1 is not addressed to warriors. It is addressed to *all* the people: you people of Gomorrah. Before you enter back into community with God, go cleanse *yourselves* (plural).

Prophets are keen on corporate responsibility, and that is something that often eludes the modern individualistic consciousness. How quick we are to say, "Don't blame me. I didn't vote for the guy." Or, "Don't blame me. I'm Brethren. I opposed this war from the beginning." When all others have washed their hands of responsibility, the only ones who stand in need of being cleansed are the soldiers, who are actually among the first victims of the whole bloody system. Isaiah's message is clear, not just for the soldiers but for all the residents of Gomorrah. If you are not engaged in ending bloodshed, then you are engaged in shedding blood.

But this text is not just about stopping; the next verse is about starting. Seek justice (Isaiah 1:17). Justice is at the very heart of the prophetic mission. No, even more, justice is at the very heart of the prophet because it is at the very heart of God. Abraham Heschel wrote that the musician perceives the world in sounds and tones, the sculptor in shapes and forms, the painter in shades and hues, but the prophet perceives the world in terms of justice or injustice.[11] What is true of the ancient prophet is true of the modern as well. Martin Luther King, Jr., said repeatedly that the moral arc of the universe is long, but it bends toward justice.[12] I wish that I could share King's confidence. His statement was certainly influenced by the tradition of African-American spirituality, in which the journey is always long. When you follow the drinking gourd, you must travel far in this journey of justice, and there is sure to be suffering along the way, but hope lies in the imperceptible curve of the road as it bends toward justice. I'm not sure about that. Certainly King knew better than most that even the hope-filled journey out of slavery brought no guarantee of genuine jus-

11. Heschel, *Prophets*, vol. 1, pp. 211-12.

12. There were slight variations in King's frequent repetition of this saying. In his speech at the conclusion of the 1965 march from Selma to Montgomery, King said, "How long? Not long. Because the arm of the moral universe is long but it bends toward justice." In his sermon at the National Cathedral in 1968, King said, "We shall overcome because the arc of a moral universe is long, but it bends toward justice." King, *A Testament of Hope: The Essential Writings and Speeches of Martin Luther King, Jr.*, ed. James M. Washington (San Francisco: HarperSanFrancisco, 1991), pp. 230, 277.

tice. Slavery and brutality reassert themselves in bewildering guises that leave us wondering if the journey is uphill or down. I believe that justice will reign in the world only as a gift from God, only in the new heaven and new earth that will come, not because we have made our way along that bending road toward justice, but because of a radical, disruptive intervention by God. It is what the Bible calls the second coming. Maranatha. Nonetheless, whether it comes by radical disruption or journey along the road, in the meantime, we are called to seek justice, to *do* justice. If there is no doing, there is no justice. In Jeremiah 22:15-16, knowing God is equated, not with subscribing to certain beliefs, but with doing justice.

What is this justice that is the concern — no, the obsession — of the prophets? Without hesitation, we can say what justice is not. Justinian's *Institutiones* begins with the statement, "Justice is the firm and continuous desire to render to everyone that which is due."[13] In contrast, the prophetic commitment to justice has nothing to do with carefully balanced scales and objective criteria by which there may be a dispassionate evaluation of what is due to whom. In the prophets, justice is passionately arrayed against the mighty and in favor of the poor and the needy who are being trampled under the "system of justice" (Amos 8:4-6). In the prophets, justice is not a system for maintaining order. Like torrents of water, justice is unruly, defying all order (Amos 5:24). It is powered by the passionate fury and the compassionate love of God.

So in the Bible, justice is not sponsored by some blindfolded goddess who holds up the balanced scales; it is demanded by wild-eyed prophets who see all too clearly the disparity between rich and poor. Justice is not administered by heavy-robed judges who spend country club weekends cavorting with the ruling class; it wells up from underneath, there in the dusty streets, there by the gates of the city, there in the cry of the dispossessed. There are no bureaus of justice, no departments of justice, no halls of justice, no systems of justice; there is only the mighty stream that washes away the very foundations of these systems designed to enforce the orders of those who incessantly rant about good order, and law and order, and order in the streets, and order in the courts, and the orders of creation. (Whenever you hear people talk about the "orders of creation," watch out! It usually means that they are quite comfortable with their current social status, and therefore, they believe that God has nailed it down to be that way forever.)

13. Quoted by Heschel, *Prophets*, vol. 1, p. 209 n. 18.

Without hesitation, we can say what justice is not. For the prophet, justice and bloodshed are irreconcilable. In today's text, the evil must stop and the blood must be washed from our hands before we can even think about seeking justice (Isaiah 1:15-17). In Isaiah 5:7, violence is presented as the very antithesis of justice. God came expecting justice and saw only bloodshed. It is precisely this irreconcilability of violence and justice that the powers will not admit — indeed, cannot admit, because if violence is deprived of the claim that it is deployed in the pursuit of justice, then it loses all appeal. Wars, beheadings, electrocutions, bombings, hangings — these are not elevated enterprises. The only way to try to elevate violence is to claim that it is actually in pursuit of something quite elevated — justice, freedom, liberation, humanitarianism, peace. All warriors can play that game. What are the criteria, then, by which we can do a comparative evaluation of America's claim to be fighting for peace and justice, versus Stalin's claim to be building a bright tomorrow for Soviet workers, versus Hitler's claim to be liberating the German people in Sudetenland, versus Osama bin Laden's claim to be freeing the holy land from crusaders, versus other claims *ad infinitum?* Isaiah offers the word from God, which is the one standard of evaluation: where there is violence, there is no justice.

But to know what is not justice is not to know what justice is. "Seek justice," says the God of Isaiah, as if justice were in hiding. Where are we to seek it? For people of religious proclivities, the answer seems clear. If it is justice that we seek, then it is to the God of justice that we must turn to bolster our understanding, to refine our definition, and (perhaps eventually) to do a little justice. But no, that is exactly the path that has been closed to us. Recall that, at least for now, God is not listening. This God has a belly full of our prayers, our hymns, our offerings. Religion has become, not a conduit, but an obstacle to communing with God. So the question reasserts itself. If it is justice that we seek, where are we to turn?

Isaiah tells us in the very same verse: ". . . seek justice, rescue the oppressed, defend the orphan, plead for the widow" (1:17). To seek justice has nothing to do with climbing up to God. To seek justice is to climb down the social ladder and to stand alongside the people who are being battered and dispossessed by the upward momentum of the Great Society. Our relationship with God is at stake in our relationships with these sisters and brothers at the bottom far more than it could ever be at stake in our acts of religious observance, in our prayers and confessions, in our songs and sacrifices. But this is not about charity. This is about justice. This is about renouncing and turning away from our complicity in oppression.

One peculiarity of concern for justice in ancient Israel was the manner in which it was influenced by what can only be called "lists" of people
who were in misery and who were suffering injustice. These were people
to whom God had granted a special claim on the conscience, compassion,
and resources of Israel. These lists became formulaic, recurring again and
again in Scripture. The earliest list of those who suffered injustice included
the widows and the orphans who are cited by Isaiah, but also the aliens
and those who were strangers in the land.[14] But one amazing facet of Israel's formulaic lists of those who were oppressed is that over the span of a
thousand years — a thousand years, mind you, from the earliest oral traditions of the Bible to the Jewish writers of the New Testament — not one
group was ever dropped from the list. After a thousand years, we find the
Gospel and epistle writers still demanding justice for the widows (for examples, Mark 12:40; 1 Timothy 5:16), the orphans (James 1:27), and the
aliens (Hebrews 13:2). The list never contracted. On the contrary, the list

14. The earliest list of *personae miserae* was comprised entirely of people who had been
rendered poor and vulnerable because family ties had been severed. In a patriarchal culture,
widows and orphans were left without formal claims to land or other means of subsistence.
The immigrant was totally bereft of the security provided by ties to extended family or
tribe. As Christiana van Houten notes, the call to do justice to the *personae miserae* made its
way into the legal codes of Israel and Judah, but these laws cited no punishments for failure
to do justice. Instead of punishments, the motivation clauses referred to choosing righteousness, and they also referred to history. Never forget, these laws said (e.g., Deuteronomy
24:17-22), that you were once slaves and aliens in Egypt. The people were called to provide a
reflection of the justice that God had first shown to them. Van Houten, *The Alien in Israelite
Law*, Journal for the Study of the Old Testament Supplement Series 107 (Sheffield, England:
Sheffield Academic Press, 1991), pp. 50, 54.

It is a paradox (or maybe not) that the people on the list of those who suffered misery
were later included on another list, that is, the list of people who are blessed by God. The
poor, the hungry and the excluded people are cited in the beatitudes of both Matthew 5:3-12
and Luke 6:20-23. Moreover, the "Son of Man" chooses to identify so closely with these people in misery that what is done to them is done to him (Matthew 25:31-40). This biblical assertion that the poor are blessed is a total inversion of Hellenistic ideas about the role played
by the gods in the assignment of ease or misery. The classical Greek word that is often used
to refer to people who are "happy" or "blessed" is *eudaimon*, which indicates possession by a
"good demon." The demon brings good fortune, both material and spiritual. People who
suffer in misery have merely had the bad luck of lacking adequate "possession." In contrast,
biblical literature persistently conveys awareness of the role of human injustice in creating
misery. Rather than *eudaimon*, in the beatitudes Matthew and Luke use the Greek *makarios* to
refer to those who are "blessed." See F. Hauck, "*makarios*," in *Theological Dictionary of the New
Testament*, vol. IV, ed. Gerhard Kittel, trans. Geoffrey W. Bromiley (Grand Rapids: Eerdmans,
1967), pp. 362-64, 367-70.

was always expanding, like a growing consciousness of the need for justice. In addition to the widows, orphans, and aliens who had been left impoverished by disruption of family support, the list expanded to include all others who were hungry and dispossessed. It expanded to include the sick, the lepers, the lame, the blind. It expanded to include the captives and the prisoners. And a thousand years later, the good Jewish rabbi, Jesus, kept that long list intact and expanded it still further to include those who had been cast out of the community as people of ill-repute — the lawbreakers, the demon-possessed, the prostitutes.[15] Before, these impure

15. In Matthew 21:31-32, a saying is attributed to Jesus that is breathtaking for its courage and for its total reversal of commonly held social mores: Jesus tells the chief priests and elders that prostitutes will enter the kingdom of God before them. The Greek word for "prostitute" is *pornē,* but the use of the word evolved to include adulterers and any people who engaged in extramarital sex. Friedrich Hauck and Siegfried Schulz, *"pornē,"* in *Theological Dictionary of the New Testament,* vol. VI, ed. Gerhard Kittel and Gerhard Friedrich, trans. Geoffrey W. Bromiley (Grand Rapids: Eerdmans, 1968), pp. 579-95. Matthew portrays Jesus as radically altering the idea of sexual sin so as to place those who are impure in fleeting thoughts on the same level as the *pornē* who lacked purity in deed (Matthew 5:27-28; 15:18-20).

Luke 7:36-50 is a text steeped in impurity, a text in which Jesus is portrayed again as including prostitutes on the list of those who have suffered unjust rejection by the community. Jesus is dining at the home of a Pharisee who is appalled when a woman who is a "sinner" enters the house to wash the feet of Jesus and to anoint him with oil. Eduard Schweizer explores the complexity of this text, but he agrees with most scholars, who conclude that this sinner woman was a prostitute. Schweizer, *The Good News according to Luke,* trans. David E. Green (Atlanta: John Knox Press, 1984), pp. 137-41. In the parallel texts in Matthew 26:6-13 and Mark 14:3-9, the unclean person is not the woman but the host, Simon the leper, and the primary complaint against the woman had to do with the cost of the ointment she was using to anoint Jesus. In John 12:1-8, the host is Lazarus and the woman is identified as "Mary" (Magdalene?), but neither of these are portrayed as unclean. A conflation of the text in John 12 with that in Luke 7 may have contributed to the ecclesiastical identification of Mary Magdalene as a prostitute, yet none of the Gospels identifies her as a prostitute. The Gospels present Mary Magdalene as a follower of Jesus and as one of the first witnesses to the resurrection. The later ecclesiastical portrayal did not emerge from empathy for prostitutes but from deep-seated misogyny, as noted by Susan Haskins, *Mary Magdalen: Myth and Metaphor* (New York: Harcourt, Brace & Company, 1993).

Paul must be described as resistant to the inclusion of prostitutes on any list of those who suffer injustice. He insists repeatedly that the church — the body of Christ — should not be joined with *pornai.* Yet Paul concedes that even prostitutes can be "washed" and "sanctified" (1 Corinthians 6:9-11).

Just as Israel's regard for the alien was shaped by history, the story of Israel's past served to bolster communal awareness that even prostitutes must be treated justly. In Joshua 2:1-21, a prostitute named Rahab provided shelter and hiding space for Israelite spies

people had been perceived as a threat to the very existence of the community. With Jesus, these unclean people are to be cleansed by the embrace of the community that had once rejected them. They are a gift insofar as they provide an opening for the community to actualize the only reason for its existence, which is to serve as a reflection of the justice and mercy of God. Justice becomes the cleansing water, not only for the people on the list, but for the whole community. The scarlet sins pervade the whole community and not just those who suffer ritual impurity, but with justice, they will become pure as snow (Isaiah 1:18).

This formulaic list might strike us as very odd. If we are setting out to find injustice, we don't need a list because we have the media. We have *Newsweek* and ABC and CNN, and there between the celebrity profiles and the beer commercials, we can tell you where the horror is: there is genocide in Darfur, and there is suffering under the military regime in Burma, and there is Katrina with its lessons about racism and poverty in America, and there is the disappearing Amazonian rainforest, and there is Tibet, and there is that earthquake, and even though I forget where that was, don't forget to boycott sweatshops. Frankly, our media-driven minds have trouble maintaining focus for a thousand seconds, let alone a thousand years. Please don't misunderstand. I like a good boycott as much as the next guy, and I genuinely love the relief work of Mennonite Central Committee and the Global Ministries of the Church of the Brethren General Board. May that work continue for a thousand years and more. But it would be a profound misunderstanding to assume that injustice descends like a natural disaster that no one could have seen coming. Injustice is not like breaking news emerging full-blown from the latest hot spot. Injustice is a by-product of living in Gomorrah, a consequence of complicity with a filthy, rotten system. We need an expanding consciousness of it, an expanding list. We need expanding compassion, expanding resistance. And if Isaiah seems insistent on our need to encounter these people who suffer oppression, it is because that is the only path to a renewed encounter with God. This text in Isaiah 1 is deeply resonant with the words of Jesus in Matthew 25. Do it to one of the least of these and you do it to me. The nearest we will ever get to seeing the face of God on this planet is to look into the face of a sister or brother in need — in need of justice.

---

who had been sent by Joshua to Jericho. When Jericho was destroyed, Rahab and her family were the only ones who were spared (Joshua 6:17, 22-25). Rahab the prostitute is remembered as a model of righteous works (James 2:25-26), a model of faith (Hebrews 11:31).

Let me close by telling a story about a man I knew years ago in Washington, D.C., a guy named Joe. Actually, I need to tell you this story because of an odd experience I had while working with this text from Isaiah 1. I was checking out some commentaries and jotting down some notes, and this guy Joe kept popping into my mind. That was odd because I must confess that, in the last few years especially, I've rarely remembered him. But these memories kept surfacing until I was driven to reread a diary that I was keeping at the time, and there was Joe. There was something in these verses — blood on the hands, wash yourselves, seek justice — that culled up all these memories of him.

Now, I don't know about you, but I've been in a few ritually unclean spots in my life. After I graduated from seminary (and come to think of it, seminary itself is a little ritually unclean), I joined Brethren Volunteer Service and went to work with the Community for Creative Nonviolence in Washington, D.C. I was there and at a sister community in Baltimore between the mid-1970s and early '80s. The community had a free kitchen, a free medical clinic, a hospitality house for homeless people, and a meeting room for engaging in Bible study and for hatching antiwar conspiracies. The community houses were located on the corner of 14th and N Streets. At the time, it was known as a "bad" section of town, but just barely, because directly across the street there was the start of a gradual transition of neighborhoods that went all the way out to the wealth of Georgetown.

My first night at the community, I was astonished to discover that, soon after dusk, the sisters were working the corner of 14th and N. Up to that point, as far as I knew, I had never seen a prostitute plying her trade. That first night, I turned off the light in my room and I watched them for what must have been hours. But honestly, it wasn't titillating for me. It was more like watching a National Geographic film about some exotic culture. The cars would go driving by slowly, and those cars weren't from the poor side of town. The sisters would start calling out, "Hey, baby. Hey, honey." Every so often, a car would pull over, the window would go down, a sister would lean in through the open window and some sort of negotiation would commence — over price, I guess. Sometimes a sister would jerk her head back out of the car and step back onto the sidewalk and cuss at the guy: "You sorry-ass mother . . ." From "baby" and "honey" to "sorry-ass mother" in sixty seconds or less.

The next morning, I was talking to Ed Guinan, one of the founding members of the community, and in full naiveté, I asked, "Ed, did you know that there are prostitutes working that corner out there?" Ed said, "Sure.

They come into our medical clinic all the time. There are some pretty sad stories that some of them have to tell, but they're really a bunch of great women. Would you like me to introduce you to some of them?" I replied nervously, "Maybe later, Ed."

Joe was a white guy in his 70s who had been living at the community for years by the time I got there. He had come from Louisiana to live with some family members in D.C., but they quickly made it clear that they didn't want him around. So, Joe ended up homeless on the street until some community members invited him into the hospitality house, and he just stayed. Joe was a quiet guy, and he was a little bit grumpy. Over the years, he assumed responsibility for two main jobs around the house, and he didn't want anyone to interfere with his work. First job: Joe got up at four in the morning and started the coffee. Second job: Joe was in charge of the evening sandwich line. Breakfast and lunch, the free kitchen was open, but not in the evening, so that's when Joe handed out free sandwiches made of stale, donated bread and nondescript lunch meat. He gave out close to a hundred sandwiches each evening between five and six o'clock. The only assistance with the sandwich line that Joe would accept from the rest of us was help in carrying out the table, the chair, and the trays of sandwiches. Joe sat out there on the corner of 14th and N every evening for one hour on the nose. The line started forming early — maybe quarter to five — but Joe never handed out sandwiches early, and if you showed up a minute or two after six, all you'd get from Joe was, "Well, maybe tomorrow night you'll be on time."

Now, I never dared to interfere, but there were a few times when I saw Joe making his sandwiches. I'd be sitting in the next room, pretending to read a book, but I'd actually be glancing over the pages to watch Joe working in the kitchen. He'd start the whole process by washing his hands as if he were the most meticulous of surgeons. He'd be at the sink washing and scrubbing and rinsing and washing again. He'd dry his hands on a nice, clean towel, and then he'd light up a cigarette, plop a dirty ashtray on the kitchen table and start spreading mustard.

It must have been about a month after I had arrived at the community that I was walking through one of the living rooms and I happened to notice Joe sitting there and looking out the window at the traffic. So I went over, pulled up a chair, sat down next to him, and said something like, "Hey Joe, how are you doing?" The man said nothing. He was right there, so I knew that he had heard me. Was he trying to tell me to buzz off? As silent minutes passed uncomfortably, I wanted to get up and leave, but I just continued to sit there, and the two of us just continued to look out the window. After what seemed like forever, out of the blue, Joe said, "So I guess you want to know why I was in prison." I said, "I didn't know you were in prison, Joe." And then we were quiet again.

When Joe broke the silence a second time, he didn't talk for long — three or four minutes, maybe — but it was the most I had ever heard him talk about anything. He had done twenty-five years in Angola Prison in Louisiana for killing a man. There was a bar fight and a knife. Joe said that he didn't even remember killing the man, and then he added that there was a lot that he didn't remember from those days when he had been going from one alcohol blackout to the next. But even though he didn't remember doing it, Joe knew that he had killed the man because of the blood on his hands. And then he started talking about his sandwiches — about how, if he had taken a life, maybe sometime one of those sandwiches would be enough to help somebody make it through the night. Maybe one of those sandwiches would help to save a life. And then he was quiet again. And so was I, which wasn't easy because, you see, I'm a verbal person, and so many stupid things were running through my head that I could have said: "Joe, this doesn't make me think less of you." "Joe, the killing was due to the alcohol, so don't be so hard on yourself." "Joe, God still loves you." But Joe didn't need to hear any of that from me. What Joe needed in life was precisely what he was already doing — washing his hands and making sandwiches. So I said nothing. We sat there looking out the window for a few minutes more. When I got up to leave, I took a risk, or at least it felt that way. As I brushed past him, I put my hand on his shoulder — not too long, mind you — and then I left.

Washing can take any number of forms. There's the cleansing of baptismal immersion, and there's the Church of the Brethren service of footwashing. In contrast, there is the Gospel depiction of Pilate washing his hands (Matthew 27:24). Pilate's was a cynical act, performed not for the cleansing of guilt but for an assertion of innocence. Said Pilate, "I am innocent of this man's blood." This is not the cleansing that Isaiah demands. Isaiah's washing is performed at the midpoint between the confession of past failures and the will to begin anew. We wash because we want to set out on a new path. We wash because we want reunion with community and with God. We wash because there is work to do, there are sandwiches to be made.

The night that Joe died was a night like any other. I don't know who helped him set up the chair and table and piles of sandwiches that evening, but he was out there at five o'clock, not a minute sooner, I'm sure. It was late autumn, so the D.C. evening was probably a little crisp, and at five o'clock, it was already getting dark. Those glaring, city street lamps were probably shining down on Joe and his sandwich line. When Joe came back inside at six o'clock sharp, I'm sure he did what he always did; he ate one of the sandwiches he had fixed himself, and then he went up to his room for the night. The first sign that something wasn't right was the next morning when the coffee wasn't made.

I don't know if it was out of coincidence of timing or out of respect for Joe that the sisters always waited to take that street corner until Joe had done the sandwich line. But when it got dark early, they were out there soon after six. "Hey, baby. Hey, honey." Somehow, these impure women made it onto the list of those who suffer injustice, those who have a special claim on our conscience. On that last night, Joe would have been able to hear their voices from up in his room. "Hey, baby." And I hope that he did hear them, like some unwashed angels calling him to come home. "Hey, baby." Amen.

2. Radio Questions

Q *How did you come to espouse nonviolence? Was it the result of gradual changes in your life, was there a conversion experience, or did you simply grow up surrounded by pacifists?*

A In a culture of violence, I believe that no one grows up simply surrounded by pacifists. That may have been possible in an earlier era, before the rise of global monoculture.[1] There may still be some enclaves of indigenous cultures in which young people grow up learning that violence is not a solution to problems. Some Jains, Buddhists, and Hindus are taught the virtue of *ahimsa* from an early age, and of course, many Amish, Mennonite, Brethren, and Quaker children are taught that nonviolence and reconciliation are intrinsic to a life of discipleship. But the dominant culture persistently intrudes with proselytizing messages about the necessity, efficacy, and virtue of violence.

So conversion is essential — that is, conversion onto a path other than the lifestyle that is established and enforced by the dominant culture. In speaking of "conversion," however, I am not using the term in the sense that some Christian evangelicals talk about "converting" nonbelievers to Christian religious practices and doctrinal affirmations. Ever since the

---

1. Monoculture is the product of what Immanuel Wallerstein calls the "world-system" of global capitalism. According to Wallerstein, the world-system emerged from the struggles of sixteenth-century Europe and was propagated first through colonialism and more recently through global commerce and communication technologies. Wallerstein, *Utopistics, or, Historical Choices of the Twenty-first Century* (New York: The New Press, 1998), pp. 1-33.

Questions and responses prepared for an interview with students, WWEC FM, Elizabethtown College, November 5, 2007.

days of Constantine, mainstream Christianity has forged easy accommo-
dations with hegemonic cultures.[2] In the introduction to his book on war
and peace in world religions, comparative religions scholar John Ferguson
observes that no religion is more pacifist in its origins than Christianity,
and at the same time, no religion has been responsible for more bloodshed
in its history.[3] The essential conversion that must take place is not that of
winning over nonbelievers and adherents of other religious faiths, but that
of converting Christians away from our religion and onto the path of following Jesus. Led by the Spirit, this conversion is not an event that takes
place at only one point in time; it is a movement that entails ongoing
struggle for any of us who seek to be disciples.

I grew up here, in Lancaster County, at a time when this was still a rural area. Today, Lancaster County is being "developed," a happy word that
covers up all sorts of horrors and losses. But even during the time when I
was growing up, Lancaster County was a place of mighty contradictions.
On the one hand, Anabaptism flourished here, and the awareness of alternative lifestyles was as near as the horses and buggies, the prayer bon-
nets, and the Ephrata Cloister with its radical, communitarian vision. On
the other hand, the politics in the county was very conservative and thoroughly infused with patriotism. Lancaster County had its own peculiar
version of pretending that loyalty could be given to both God and country without the need to experience any tension. For me, the tension was
enormous.

Some of my earliest inklings of the gospel call to nonviolence may
have been passed along by my grandparents, who had been Mennonites. I
have distinct memories of my mother's mother preparing meals for the
hoboes who were, at the time, still wandering the back roads of Lancaster
County. Later, the sermons and actions of Martin Luther King, Jr., contributed to my awareness that biblical peace and reconciliation need to be expressed communally and socially and not just interpersonally. I hope that
my conversion is continuing.

2. The church is able to become a pillar of society only insofar as the tension between
gospel and social order is ignored, sublimated, or erased. The successful eradication of this
tension gives rise to what H. Richard Niebuhr called "the Christ of culture." Niebuhr, *Christ
and Culture* (New York: Harper & Brothers, 1951), pp. 83-115.

3. John Ferguson, *War and Peace in the World's Religions* (New York: Oxford University
Press, 1978).

Q *You refer to the conservative politics of Lancaster County. Do you consider your-self to be a leftist?*

A I'm not sure that these designations — left wing and right wing, lib-eral and conservative — have much meaning anymore, if they ever did. The history of the left wing–right wing vocabulary can be traced to assem-blies in pre-revolutionary France in which the strong monarchists sat to the right of the king, while those with sentiments that were more republi-can sat to the king's left.[4] Then along came Marxism, which is certainly opposed to monarchy, but insofar as Marxists favor communal rather than private ownership, the "left" was suddenly associated with big gov-ernment, while the "right" was identified with defense of the individual, private ownership, and curbs on government power. Yet today, President George W. Bush is described by many as a "right winger," even though he has presided over a government in which spending and deficits have soared, and he has advocated government intrusion into private lives on issues as personal as human reproduction, gay marriage, medical mari-juana, and the content of your telephone conversations. I think that a true conservative would want to prevent government intervention in such matters and would want to cut government spending by starting where it's the most bloated, that is, with the military.

I must confess to having anarchist sympathies. Some people would categorize communitarian anarchism as left wing extremism and individ-ualistic anarchism as right wing extremism. I don't know. Maybe the two converge. It is clear to me, however, that these conventional, political cate-gories are irrelevant to discipleship. To live in the presence of the reign of God, to love enemies, to feed the hungry, to visit the prisoners, to take all that you have and give it to the poor — is that left wing or right wing? It is radical in a way that transcends all such political orientations.

Q *What would you say are some aspects of peacemaking that are especially relevant to college students?*

A Militarism has always been a prominent feature of American society, ever since European settlers came armed with visions of building a shin-ing city on a hill. They perceived themselves as being on a mission from God, a mission in which not even genocide was precluded. But militarism has reached a feverish pitch in the days since World War II, and it has been

4. Hugh Graham, *The Vestibule of Hell: Why Left and Right Have Never Made Sense in Politics and Life* (Toronto: Stoddart Publishing, 2001), pp. 2, 17-19.

refueled by rage and fear since September 11, 2001. In the past few years especially, the federal government has gone looking for institutions that have been somewhat impervious to militarization, and that has included some colleges and universities. Unlike Elizabethtown, some schools already have facilities for Reserve Officer Training Corps and some hold major contracts for military research. In order to make the remaining schools less independent of the armed forces, the government has passed laws requiring that colleges and universities host military recruiters, and if they refuse, the schools face the loss of federal aid and grants.

It's not only institutions but also individual students who are faced with a financial carrot and stick. Males who do not register with Selective Service at the age of eighteen can be denied government-sponsored education assistance. When I was a student, refusal to cooperate with the draft carried the risk of prison, but not the additional risk of being denied access to formal education. Today, there is registration but no draft. It's interesting to me that the people who are calling for a reinstitution of the draft are not, for the most part, Republicans but Democrats like Congressman Charles Rangel of New York. One of Rangel's points is that young people who join the military today are often from poor families — kids who can't afford college and who face the choice of joining the U.S. Army or being unemployed. Some politicians who oppose reinstitution of the draft probably suspect that college campuses would not be so silent today if students faced the imminent prospect of being drafted.

But the absence of a draft does not alleviate the seriousness of the questions that students face, including the question of whether to register with Selective Service. In addition, since college is not a moratorium from life, students face the same questions confronting all adults about whether to resist the militarism in our society. I really like the efforts of some students at Elizabethtown to gather together a community of peace activists, to open dialogue on the campus, and to work toward an ongoing, nonviolent presence at the local military recruitment office.

Q   *Do you believe that nonviolence is the best response in all situations?*
A   It depends, of course, on what you mean by "best." Nonviolence can get you killed. So no, nonviolence is not always the safest course of action and it is not always the most effective course of action, but I believe that it is always the path laid out by Jesus.

Some people claim that militarism and pacifism are two extreme positions on opposite ends of a single continuum. At one extreme, the militarist contends that force holds the promise of solving all manner of problems, while at the other extreme, the pacifist contends that violence is never an acceptable response. For those who maintain that these are two extremes along a single continuum, there are plenty of options in between. Over toward the militarism end is the so-called "just war" position,[5] while those tending toward pacifism would allow for the use of force in rare instances — say to prevent genocide or to defend a loved one.

I don't believe the continuum idea is valid because I don't believe that violence and nonviolence are essentially related to one another in a way that can be measured by gradations. As the "non" in front of "nonviolence" suggests, they are related to one another as negations rather than gradations. I do not believe that the way to move from violence to nonviolence is gradually to shave away a little bit of violence until I wake up some morning to discover that I've become a pacifist. Nonviolence differs from violence in its very basic insistence that people may never be used as means to an end. If I start from a position that espouses the acceptability of violence in certain circumstances, I can't get there from here. I can't get to nonviolence through gradual transition. It requires a leap — a leap of faith.

In speaking of this leap, I don't mean to suggest that conversion takes place only as a blinding flash. Even Paul's road to Damascus (Acts 9:1-31) was a road, with preparatory moments along the way and with uphill struggles that followed the time of revelation. One could even say that conversion is the beginning of struggle, not the end of it. With Paul, the initial outward manifestation of his conversion was that he ended his persecution of the Jewish followers of Jesus. It was not that he eased the persecutions a little bit at a time, and it was not that he changed the identity of those whom he was persecuting. He ended the violence. Conversion is ongoing and ever new, and with nonviolence, it is the newness that must be emphasized. Whatever preparatory moments there may be, one does not embrace nonviolence by gradually limiting the circumstances in which violence is endorsed. But again, the struggle is ongoing. One can never arrive at a point of saying, "Now I am truly nonviolent. Now I am most unlike the militarist." Such an arrogant assertion is not only unloving; it employs the spirit of violence by treating people as nothing but

5. I associate the just war position with militarism because I agree with Robert W. Brimlow that there has rarely been a war in history in which both sides could not claim varying degrees of justification under traditional just war criteria, no matter how strained the pretenses. Brimlow, *What about Hitler? Wrestling with Jesus's Call to Nonviolence in an Evil World* (Grand Rapids: Brazos Press, 2006), pp. 38-56.

means — means of comparison and means for the assertion of one's own righteousness.

Q *You know the question that's asked of every pacifist, and I'll ask it of you. What do you do if someone is attacking you? Or, a dilemma that might be even greater, what do you do if someone is attacking a loved one?*
A Pacifism should not be misunderstood as mere passivity, and pacifists especially should never lapse into that misunderstanding. To stand by and do nothing while others are being attacked is to assent to violence. Without attacking the attacker, it is possible to interpose oneself in defense of the person being attacked.

Joan Baez had a great essay in which she showed how zealous proponents of violence are in trying to prove that, when push comes to shove, pacifists are hypocrites. Baez was asked what she would do if someone were attacking her grandmother:

> "Attacking my poor old grandmother?"
> "Yeah. . . . Say he had a gun, and he was about to shoot her. Would you shoot him first?"
> "Do I have a gun?"
> "Yes."
> "No. I'm a pacifist. I don't have a gun."
> "Well, say you do."
> "All right. Am I a good shot?"
> "Yes."
> "I'd shoot the gun out of his hand."
> "No, then you're not a good shot."
> "I'd be afraid to shoot. Might kill grandma."[6]

And it goes on like that, trying to create the scenario in which the pacifist would have to admit, "I'd go on a murderous rampage. I'd kill everyone in sight."

As Dale Brown observes, such hypothetical scenarios can cut both ways:

> . . . you arrive suddenly on a terrible scene. A group of children are playing. A man is pointing a gun in their direction. If you shoot him, you

---

6. Joan Baez, "Three Cheers for Grandma!" in John H. Yoder and others, *What Would You Do?* (Scottdale, Pa.: Herald Press, 1983), p. 62.

will save the children. If you fail, you may be responsible for their death. You shoot. The man is dead.

As long as it is hypothetical, however, why not add a bit more? There was a ferocious bear coming up the hill which the man could see and you could not. He was actually going to shoot the bear in order to save the children. Since your shot killed him, however, the bear mauled several children to their death. Tragically, you only had one shot.[7]

As both Brown and Baez note, all of these hypothetical scenarios ignore the very real violence already prevalent on our planet. They steer us away from questions of what we are going to do about that.

Nonetheless, there are serious aspects to these questions about what pacifists can do in defense of loved ones. We ought to put aside the sexism of these hypothetical scenarios in which the victims are inevitably either women or children. We may never assume that our loved ones are inanimate objects who do not have responses of their own, but still, I suspect that many pacifists have thought about this question. Dorothy Samuel has produced books, articles, and videos recounting actual instances in which potential victims responded to assailants with nonviolent creativity and surprise that evoked hesitation and wonder rather than attack.[8] Unfortunately, I suspect that fewer pacifists have questioned the common practice of calling the police in times of crisis. If I refuse to wield the gun, is it a mere gambit at personal purity that would allow me to call upon others to wield it on my behalf?

I hope that all pacifists give consideration beforehand to potential responses in the face of personal assault against self or others. For pacifists engaged in public witness, I hope that there is always careful discussion beforehand about how to respond if adversaries become angry or aggressive. But this is not the way in which violence intrudes into the lives of most of us. Some folks might want to sit back and say, "I'm not in the military. I'm not working for Halliburton or Blackwater or one of the big military contractors. I'm not killing anybody." And yet, over one-third of every tax dollar that we pay goes for military purposes. We end up praying for peace while paying for war. I know people who are engaged in several forms of tax resistance. Some refuse payment of a por-

---

7. Dale W. Brown, "Why Not Add a Bit?" in Yoder, *What Would You Do?*, p. 69.

8. For amazing examples of nonviolent response to personal assault, see Dorothy T. Samuel, *Safe Passage on City Streets* (Nashville, Abingdon Press, 1975).

tion or all of their federal taxes, but of course, the Internal Revenue Service eventually catches up with them and puts a lien on property, bank accounts, or paychecks. Others choose to live below the taxable income level. But total noncomplicity in paying for war is impossible. Every purchase that we make from gasoline to food means that we are helping to pay for someone's taxes somewhere along the production and marketing line. So what does nonviolence require of me? Is it enough that I refrain from carrying a gun and that I join in occasional peace rallies, or does it require something more fundamental? Does it require a change in lifestyle?

Q   *If the question that pacifists hear most often pertains to the defense of Grandma, the Hitler question is certainly a close contender. What do you do about Hitler?*
A   Since the end of World War II, the United States has been involved in dozens of wars and military incursions, many of which have not gone well, even from a military perspective. The Korean War was fought to a standstill. The Vietnam War was an unmitigated disaster, with over a million people killed in Southeast Asia before the United States withdrew in disgrace. The U.S. was driven out of Lebanon in the 1980s and out of Somalia in the 1990s, and now there are the quagmires in Afghanistan and Iraq. It's no wonder that proponents of American military might look back with longing at the Allied military victory of World War II, "the good war." What's more, the adversaries in that war seemed worthy of the demonization that is part of all war propaganda. With the exception of neo-Nazis, not too many people could paint Hitler in a favorable light. Therefore, persistently since World War II, U.S. presidents and war propagandists have sought to depict each new U.S. adversary as a reincarnation of Hitler. One of the earliest such efforts was in the 1950s when Secretary of State John Foster Dulles called Egyptian President Nasser "Hitler on the Nile." Panama's Manuel Noriega was portrayed as Hitler, and so was Serbia's Slobodan Milosevic. The elder and the younger Bush and the Clinton between them all called Saddam Hussein "Hitler."[9] The most recent emergence of Hitler is in Osama bin Laden and his gang of "Islamo-fascists." All of this heated rhetoric serves to stoke the fires of war. Any reluctance to confront militarily each new manifestation of Hitler is portrayed as the same "appeasement" that gave Nazi Germany open access to Czechoslo-

9. These and other examples of the Hitler analogy are cited by Michael Parenti, *Against Empire* (San Francisco: City Lights Books, 1995), pp. 91-92.

vakia and Poland. I reject the claim that Hitler has been reincarnated in anyone, as well as the claim that talking with adversaries constitutes appeasement. In a world that is heavily armed, the refusal to talk makes war a virtual certainty.[10]

Proponents of military intervention have a habit of creating conflicts and then saying to pacifists, "What are you going to do about it?" After toppling the government of Iraq, fueling sectarian violence, disarming and then rearming Sunni militias, proponents of the war in Iraq say to antiwar folks, "If we pull out now, there will be a bloodbath. What are you going to do about it?" The first thing to do is not to create the conditions that make a bloodbath more likely.

From a pacifist perspective, I think one of the first things to do about Hitler is not to fight World War I. It was the war during which Hitler himself became enamored of warfare, and his subsequent rise to power was facilitated by saddling a defeated Germany with the economic hardships imposed by the Treaty of Versailles. In this exercise of what might have been, in the unlikely event that Hitler still would have come to power in the 1930s, the nations that were already alerted to his militaristic and anti-Semitic rhetoric could have moved immediately to impose economic embargoes that (unlike those against Iraq in the 1990s) would have precluded rearmament while not depriving the population of food and medical supplies. In the real world, this did not happen because Hitler had prominent supporters in the U.S. and in the other nations that would eventually be allied against him, and also because strong U.S. isolationist sentiments opposed, not only military intervention, but any response whatsoever to "foreign" affairs. What was absolutely unconscionable was the refusal to

---

10. The pacifist Rabbi Abraham Cronbach wrote, "Like the man in the jest who so feared death that he committed suicide, nations wage war because they dread war. One nation's military preparedness inspires other nations with the terror of what might befall them should war occur; and with their fear arises the inclination to hasten war before the menace grows.... In brief, preparation for war takes the lead among the causes of war. It is a deadly link in a vicious circle."

Cronbach was a remarkable figure who tried to practice the pacifism that he preached. In 1935, he approached the American Friends Service Committee with a proposal that they host a dialogue between Nazis and representatives of the Jewish community. While the Quakers took his hopes for Jewish and Nazi reconciliation seriously, not many others did. Following World War II, Cronbach wrote, "Of all the outrages against the Jews committed by Hitler, none is more calamitous than this: he has banished from the hearts of many of us the will to peace." Cronbach's writings are quoted by Evelyn Wilcock, *Pacifism and the Jews* (Gloucestershire, England: Hawthorn Press, 1994), pp. 123-24, 130.

rescue Jews. The pacifist response to Hitler would demand that the boatloads of Jewish refugees from Europe be welcomed rather than turned away.[11]

If Hitler would have been able to come to power without the backdrop of World War I, and if he would have been able to retain his grip on power in the face of embargoes and international support for the Jews of Europe, pacifists would not have rested. Indeed, in the real world, pacifists did not rest. While their stories are too little told, nonviolent activists were working against the Nazi threat inside Germany and in adjacent countries. What would have been the result if the Allies had devoted their billions of dollars in wartime spending (hundreds of billions in today's dollars) to supporting and strengthening movements of nonviolent resistance to the Nazis? Some public protests were already taking place in the very heart of the Reich. In 1943 in the streets of Berlin, over 600 women rallied to demand that their Jewish husbands be released from custody, and their protest was successful![12] In Germany and in occupied France, some non-Jews sought to impede the roundup of Jews by wearing the yellow star that the law required all Jews to wear.[13] The White Rose group was surreptitiously distributing anti-Nazi literature inside Germany.[14] The Confessing Church was publicly opposing Hitler's takeover of the German churches.[15] In the Netherlands,

---

11. The alarming story of America's refusal to aid these refugees is told by Arthur D. Morris, *While Six Million Died: A Chronicle of American Apathy* (New York: Random House, 1968). While modern wars are often fought under humanitarian guises, it is far from clear that war is a preventive measure against genocide. In view of the fact that many genocides have occurred in the context of civil wars or wars between nations, some scholars have begun to explore the manner in which war exacerbates intra- and inter-communal tensions and creates a fertile ground for genocide. As Robert Melson comments, "Wartime conditions heighten feelings of threat, permit administrative measures that would not be tolerated otherwise, and provide a cover from external interference and condemnation." Melson, "Provocation or Nationalism? A Critical Inquiry into the Armenian Genocide of 1915," in Frank Chalk and Kurt Jonassohn, *The History and Sociology of Genocide: Analyses and Case Studies*, published in cooperation with the Montreal Institute of Genocide Studies (New Haven: Yale University Press, 1990), p. 285.

12. Peter Ackerman and Jack DuVall, *A Force More Powerful: A Century of Nonviolent Conflict* (New York: St. Martin's Press, 2000), pp. 236-38.

13. Gene Sharp, *The Politics of Nonviolent Action*, part 2: *The Methods of Nonviolent Action* (Boston: Porter Sargent Publishers, 1973), p. 136.

14. Inge Scholl, *The White Rose: Munich, 1942-1943*, trans. Arthur R. Schultz (Middletown, Conn.: Wesleyan University Press, 1983).

15. Many excellent accounts of the German church struggle have been written by authors that include Karl Barth, Arthur C. Cochrane, Helmut Gollwitzer, Guenter Lewy, Mar-

the Nazi occupation was opposed with public demonstrations, strikes, and nonviolent sabotage of facilities that the Nazis hoped to use for arms production. In occupied Denmark, in a spontaneous and courageous effort by common folks, fishing boats and other vessels were used to ferry thousands of Danish Jews to safety in Sweden.[16] These are just a few examples of how it is a false dichotomy to claim that Hitler had to be opposed by violence or by nothing at all. If there had been a massive influx of outside support for these efforts, then the possibility that Hitler could have been toppled by a movement of noncooperation and nonviolent resistance might have been more than a pacifist pipe dream. This is not to say that no one would have died. White Rose activists and Confessing Church leaders were exiled, imprisoned, or executed. Nonviolence is dangerous.

But what are the dangers of the military option? Along with the horrible suffering of combatants and noncombatants alike, the outcome can be deceptive, even for the victor. Jacques Ellul wrote, "That violence is so generally condoned today shows that Hitler won his war after all: his enemies imitate him."[17] It has become an accepted practice in warfare to incinerate cities as Hitler had done. The state has acquired unprecedented power as Hitler had wanted.

Of course, both of these questions — What do you do about Hitler? How do you defend loved ones? — come out of a presupposition that nonviolence ought to be about effectiveness. The questions invite us to demonstrate that nonviolence is more effective than violence. Effective at doing what? Effective at defending lives? Effective at securing freedom? The war in Iraq demonstrates once again that violence is ineffective at achieving these goals.

For some people, however, the validity and importance of nonviolence have little to do with calculations about effectiveness. For some people, nonviolence is rooted in faith, and let me confess that I am this type of pacifist. Whether it works or doesn't work, nonviolence is part and parcel of the effort to be a disciple of Jesus. It is there in the Sermon on the Mount — being peacemakers, loving enemies, turning the other cheek. It is there in the way of the cross — putting away the sword, accepting suffering

---

tin Niemöller, and Gordon Zahn. One book that draws on all these accounts is by J. S. Conway, *The Nazi Persecution of the Churches, 1933-45* (New York: Basic Books, 1968).

16. A summary of the nonviolent resistance in the Netherlands and Denmark appears in Ackerman and DuVall, *A Force More Powerful,* pp. 207-36.

17. Ellul, *Violence: Reflections from a Christian Perspective,* trans. Cecelia Gaul Kings (New York: Seabury Press, 1969), p. 29.

rather than inflicting it. It is there in the resurrection — proclaiming the defeat of death, overthrowing the violent intentions of the principalities and powers.

Q   *Since you just acknowledged that, for you, nonviolence is based in faith, to what extent can you expect others to live nonviolently if they do not share your faith commitments? If the way of Jesus entails risk and suffering, how can you expect nonbelievers to assume those risks? If you believe that peace is the way of the gospel, can you urge Americans to disarm even if they do not believe in that gospel?*

A   Those are important questions, and without wishing to evade them, let me start by observing that very similar questions could and should be posed to proponents of military action. Confidence in the efficacy and justifiability of violence also entails a series of what must be described as faith assumptions. How can one assert that the lives taken in a war are of only relative worth and that they may therefore be sacrificed to a cause that is theoretically greater? Such an assumption cannot be proven by scientific inquiry. Violence and the rage behind it are not rational phenomena, not even if they receive the sanction of governments. It is noteworthy that Sun Tzu, the classical Chinese philosopher who is still studied at West Point, wrote about *The Art of War,* not the science of war. How can the proponents of particular wars require that we should all share in the risks and the costs even if we do not share in the emotions and the faith assumptions that are clearly factors in all resorts to violence? The answer, I believe, is that they should not, nor should I bring similar expectations related to nonviolence.

Traditionally, some (not all) Anabaptists have resolved this dilemma by withdrawing into communities in which it has been possible to practice discipleship without expecting that the world would do likewise. I like the communitarianism of that, and I certainly agree that the world is not particularly concerned about discipleship, but the danger with this version of Anabaptism is that the *witness* to the reign of God can be obscured by isolation. When it is grounded in faith, nonviolence is about *witness* rather than politics.

I would never run for public office, even if I held illusions that people would be foolish enough to vote for me. For numerous reasons, discipleship is totally antithetical to ideas about winning the reins of power so that a certain version of faith can be imposed upon the world. One reason has to do with the nature of discipleship. Discipleship is not about leading; it is about following Jesus (Luke 22:24-27 and parallel texts). A second reason has to do with the nature of power. We do not control power; it controls us. A third reason has to do with the very dilemma that we are discussing here. Discipleship entails risks, and those risks ought to be assumed only if one has been called to do so, not forced to do so.

If I believe that the way of Jesus would be to shut down the Pentagon and throw open the prison gates, I am certainly free to — indeed, called to — tell the world about that faith. But that does not mean that I am called to wheedle my way into the halls of power or to nurture illusions that I am the one who will make that happen. The very essence of coercive power is to be in a position to force other people to assume the risks associated with a course of action that is contrary to their faith and their will. Here, I suppose my anarchism shows through. Faith and coercive power are incompatible.

3. Old (Anti) War Stories

Why do we look back? In a few minutes, I'll be telling some stories from 1976. That certainly qualifies as old, but I hope this is not an exercise in mere nostalgia. We look back to see what has changed and what has not. We look back for information and inspiration that might help to shape our ongoing journey. With his oral history projects, Studs Terkel was an excellent example of that. For Terkel and the people he interviews, looking back was not wistfulness for events that were over and done; it was fire for the ongoing struggle.[1]

For me, looking back is not nostalgia because many of the people who were friends back there and then are still friends to this day, and for that I am thankful. Together, we are still on the wrong side of the law occasionally. (Or maybe it's the right side. I forget who the law is supposed to be defending.) At our best, we are malcontents. Some folks reckon that, if you don't feel at home in the world, it's time for psychotherapy. Instead, my friends and I reckon that, if you start to feel too comfortable, that's the real danger sign. We challenge one another as only friends can do.

As we look back to past forms of activism to see what might be of help in the ongoing struggle, what are the criteria by which we evaluate? I believe that one of the least interesting tools of evaluation is that of trying to assess whether our activism is current in terms of trends, styles, and fashions. I'm sure that many people here have heard the dismissive comments, "Oh, that's so '60s," or "That kind of protest went out with the

---

1. For a relevant example of his work, see Studs Terkel, *Race: How Blacks and Whites Think and Feel about the American Obsession* (New York: Anchor Books, 1993).

A talk prepared for a gathering of reminiscence by peace activists and friends from college days, Brethren Heritage Room, High Library, Elizabethtown College, November 5, 2007.

'70s." In response, we must acknowledge that we are unlikely candidates for the pages of *GQ* or *Women's Wear Daily*. But instead of asking if our activism is in fashion, we must ask ourselves if we are struggling to be peacemakers (rather than simply troublemakers) and to love enemies (rather than to defeat them). Such efforts were not "P.C." even in 30 C.E.

Another evaluation tool of which I am little enamored is that of effectiveness. Did it work? Was it successful and will it work again? The 1960s and '70s movement for peace in Southeast Asia was more visible and vigorous than today's movement against the war in Southwest Asia, but some judge the movement against the war in Vietnam a failure because the war was not ended sooner. Others argue that the movement was successful at pressuring Johnson and Nixon into participation in the Paris peace talks; horrors were prevented that might have driven the death toll above the million who had already died in Vietnam, Laos, and Cambodia. But can either peace movements or warriors plausibly claim to be effective based on having averted greater horrors that might otherwise have occurred? Such claims are firmly within the realm of the hypothetical. Yet somehow, an aura of objectivity surrounds those who claim to be measuring effectiveness, and in modern discourse, objectivity is valued as much as pragmatism. Effectiveness can be measured in ways that faithfulness cannot. Or can it? Neither effectiveness nor faithfulness can be taken into the laboratory for measurement without first posing a whole litany of questions that require subjective answers. Effective or faithful according to what standards and according to whose judgments? What is regarded as effective or faithful by Amish farmers might be regarded as woefully inadequate by Pentagon generals or Wall Street brokers. But more to the point, both effectiveness and faithfulness are less tools of evaluation than they are contrasting models for living in the world. To be effective is to look to the world for an indication that one's life has been well-lived. To be faithful is to be guided by narratives that are happily out of sync with most of the world most of the time.

Many would agree with Gene Sharp that Gandhi and King were especially effective practitioners of nonviolence.[2] India won its independence.

2. In the preface to his book on Gandhi, Sharp credits both Gandhi and King with "refinement" in the application of the "technique" of nonviolence. Gene Sharp, *Gandhi as a Political Strategist, with Essays on Ethics and Politics* (Boston: Porter Sargent Publishers, 1979), pp. xiv-xv. As I read Sharp's books, I routinely argue with his perspectives, including his description of nonviolence as "technique," but these are the arguments of a grateful reader. Sharp has rescued numerous stories of nonviolence from near oblivion, and at great personal risk he has met

Civil rights legislation was enacted. Yet, neither Gandhi nor King gave glowing assessments of their own successes. Toward the end of his life, King recognized that legislation had done little to alter racism and segregation patterns in the North or in the South, that economic exploitation of groups like the sanitation workers continued unabated, and that the nonviolent movement was having no discernible impact on America's proclivity for violence abroad.[3] For Gandhi, in his last two years, he was dismayed by the fraternal and sororal warfare between Muslims and Hindus, by the division of one people into India and Pakistan, and by the inauguration of an Indian national government that immediately opted for police and military structures that were indistinguishable from those of other nations.[4] Still, both Gandhi and King were aware that nonviolent actions have an integrity of their own independent of whether they meet with what the world would call "success."

An added dilemma with adopting effectiveness as the criterion by which to judge nonviolent activism is that this is precisely the standard insisted upon by the powers that be, by the technological society, by the empire itself. If the goal is good, we are told, then the only concern we need to have regarding the means is whether they are effective in getting us there. By relegating the means to insignificance, we arrive at the Orwellian notions that freedom can be produced by means of invasion and conquest, or that peace can be produced by means of war. Going to war for peace is sometimes recognized for the oxymoron that it is, but going to war for

---

with revolutionary groups to urge that they organize movements of non-cooperation rather than armed struggle.

3. James H. Cone contends that, while King never surrendered his hope for "the beloved community," during his final months, he had a growing awareness of what Malcolm X called "the American nightmare" rather than "the American dream." See Cone, *Malcolm & Martin & America: A Dream or a Nightmare?* (Maryknoll, N.Y.: Orbis Books, 1992). For a contrasting view that differs with what he calls "the radicalization thesis," see Michael G. Long, *Against Us, But for Us: Martin Luther King, Jr. and the State* (Macon, Ga.: Mercer University Press, 2002).

4. At a prayer gathering on September 26, 1947, Gandhi said, "There was a time when India listened to me. Today I am a back number. I have been told I have no place in the new order, where we want machines, navy, air force and what not. I can never be a party to that." *The Penguin Gandhi Reader*, ed. Rudrangshu Mukherjee (New York: Penguin Books, 1993), p. 279. Respectful though he is of Gandhi's vision, Richard G. Fox writes, "Finally, for Gandhi, in 1948 comes a martyrdom that many see as a deus ex machina, saving him and his utopian vision from further embarrassment in a world that no longer had any real place for them — and may never have had, except perhaps momentarily in the struggle against colonialism." Fox, *Gandhian Utopia: Experiments with Culture* (Boston: Beacon Press, 1989), p. 5.

freedom is equally oxymoronic. War is *always* the enemy of freedom. War always means more repression at home and abroad, more surveillance, more restriction on movement across borders, more imprisonment, more covert intrusion of government into our lives — and that's just to cite some of the decreased freedom in terms of civil liberties. In terms of more basic freedoms, like the freedom simply to live, absolutely nothing on the planet does more than war to spread homelessness, starvation, communicable diseases, and weapons that will kill for years to come. War is the enemy of both peace *and* freedom.

Of course, there could be an interesting argument on the relative "effectiveness" of violence versus nonviolence, an argument in which proponents of militarism may not assume that the outcome is predetermined. They would certainly cite the "good war" and the overthrow of Nazi tyranny, to which proponents of nonviolence would respond with the contrary citations of the quagmires in Vietnam, Iraq, Somalia, and Lebanon — orgies of violence leading precisely nowhere. But for now, that is not an argument in which I wish to engage because I believe that the standard by which we judge nonviolent activism must be something other than that. "Does it work?" is the appropriate question for judging cars, computers, and other consumer products. Does it do what I want it to do, and if not, is there a money-back guarantee?[5] With nonviolence, we surrender control and there are no guarantees. In evaluating nonviolent actions, rather than applying standards of efficacy, I believe that it can be helpful to apply standards that draw upon faith. There are many possible questions that are relevant when evaluating actions from a faith perspective, but briefly, allow me to cite just three of these.

1. The question is not "Does it work?" but "Is it truthful?" Forgive me, friends, for referring to "truth," a word that grates on our modern/postmodern ears. I am often struck by how very modern Pontius Pilate sounds in the Gospel of John when he contemptuously asks Jesus, "What is truth?" (18:38). For those whose faith is shaped by gospel, truth is embodied in Jesus, embodied as love, but this love does not equate with being nice. Love of the adversary is never easy or pretty; it is "a harsh and dread-

---

5. Ironically, these questions that seem most appropriate to ask about consumer products are precisely the ones that advertisers do not want to ask. In the world of corporate advertising, the decision to buy a car has little to do with practicality. The car is a source of happiness and pride. It is a member of the family. Buy this car and you are having a love affair. While you possess the car, you are also possessed by it. See Jean Kilbourne, *Can't Buy My Love: How Advertising Changes the Way We Think and Feel* (New York: Touchstone, 2000), pp. 95-107.

ful thing."[6] Love of justice may take forms that would be considered rude by conventional standards — the smashing of pottery (Jeremiah 19), the overturning of tables (Matthew 21:12; Mark 11:15; John 2:15) and, one might add, the sit-ins at lunch counters, the destruction of draft files. But while love may abide actions that transgress good etiquette, it cannot allow for dehumanizing verbal or physical assaults on other people. For people of faith shaped by gospel, an action must be evaluated according to whether it affirms life. Does this action witness to the resurrection? Does it witness to the repudiation of death in all its forms?

2. Does this action build community? There have been some wonderful, nonviolent radicals who were freelance individualists in their activism — to name just one, Ammon Hennacy, who was loosely affiliated with the Catholic Workers.[7] Nonetheless, community is vital to action grounded in faith. In a little while, I want to say more about the importance of community in shaping and sustaining nonviolence. For now, just let me say that the times I remember best from college were those not infrequent times when Gene Clemens would invite groups of students and others to pile into his VW bus, and off we would go to an antiwar march in Washington, to a forum in Lancaster, to a peace gathering in Harrisburg. Surrounded by sisters and brothers in these little ad hoc communities, I was given encouragement and freedom to be — how to say it? — better than myself.

3. Does the action concede as little as possible to the powers that be? To some extent, of course, the nonviolent action is addressed to the powers, as well as to other people and to self. In some sense, too, I am subject to those powers as I am shuffled off to jail or simply ignored. I want to beware, however, that my plea for peace entails none of the militarized logic that has sometimes fueled liberal dissent. In the past, some liberals opposed plans to construct the B-1 bomber because the need for it was obviated by the Pentagon's fleet of B-52s. More recently, some liberals opposed the war in Iraq because it distracted from the ongoing war in Afghanistan and from the effort to "get" Osama bin Laden. There is no advocacy of peace in such arguments. I must confess my own bias that involvement in electoral politics is rarely a form of peace activism. Supporting a candi-

6. In Dostoyevsky's *The Brothers Karamazov*, Father Zossima says, "Love in action is a harsh and dreadful thing compared to love in dreams." In her own work, Dorothy Day persistently reminded herself of this saying. Cited by William D. Miller, *A Harsh and Dreadful Love: Dorothy Day and the Catholic Worker Movement* (New York: Image Books, 1974), p. 25.

7. See Hennacy, *The Book of Ammon* (Salt Lake City: Hennacy, 1965).

date who believes in trimming the Pentagon budget so that there can be a "leaner, meaner fighting force" is a huge concession to militarism.

When I think back on old antiwar stories, an important year for me was 1976. Of course, '76 was also America's bicentennial year, but I wasn't there for most of that celebration. I wasn't there when the tall ships from around the world sailed into New York harbor, and I wasn't there in Philadelphia when they rang the Liberty Bell, and I wasn't there for the greatest fireworks display in human history. To me, the most interesting commentary on the Spirit of '76 was unveiled in an ad campaign launched that year by a chain of fried chicken restaurants: "Now we give you freedom of choice — regular or extra crispy!" Call me cynical, but I was sitting over in my vegetarian corner thinking, "Either way, it's still just dead bird, right?" Nevertheless, the fried chicken chain must be credited with a degree of insight regarding the meaning of "freedom" in American political discourse. The two political parties offer voters options that are scarcely more divergent than regular or extra crispy.

There are three places that stand out in my memory from 1976. First place, I remember standing inside a garbage dumpster near Jessup, Maryland. Located midway between Washington, D.C., and Baltimore, Jessup was home to one of the largest produce terminals on the East Coast. At the time, I was involved with the Community for Creative Nonviolence in D.C. and with the Jonah House community in Baltimore, and we had a free kitchen in each city. What my friends and I were doing inside the dumpsters was salvaging food for the kitchens. There were over fifty wholesalers at Jessup, and over a hundred dumpsters, some of them so huge that climbing in was no easy feat and getting back out was no sure thing. As a seasoned dumpster diver I can tell you that, while rotting onions smell awful, the main hazard was from the rotting lettuce which, on a cold winter morning, left your hands numb from the rotting slime. But in fact, much of the produce in those dumpsters was not rotting at all. If a ten-pound bag of potatoes split open, it was cheaper for the wholesaler to throw it away than to pay employees to repackage it. If there was one rotten apple in a bag, the whole bag went into the dumpster. After the back of our pickup truck was full of produce, we would go back to the kitchens, give all the fruits and veggies a thorough bath, and prepare some downright *haute cuisine*.

In my years of dumpster diving at Jessup, most of the wholesalers were friendly. They knew what we were doing, and some would even direct us to dumpsters where they knew that there would be good pickings on certain mornings. But one thing that always seemed odd to me was the attitude of a few wholesalers that we should not go near their dumpsters because that garbage was their private property. What can you say to that? You depart in peace.

What has changed since 1976? There are not fewer hungry or home-less people. There are more. There is not less garbage. There is more. But one thing that has changed is that the odd attitude that garbage is private property has carried the day. In most locales today, dumpsters are locked. In our hyper-capitalist society, we have the absolute right to deprive oth-ers of the use of whatever property we do not need or want. Our right to waste trumps the ability of others to survive.

The second place I remember being in 1976 was inside the Pentagon, inside the veritable belly of the beast. Some friends and I from Jonah House availed ourselves of the rare public access provided by the Penta-gon Bicentennial Tour. The tour route was rather vacuous, winding its way past a chapel and down halls lined with the portraits of stern-faced gener-als, but the tour line also happened to go by one office of interest to us, the office of the Undersecretary of the Navy for Research and Development. A glance through a window in the office door showed file cabinets with large combination locks, but the drawers were ajar, perhaps so that office staff didn't have to unlock and relock drawers as they went about their work. The Navy Undersecretary's office was of interest because it was the site of planning for the Trident nuclear submarine, a weapons system that has since been built. As initially proposed, the Trident could serve as ei-ther a first-strike weapon or a hand from the grave, that is, a doomsday weapon that could still be used even after all land-based weapons had been turned to dust by nuclear assault. Each Trident was to be two football fields long and four stories high with the capacity to deliver 408 indepen-dently targetable nuclear warheads, which is to say, 408 incinerated cities. Our friends with the Atlantic Life Community were busy with nonviolent protests at the Electric Boat Company in Groton, Connecticut, where the Trident was being assembled. Our friends with the Pacific Life Commu-nity were busy with nonviolent protests in Bellingham, Washington, where the Trident was to be based. So, in honoring our friends, it seemed only right that we should get busy inside the Pentagon.

Three co-conspirators and I went for a second tour of the Pentagon. Two of my friends had small, handmade banners tucked beneath shirt and blouse. Outside the Undersecretary's office, they knelt in the hallway, un-furled the banners, and started praying that the Trident and its warheads would never be used. The other friend and I had bottles filled with our own blood stuffed down the crotch of our pants. Security grabbed my friend outside the office, but I was able to reach the filing cabinets. Blood joined weapons plans. With deed done, the first person to speak to me was a white, female employee in the office who said, "You're nothing but poor, white trash." I wish I had had time to respond. I would have wanted to tell her that my intent had not been to ruin her day. I would have wanted to tell her that I was not claiming moral superiority because, what with our tax dollars and other complicities, we're all working on war machines. I would have wanted to see if even a little of her anger would have mellowed if I had told her about dumpsters and about rotting onions and about how I was trashy in ways that she couldn't even imagine. I would have wanted to buy her coffee, but the handcuffs arrived.

What has changed since 1976? The Pentagon's work proceeds at a more feverish pace than before. The public access to the building has certainly changed. There are no more tours for the likes of me. Certainly the files have changed. If paper mattered in 1976, today it's the computers and the CD-ROMs and the hard drives that have the combination locks. But for nonviolent protest, I think the symbol of blood has changed as well. Thirty years ago was an era of innocence regarding HIV and other blood-borne dangers. Today, if people were to see blood on files, they would be less likely to reflect on the deadly nature of military planning than on the presence of a biohazard. For nonviolent action, the symbols and forms of engagement must be carefully chosen. Some old symbols become new. I like the way in which some of my friends have resurrected the prophetic vision of beating swords into plowshares (Isaiah 2:4; Micah 4:3) as they trespass on military bases and deliver hammer blows to bombers and missile silos. I like the joyful disruption of good order — the blockade, the sit-in, the refusal to stay confined to free-speech zones.

Along with weighing the coherence of symbols, we must also consider the fundamental questions that have been raised in the debates among pacifists and antiwar activists over the types of civil disobedience that result in damage to property. This type of disobedience is not new. Groups who have engaged in it in the past include the slaves who sabotaged the farming implements of the slaveholders and the rebels who tossed tea overboard in Boston harbor. But even though these actions lend an aura of historical respectability to this type of disobedience, neither the slaves nor the rebels were necessarily espousing nonviolence, and therefore, there was no particular need for them to evaluate their actions by the standards that certainly apply if one seeks to be a nonviolent activist.

Regarding actions such as the defacement of public property, the destruction of draft files or weapons files, and the hammering of bombers and missile silos, two important questions have been posed. Without assuming that my own actions escape moral culpability, allow me to cite these two questions and trace the contours of the debate: (1) Can a truthful witness ever entail any degree of secrecy? If anything is hidden (like I was hiding the bottle of blood), does that constitute deception and does it make a lie out of whatever action ensues? (2) Is property destruction itself a form of violence? These are serious question. Since secrecy, lying, and violence are tools in the service of the powers, reliance on these methods would only serve to reinforce empire rather than to resist it.[8]

(1) The communities of which I have been a member have routinely and intentionally opted for openness and transparency, sometimes to the detriment of the actions we had planned. In the late 1970s in Baltimore, our community was involved in a campaign for the conversion of Johns Hopkins Applied Physics Laboratory (APL) to nonmilitary work. We were thankful that several workers from APL joined our campaign and participated in all of our meetings, even though it eventually became clear that at least one of these workers was attempting to foil our efforts. On the very morning that we had planned to scale the APL water tower and unfurl a banner, access to the tower was blocked. In reaction, we did not seek to identify and exclude the informer. We just continued with our work of trying to convert ourselves, the informer, and the APL.

While lying is never justified, are there circumstances in which one may retain silence about intended actions without having that constitute deception? If silence and privacy are not judged to be wrong in and of

---

8. Even the vocabulary of "resistance" is not without controversy. Does the call to discipleship lead to "nonresistance," "nonviolent resistance," or both? Scripture is rich and varied, but in the New Testament, nonresistance is often advocated in texts pertaining to relationships with human adversaries (e.g., Matthew 5:38-41), while the calls to resistance (e.g., James 4:7; 1 Peter 5:8-9) are applicable in relationship to powers, spirits, and evil personified as the devil. This differer.:iation would be fully congruent with the admonition in Ephesians 6:12 that the struggle is not against enemies of flesh and blood but against rulers, authorities, and spiritual forces. On the text from Ephesians, see Walter Wink, *The Powers*, vol. 1: *Naming the Powers: The Language of Power in the New Testament* (Philadelphia: Fortress Press, 1984), pp. 84-89.

Among abolitionists in nineteenth-century America, the term "nonresistance" was especially appealing to advocates of perfectionism. Yet William Lloyd Garrison, founder of the New England Non-Resistance Society, joined ranks with Henry David Thoreau, author of "Resistance to Civil Government." Henry Mayer, *All on Fire: William Lloyd Garrison and the Abolition of Slavery* (New York: St. Martin's Press, 1998), pp. 249-51, 414-15.

themselves, may they sometimes be put into the service of a greater un-veiling *(apokalypsis)*? Put aside, for now, my own stumbling around in the Pentagon. Allow me to cite some examples that are less suspect, more courageous, and more loving. In antebellum America, in response to the Fugitive Slave Act, some Northern abolitionists sheltered and aided es-caped slaves as they made their way to freedom. Since the Fugitive Slave Act had stipulated that providing shelter was illegal and that all escapees must be returned to slavery if they were apprehended, the underground railroad was a secretive endeavor. Was it also deceptive? Even if it provided the concrete service of aiding sisters and brothers who had escaped the horrors of slavery, does a good goal justify deceptive means? In fact, I be-lieve that the underground railroad was a marvelous creation that, while secretive, totally subverted the self-deception of a slaveholding society. The secretive railroad helped to unveil the reality that it was deceptive to pretend that the evil of slavery could persist in a society that had any illu-sions of being free. Jesus himself comes in the secretive guise of the fugi-tive. To break silence, to obey the law, the abolitionists would have had to deceive themselves into thinking that it was not Jesus who was visiting when escapees arrived in need of water, food, and shelter.

When my friends Dan and Phil Berrigan joined with others in burn-ing draft files in Catonsville, Maryland, I believe that they performed the service of unveiling the deadly nature of the empire.[9] One could not per-sist in the illusion that life went on as usual while death rained down on Southeast Asia. *Apokalypsis:* burning papers was highly felonious and na-palming children was no crime at all. Such imperial values need to be un-veiled and overturned, like tables in the temple.

In Acts 5:29, the apostles said, "We must obey God rather than any hu-man authority," and in Romans 13:1, Paul wrote, "Let every person be sub-ject to the governing authorities . . ." The texts collide in interesting ways. Since Paul goes on to write that all authority is from God, would he con-tend that the "governing authorities" were not the "human authorities" whom the apostles disobeyed? Is subjection something other than obedi-ence? Or did Luke and Paul simply disagree? At the moment, I have no wish to add to my crimes by committing exegesis. But in brief, let me observe that my friends and I have tried to follow Paul's admonition to be in subjec-tion. When we have committed acts of civil (or uncivil) disobedience, we have not tried to escape arrest or legal consequences. We have gone into

9. See Daniel Berrigan, *The Trial of the Catonsville Nine* (Boston: Beacon Press, 1970).

court to acknowledge openly what we did and why we did it. For us, to try to escape undetected or to try to avoid courtroom self-incrimination would entail too little subjection and too much concealment.[10]

(2) Is the intentional damaging of property itself a form of violence? People of good faith differ. I hope that it is in good faith that I understand concerns about violence and nonviolence as applying specifically to our relationship with other living beings.[11] If I am more open on the question of how we relate to inanimate objects, some of my friends regard my stance on not killing or physically assaulting other living beings as quirky and overly fastidious, even as it is inconsistent in practical application. I do not intentionally kill insects, but I am certain that my car kills them as I drive down the highway. I do not eat meat, but I feel certain that I would use physical force against a nonhuman animal that was attacking a person if doing so would save a human life. So I confess to being a "speciesist" who values human life most highly, but who nonetheless tries to live out a faltering respect for all living being.[12] But then my friends point to still another inconsistency, namely, the broccoli that I eat is living too.

Nonetheless, even though I understand the principles of violence and nonviolence as applying specifically to our relationships with other living

10. One author writes that it is integral to the very definition of "civil disobedience" that "participants do not try to avoid the consequences of the action." Per Herngren, *Path of Resistance: The Practice of Civil Disobedience* (Philadelphia: New Society Publishers, 1993), p. 9.

11. Clearly, there is no universal agreement on the distinction between property damage and violence against people. The Federal Bureau of Investigation definition of "terrorism" reads as follows: "Terrorism is the unlawful use of force against persons or property to intimidate or coerce a government, the civilian population or any segment thereof, in furtherance of political or social objectives." Since the definition stresses unlawfulness and includes actions against property, a liberal application of the definition could classify Plowshares activists and me as terrorists. Of course, in an earlier day when Britain was determining lawfulness, Boston Tea Party participants would have qualified as well. The FBI definition is quoted by Robert W. Brimlow, *What about Hitler? Wrestling with Jesus's Call to Nonviolence in an Evil World* (Grand Rapids: Brazos Press, 2006), p. 89.

12. Tristram Stuart observes that vegetarianism in the West owes less to Christianity than to the European encounter with Eastern spiritual traditions. Within Christianity, vegetarianism has not been absent, but, except for the practice of refraining from eating meat on Fridays, it has usually been associated with fringe groups of ascetics and heretics, such as the medieval Cathars. Augustine, whom Stuart calls "the anti-vegetarian," argued that the Gospel accounts of Jesus casting evil spirits out of the Gerasene demoniac and into a herd of swine (Matthew 8:28-34; Mark 5:1-13; Luke 8:26-33) indicated that the effort to refrain from killing animals is superstitious and injurious to faith. Tristram Stuart, *The Bloodless Revolution: A Cultural History of Vegetarianism from 1600 to Modern Times* (New York: W. W. Norton, 2007), p. 151.

beings, the willful damaging of property can constitute a form of psychological violence. Nonviolence requires not only that I refrain from physically assaulting other people, but also that I approach them with respect. I recall that, at one Pentagon antiwar demonstration, I confronted another protester who was yelling at Pentagon employees and calling them "Baby killers." Peace witness must be more loving than that. Nonviolence requires that we strive to rid ourselves of self-righteousness and approach adversaries with a full affirmation that they are precious children of God. Since damaging property carries the risk of constituting an emotional assault, I believe it is important to pose three questions that might help to mitigate the risk: Is my symbolic action intended to mark, damage, or destroy public property that is (at least in some sense) owned by all of us rather than personal property, the damaging of which would carry a greater risk of emotional assault on the owner?[13] Is my action directed against objects that are instruments of death or that are specifically intended to increase the capacity for violence? Is my action carefully planned to avoid the possibility of physical injury to any person other than myself? An affirmative answer to each of these questions would clearly preclude actions such as spray-painting my neighbor's house (or even my neighbor's gun collection), smashing storefront windows, or us-

13. Per Herngren is certainly correct in observing that our attitude toward material objects is distorted by a capitalist ideology in which property rights are sacrosanct. The rights of government and individuals to own weapons supersede the right to life of the people against whom the weapons will be used. In capitalist societies, too, there is a third category of property ownership with which to contend, that is, property owned by corporations; this is property that is neither "personal" nor "public." At various stages in the production process, are weapons components owned by governments or by military contractors? Herngren, *Paths of Resistance*, pp. 65-66.

I do not deny that property damage can have an emotional impact on people even when it is not their own personal property that is at stake. Indeed, that can be part of the intent of the action. In 1982, some friends and I held a "Bake Sale and Free Gun Smashing" in Wisner Park in Elmira, New York. We publicized the event: come buy some baked goods (with proceeds going to international famine relief), bring along your guns, and we will smash them for free. Our action was met with a mixture of good-humored support and angry indignation. Local gun dealers took out newspaper advertisements to inform the public that unwanted guns should be sold, not smashed. The police showed up to inform us that it was a crime to obliterate the serial numbers on registered weapons. We sold scores of cupcakes, but one old hunting rifle was the only gun we got to smash. With a note of explanation, we sent the proceeds to Mennonite Central Committee, and in return we received a thank you letter that included the bemused observation that it was the first time that MCC had ever received a contribution from a gun-smashing bake sale.

ing explosives that could increase destructiveness and risk to human life. But affirmative answers would not have precluded nonviolent activists from using hammers to smash the gas chambers at Auschwitz, and who of us would not fervently wish that such an action had been possible?

But put aside hyperbole that includes unrealistic visions of nonviolent activists at Nazi death camps. In our own mundane setting, why engage in actions that carry the risk of moral culpability? As indicated by the litany of questions in the preceding paragraph, nonviolence is not intrinsic to property destruction. If there are rare instances in which damage to property may be a form of nonviolent witness, these are hemmed in by all sorts of questions about motivations and attitudes and definitions of property and so on. Why not adhere to the safer paths that entail less risk of moral culpability — less risk that we are engaging in violent actions that are simply covered by the platitudes of nonviolence?

It is certainly true that damaging property is not intrinsically nonviolent, but then again, neither is speaking or carrying banners or holding vigils or writing letters to elected representatives. Nonviolence is an ongoing struggle to convert oneself into the service of life rather than death. But even as we struggle with ourselves, we must resist the temptation to focus on illusions of personal purity. There is a deceptive quality to the search for the safest path of action that will ensnare us in the lowest possible moral culpability. What path is safer than being quiet and doing nothing? And yet, in a culture of violence, death thrives on our quiescence.

My breach of good decorum at the Pentagon determined the third place that I remember being in 1976, namely, in jail. Nonviolence is not confined to the moment of protest. The struggle to be nonviolent must continue in jail, just as it must continue in the workaday world. It cannot be just a Sunday-go-to-meeting phenomenon. There is a dailiness to the effort to witness to faith, to resurrection, to peace. With nonviolent actions, we are in danger of elitism whenever we neglect the daily for the flashy. Most middle-class people (let alone poor people) cannot afford to jet-set their way to a week at Camp Casey in Crawford, Texas, or to the next huge rally in Washington, D.C. For most people, risking months or years in prison would threaten not only their own well-being, but that of dependents as well. For people with large families, it would be very difficult to live intentionally below the taxable income level to avoid paying for war while praying for peace. Simplifying lifestyle, limiting income, risking imprisonment, devoting time to feeding the hungry and protesting militarism — all of these become more feasible in the context of the intentional community and the literal communism recommended by the book of Acts (4:32-37). I could risk jail only because there was an intentional community of people with whom I shared everything — a community that encouraged me to go and a community that would welcome me back home. There are multiple ways to avoid the dangers of elitism. One is respect for the local. Peace activism cannot be defined by our ability to fly off to Crawford or to raise a ruckus in a Pentagon office. It must happen here. It must happen daily. But another way to repudiate elitism is to enter into genuine community, genuine *ecclesia*. Community might take different forms in various settings, and the formation of it is certainly difficult in a culture of individualism, but I believe community is vital to nonviolence.

So off to jail went I. In passing, let me observe that I am unlike most people locked up in America's cages, but that's not because I am nicer than they are, nor because mine was a less dangerous form of criminality. I must insist that I was a common criminal and that I have remained, at least to some degree, unrehabilitated. But I am different from most of my caged brothers and sisters in that I am not poor and I am not black or brown. Jimmy Carter and Gerald Ford were the presidential candidates in 1976, and it was a memorable experience to be locked up while watching a presidential debate. The TV was blaring, as it always seemed to be in jail. I was surrounded by black men, and we were looking out between the bars, watching two white guys talk about freedom.

One thing that has changed dramatically since 1976 is the size of the prison population in the United States. Nearly one percent of all people in the country are now imprisoned, the highest per capita rate in the world. In many societies, there is a rough but disturbing correspondence between rates of imprisonment and levels of militarism. Russia and China also have high rates of both incarceration and military expenditure, but in neither case do they approach the alarming levels of the United States. Do the powers believe that happiness will flourish once evil has been sufficiently contained and control has been effectively established at home and abroad? Are the American people more evil than the people of other nations, thus giving rise to the need for more containment and control?

I certainly do not believe that the American people are evil. Indeed, I don't even believe that American power is more evil than the power of other nations. There's just more of it. The effort to establish containment and control takes a horrible toll in wasted resources and wasted lives. And perhaps it is this waste that constitutes an uncanny interconnection of dumpster, Pentagon, and jailhouse.

4. Peacemaking and Prison Abolition

Can you think of any laws that you would violate as a matter of principle? I'm not asking about laws that we might violate out of convenience if we thought that there was a low risk of getting caught. Who of us has not gone 60 in a 55 miles per hour zone when the police were out of sight? And I'm not asking about some theoretical laws in the future. I suspect that many of us have a theoretical line in the sand that we imagine would trigger our fierce disobedience if the government ever dared to cross it by, say, taking away our Bibles or our guns. And I'm not talking about laws from the past. From our safe historical distance, it's far too easy to imagine ourselves sheltering fugitive slaves or being hustled off to prison with suffragists. I am asking about laws that are on the books now and whether, as a matter of conscience, you would violate any of them.

There are plenty of laws on the books from which you could choose. Indeed, the very proliferation of laws is one of the factors that may leave us feeling befuddled at the prospect of determining whether there are specific laws that we would choose to disobey *or obey*. (At least in passing, we ought to take note of the peculiar fact that obedience is rarely regarded as an act of volition in the way that disobedience is.) For this specific locale in Pennsylvania, the volumes of federal, state, and local laws that are in effect would easily overwhelm the capacity of the college library to contain them. Even the most studious lawyers could not know one percent of the laws that are on the books. In a technological society,

---

Presentation for classes taught by Dr. Michael G. Long, Elizabethtown College, November 6 and 8, 2007.

state control is expanded through a proliferation of laws that can cover all eventualities.[1]

I can think of only four reasons why people would want to obey all these laws. (1) Some people may regard these laws as good and just. Although no one has detailed knowledge of all the legal codes, a more general familiarity with statutes proscribing murder, robbery, and so forth may contribute to the impression that these regulations are designed for our own good. (2) Some people fear the penalties for disobedience. Again, while we do not know the laws, we live in the hope that we will not run afoul of them.[2] (3) Some loyal citizens believe in law and order and are convinced that, even if some laws are silly or draconian, people may not pick and choose the laws they will obey lest the whole system come unraveled. Working carefully within the system to effectuate the amendment or revocation of certain laws is always better than defiance. (4) The last possibility, and certainly the most alarming, is that we human beings have a natural proclivity to obey authority. We need not pause to delve into the question of whether this predisposition is "natural" in a fundamental, biological sense related to brain chemicals and firing neurons, or whether instead it arises from our shared experience of having passed through infancy totally dependent on parents or other authority figures.[3] We are

1. Jacques Ellul commented on the manner in which proliferating laws reduce lawyers and judges to mere technicians who need only to apply laws rather than interpret them. There is no need for abstractions like "justice" to enter into courtroom deliberations. The proliferation of laws is both a cause and a consequence of the expansion of state power. "The state, whenever it expresses itself, makes laws. There are no longer any norms to regulate the activity of the state; it has eliminated the moral rules that judged it and absorbed the legal rules that guided it. The state is a law unto itself and recognizes no rules but its own will." Ellul, *The Technological Society*, trans. John Wilkinson (New York: Vintage Books, 1964), p. 299.

2. The Inspector said to K., "I can't even confirm that you are charged with an offense, or rather I don't know whether you are. You are under arrest, certainly, more than that I do not know." Franz Kafka, *The Trial*, trans. Willa and Edwin Muir (New York: Schocken Books, 1968), p. 12.

3. Also, we will not explore the significant question of whether the predisposition to obey authority is more pronounced in Western cultures. The classic experimental work on obedience to authority was conducted in the United States. Stanley Milgram, *Obedience to Authority: An Experimental View* (New York: Harper Torchbooks, 1975). In the United States, the land of liberty, why not obey the democratically elected authorities of this free nation? Evil could not happen here. In the early twentieth century, Germans were justifiably proud that their nation had been homeland to the world's greatest musicians, philosophers, scientists, and theologians. Why not obey the enlightened authorities of such a civilized land? Evil could not happen there.

social animals, certainly, but are we also herd animals, moving to and fro to the sounds of cracking whips and barking dogs or (more simply and pathetically) to the feel of shifting winds and public opinions?

If we conform too readily and obey too fawningly, the Western philosophical tradition offers some rather unsavory models for breaking away from the herd. For Friedrich Nietzsche and Charles Baudelaire, the route out of slavishness is found by the *Übermenschen*, the blond beasts who dare to move beyond good and evil.[4] For the Marquis de Sade and Jean Genet, the path away from conformity passes through an underworld of criminality. These are models suggesting that, to break away from the herd, one must either rise up to assert superiority to mere mortals or sink down to wallow in the mire. Since we already know that the flight of the superman crosses rather quickly into the territory of Nazism and other horrors, let us foreswear that trajectory and briefly follow the other path instead. Let us go to prison to inquire whether that can be the setting for liberation.

Can we learn a thing or two from prisoners who, no matter their moral failings, have at least shown themselves to be capable of disobeying authority? In liberation struggles of the modern era, there have been occasional efforts to overburden and clog the system of oppression by filling the prison cells with disobedient people who refused cooperation with injustice. Then, come the revolution, the Bastille is stormed, the prison gates thrown open. With Gandhi in India under British rule, with Mandela in South Africa under apartheid, going to prison was not a mark of shame but of honor. King spoke of filling the prison cell with dignity.

But several factors argue against any notion that prisoners might offer an antidote to our proclivity for obedience. First, the political context in twenty-first-century America is not one of radical or revolutionary struggle. We live in an imperial state with a politics that has been variously described as conservative, neoliberal, or even "friendly fascist."[5] Second, we live in a society of *mass* imprisonment, with a prison infrastructure that is in much better shape than the infrastructures of our transportation, edu-

---

4. Nietzsche regarded compassion and mercy as slavish instincts. I am more familiar with his writings than with those by Baudelaire. For a discussion of Baudelaire's composition, "Let's Bludgeon the Poor," see Claire Ortiz Hill, *The Roots and Flowers of Evil in Baudelaire, Nietzsche, and Hitler* (Chicago: Open Court, 2006), pp. 24-26.

5. Bertram Gross, *Friendly Fascism: The New Face of Power in America* (Boston: South End Press, 1980).

cation, or health care systems. If there are any illusions of launching a nonviolent movement of noncooperation that could overburden the prison system, the state is prepared with prisons aplenty. Third, and perhaps most obvious, the people in America's prisons today do not necessarily offer a paradigm for healthy disobedience. Once incarcerated, most prisoners will obey when they are forced to do so, and many will build up powerful reservoirs of rage and resentment.[6] The vast majority of these people will be returning eventually to live in our neighborhoods.

Along with confinement, the key to eliciting obedience from prisoners is perpetual surveillance. In the late eighteenth century, Jeremy Bentham, the father of utilitarianism, proposed a model prison that he called "Panopticon" (opticon, seeing — pan, everything). Bentham arranged tiers of cells in a circular pattern around a central tower. From within the tower, a single guard would be able to observe any of the hundreds of prisoners arrayed around him, but Bentham included a series of blinds that would prevent prisoners from knowing if they were being observed at any particular moment. Through surveillance that was theoretically perpetual, the goal was for the prisoner to internalize the policing function, to become his or her own prison guard.[7] If the lives of lawbreakers can be reformed by placing them under the gaze of authorities who never rest or blink, perhaps such scrutiny can serve to improve the character of the rest of us as well. Through security cameras in shopping malls and on busy city streets, through monitoring of Internet and phone communications,

---

6. The classic study on the psychological toll of these totalitarian institutions was conducted by Philip Zimbardo, "The Psychological Power and Pathology of Imprisonment," *Society* 9, no. 6 (April 1972): 4-8. Zimbardo traces the toll on both the keepers and the kept. If the harsh and punitive environment of the prison invades the minds and spirits of the prisoners, the same must be said of prison guards.

7. The way in which the Panopticon was supposed to foster the internalization of surveillance and control is traced in greater detail by Michel Foucault, *Discipline and Punish: The Birth of the Prison*, trans. Alan Sheridan (New York: Vintage Books, 1979), pp. 195-228. It should be noted that, if prisoners are subjected to perpetual surveillance, the prison itself is hidden from public view. While older prisons were located in or near large cities, newer prisons are located in areas that are "virtually uninhabited," the description that also applies to the locales deemed suitable for the storage of toxic waste. Is this concealment a way for society to deny its punitive nature? More likely, it is an intentional effort to render these perpetually observed prisoners invisible to the larger society. Philip Slater noted that, although our society claims to prize community and family values, the "problem people" are removed from visibility — the emotionally disturbed to psychiatric hospitals, the elderly to nursing homes, the poor to urban slums and rural hollows. Slater, *The Pursuit of Loneliness: American Culture at the Breaking Point* (Boston: Beacon Press, 1970), p. 15.

through airport watch lists and body scans, the penal ideology of perpetual surveillance has seeped through the prison walls.[8]

The prison is not a recent innovation, nor is Bentham's model the first or last proposal for prison reform. Indeed, the prison is such a magnet for reform that one cannot help but wonder if there is something about the institution that cannot be fixed. In one form or another — as a cage, as a house of detention, as a pit in the ground into which people were thrown — the prison has been around for as long as the state itself, which is to say, for five or six thousand years. During much of that time, the detention area was merely designed to hold people until the real punishments could be inflicted, punishments that might include forfeiture of property, exile, mutilation, or execution.[9] The idea that imprisonment should *be* the punishment was the product of reform. In the eighteenth and nineteenth centuries, well-meaning reformers like John Howard and Elizabeth Fry in England and Quakers and Protestant evangelicals in America proposed that, rather than hanging offenders or whipping them in the public square, lawbreakers should be sentenced to imprisonment. And what would prisoners be doing while serving their sentences? The recommendation of the Christian reformers was that the prisoners ought to be doing penance. Impose a regimen of silence, place each prisoner in an individual cell ("cell" being a monastic term referring to the rooms of monks and nuns), give each prisoner a Bible, and watch the wonderful transformation take place. In the silent halls of the first penitentiary in Philadelphia, prisoners were slowly driven mad.[10] It was time for another reform, and in keeping with the values of capitalist societies, the next reform focused on work. Per-

8. Foucault noted "the way in which a form of punitive system . . . covers the entirety of a society." Michel Foucault, *Power/Knowledge: Selected Interviews and Other Writings, 1972-1977*, ed. Colin Gordon (New York: Pantheon Books, 1980), p. 68.

9. This is not to suggest that imprisonment was always of short duration in ancient societies. As a prisoner of war, King Jehoiachin spent 37 years in a Babylonian prison (2 Kings 25:27; Jeremiah 52:31). Although pretrial detention was the most common use for the prison, Ezra 7:26 cites imprisonment along with execution, banishment, and confiscation of property as possible penalties for violation of the law.

10. David J. Rothman, *The Discovery of the Asylum: Social Order and Disorder in the New Republic* (Boston: Little, Brown and Company, 1971), pp. 79-88. While the penitentiary had been intended as an alternative to corporal punishment, American prisons quickly became the setting for physical abuse. The torture included beatings, suspensions from ceilings and walls with chains, and "water cribs" to simulate drowning. See David J. Rothman, *Conscience and Convenience: The Asylum and Its Alternatives in Progressive America* (Boston: Little, Brown and Company, 1980), p. 20.

haps what the prisoners lacked was not penance but a sufficient appreciation for hard labor. In the nineteenth century in Reading Gaol in England,
prisoners spent their days moving huge piles of rocks from one section of
the prison yard to another and then moving them back again. In America,
the Auburn and Elmira Reformatories emphasized work that would be
productive, including farming and manufacturing. To avoid the impression of slavery, however, subsequent reforms have urged that the compulsory work should be understood as "job training," and that prisoners
should also receive education and "treatment" with counseling and
psychotropic medications.[11] Prison reform is the persistent quest to find
the magic formula that will reform the prisoners into the very image of no
one so much as the reformers themselves.

But the prison system in the United States today is unlike the thing that
the reformers of earlier eras tried to tweak and prod. It is huge. It is monstrous. America has become a society of mass incarceration with over 2.2
million people locked up in jails and prisons.[12] That figure represents one
percent of the adult population of the country, but when we add to that the
numbers of people who are on probation and parole, three percent of all
Americans are under the direct supervision of the so-called "system of justice."[13] In a moment, we will look at who these people are, but first we must
be attentive to the fact that this is the highest per capita rate of imprisonment in the world. We have often heard the statistics that, with five percent
of the world's population, the United States consumes twenty-five percent
of the world's resources and produces twenty-five percent of the world's
greenhouse gases. A figure that we hear less often is that the United States
also has twenty-five percent of the world's prisoners.[14]

The U.S. per capita rate of imprisonment is far greater than that of Rus-

11. Angela Davis notes that the development and reform of prisons in the United States
has been influenced, not only by European models and precedents, but also by the American experience of slavery. When the thirteenth amendment to the U.S. Constitution was
passed in 1865, it abolished slavery "except as punishment for a crime. . . ." Davis observes
that, in the years following the Civil War, one way to deal with former slaves was to return
them to enslavement in the prison. Davis, "Racialized Punishment and Prison Abolition," in
The Angela Y. Davis Reader, ed. Joy James (Malden, Mass.: Blackwell, 1998), pp. 96-97.

12. Donna Leinwand, "Prison, Jail Populations on the Rise," USA Today (May 22, 2006):
3A.

13. Angela Davis, "Race and Criminalization: Black Americans and the Punishment In-
dustry," in Davis Reader, pp. 63-64.

14. Daniel Lazare, "Stars and Bars," The Nation 285, no. 6 (August 27–September 3,
2007): 29.

sia, China, Cuba, or any "axis of evil" country, although there are no reliable numbers for the closed society of North Korea. Where the facts and figures are available, however, there is a high degree of correlation between rates of imprisonment in a given nation and that nation's level of militarism as measured by the amount of money spent on armed forces. The U.S. spends more on the military than the next thirty highest spending nations *combined*. While not approaching the levels of the United States, China and Russia also have high levels of military spending and high rates of imprisonment. This correlation is unsurprising because the police are, in fact, the domestic military.[15] The society that seeks to control events abroad through force will do likewise at home. I am a prison abolitionist because I am opposed to militarism. I am a prison abolitionist because I believe that a society that locks up one percent of its population is not free. The prison is a totalitarian institution, and a society that is engaged in the expansion and enhancement of totalitarian institutions is not free.

And the prison system has been expanding. Last year alone, there was a two and one-half percent increase in the prison population even though crime rates had been falling for more than a decade.[16] The decade before

15. Throughout most of history, there was no differentiation between soldiers and police. Therefore, when the early church prohibited converts from bearing the sword, no distinction was made between the sword that was wielded in warfare and the sword that was wielded to maintain domestic order. In the "Apostolic Tradition" of Hippolytus, the same recommendation applied to catechumens who held the office of magistrate and those who carried the sword: ". . . let him give it up or be dismissed." Jean-Michel Hornus, *It Is Not Lawful for Me to Fight: Early Christian Attitudes toward War, Violence, and the State*, trans. Alan Kreider and Oliver Coburn (Scottdale, Pa.: Herald Press, 1980), pp. 159-60. It was not until much later that there was an effort to differentiate between military and domestic policing functions. In England, one of the earliest such efforts was the Statute of Winchester drafted by Edward I in 1283. Christopher Hibbert, *The Roots of Evil: A Social History of Crime and Punishment* (New York: Minerva Press, 1968), pp. 12-14.

In the United States, there has been a recent trend toward reintegration of military and domestic policing functions, with the FBI conducting investigations overseas and the CIA assisting with domestic surveillance. The militarization of domestic police forces was hastened in the 1970s with the creation of Special Weapons and Tactics (SWAT) teams. Today, there are routine transfers of equipment and technology from the military to civilian police forces at the state and local level. Christian Parenti, *Lockdown America: Police and Prisons in the Age of Crisis* (New York: Verso, 2000), pp. 23, 133-35.

16. Leinwand, "Prison, Jail Populations on the Rise." Since this chapter was written, there were slight reductions in the size of inmate populations in twenty-six U.S. states in 2009. For the first time in decades, a few states even closed some prisons. These changes came as states faced financial crises in the wake of the worst U.S. recession of the modern

that, the prison population was increasing as crime rates were rising. Crime increases, prisons expand. Crime decreases, prisons expand. If prisons were the solution to crime, crime rates would fall or rise with the expansion or contraction of the prison system, but the fact is, for half a century now, the U.S. has never had anything but an expanding prison system. In the U.S., the expansion of the prison system started as a response to the social unrest of the 1960s. In response to movements of resistance, the state often adopts two simultaneous strategies: (1) repression, with more police and more prisons, and (2) a response that would appear to be contradictory but is actually complementary, expansion of social welfare programs. An example of the latter in the 1960s was Lyndon Johnson's "war on poverty." Programs for the poor are not measures of government kindness but instruments of state control. As Frances Piven and Richard Cloward show in their book, *Regulating the Poor*, all the way back to early modern Europe, these welfare programs expanded during times of unrest and contracted when order was restored without regard to the actual rates of poverty in a given society.[17] The police and prison systems in the U.S. have been on a different trajectory. They expanded during a time of social unrest, and they continued to expand during the upward redistribution of wealth under Reagan, Bush I, Clinton, and Bush II.[18] In years when crime falls, police and prison bureaucrats rush to federal and state capitals to declare that they are succeeding and that they need more money so they can be even more effective in the war on crime. In years when crime rises, these same bureaucrats rush to the capitals to complain that their resources are inadequate in the face of new crime waves. So, no matter its ballyhooed success or its acknowledged failure, the penal system grows. Most publicly funded institutions do not get away with that tactic.

And most privately funded institutions do not get away with it either. In the United States, there are growing numbers of corporate-owned, for-profit prisons. This is big business, with corporate lobbyists joining pro-

era. Sasha Abramsky, "Is This the End of the War on Crime?" *The Nation* 291, no. 1 (July 5, 2010): 11-17. Abramsky optimistically wonders if this may be the beginning of a societal turn away from reliance on mass incarceration. I wish it were so, but I fear that, like other forms of miltarism, the war on crime will survive recessionary pressures.

17. Frances Fox Piven and Richard A. Cloward, *Regulating the Poor: The Functions of Public Welfare* (New York: Vintage Books, 1971).

18. Parenti argues that there is more than a coincidental link between the increasing severity of sentences and the upward redistribution of wealth. Parenti, *Lockdown America*, pp. 45-50.

fessional organizations of wardens, guards, and police in campaigning for legislatures to allocate more money for the penal system. In some states, the police and the Department of Corrections are vying with education and health care for top billing in the budgets.[19] Also part of the big money picture, some states have begun promoting prisons as providing cheap and reliable labor pools for corporations.[20] I am a prison abolitionist because I believe that big money should not set the agenda for any society.

Some prison abolitionists say that the first step in the right direction would be a moratorium on new prison construction.[21] Proponents of new prisons claim that building is another humanitarian reform designed to ease overcrowding. Such claims notwithstanding, most new prisons are already scheduled to be overcrowded before construction is complete. If you build them, they will be filled. Judges and lawmakers need to be told that there is no more room in the cages.

Earlier, I cited the falling crime rate of the past decade, but that has not applied across the board. In the past two years, as other categories of crime have fallen in the United States, there have been increases in the violent crimes of assault, rape, and murder. A spike in violent crimes is not unusual for a nation in a time of war. While theologians and philosophers dating back to Erasmus and Thomas More have hypothesized that participation in warfare contributed to increases in domestic murder rates, the first comparative, cross-national study of crime was conducted less than three decades ago by Dane Archer and Rosemary Gartner.[22] Their study examined data spanning much of the twentieth century, and while there

---

19. The police and the Department of Corrections are winning. Following a surge of new prison construction in California in the 1980s and '90s, California's colleges and universities shed 8,000 jobs while the Department of Corrections added 26,000 new employees. Mike Davis, "The Politics of Super Incarceration," in *Criminal Injustice: Confronting the Prison Crisis*, ed. Elihu Rosenblatt (Boston: South End Press, 1996), pp. 74-75.

20. One California Department of Corrections brochure encouraged potential employers of prisoners to consider the benefits of not having to provide vacation pay, medical coverage, or retirements plans, along with the added benefits of "no car breakdowns, no babysitting problems." Angela Davis observes that Americans are concerned over outsourcing jobs to Third World countries, but there is little awareness of the exploitation of cheap labor pools in U.S. prisons. Davis, "Race and Criminalization," in *Davis Reader*, p. 68.

21. Moratorium proposals are prominent in the classic work by Fay Honey Knopp et al., *Instead of Prisons: A Handbook for Abolitionists* (Syracuse: Prison Research Education Action Project, 1976), pp. 64-80.

22. Archer and Gartner, *Violence and Crime in Cross-National Perspective* (New Haven: Yale University Press, 1984).

were holes in the data for some countries during some time frames, Archer and Gartner were able to discern a clear pattern regarding murder rates. In the United States, where there are more gun dealers than gas stations,[23] the murder rates have been persistently higher than in most other nations. But for all nations, including the U.S., there was a statistically significant pattern of increased domestic murder rates during times of war.[24] While the pattern applied across the board for nations at war, the countries with the largest increases in domestic murder rates were those that were winning their wars. Archer and Gartner concluded that the state serves as a powerful model for the efficacy of violence as well as for its supposed moral justifiability.

There are a growing number of studies on the role of the state in modeling violence, but I'll cite just one more, this one having to do with capital punishment. William Bowers and Glenn Pierce of Northeastern University's Center for Social Research were able to assemble data on murders and executions in New York State between 1900 and 1963, the date of the last execution in the state. They plotted this data on timelines to see what, if anything, happened to murder rates in the month following an execution. They went into the research expecting to find no correlation between the two timelines, which would have indicated that executions did nothing to deter murders. But that's not what they found. They found a correlation between the two timelines so consistent that they were able to arrive at a statistical average. On average, in the month following an execution in New York State, there were two *additional* murders in the state. Bowers and Pierce attributed this to what they called the "brutalization effect" of capital punishment. While executions may be intended to convey the message that it's wrong to commit murder, they are actually conveying the very different message that there is nothing wrong with killing bad people, and the determination of who those bad people are is very much in the eye of the beholder.[25]

23. Noted by Richard J. Payne, *The Clash with Distant Cultures: Values, Interests, and Force in American Foreign Policy* (Albany: State University of New York Press, 1995), pp. 58-59.

24. After several years of decline in the rates of violent crime, the U.S. murder rate doubled during the war in Vietnam. Archer and Gartner, *Violence and Crime in Cross-National Perspective*, p. 68.

25. William Bowers and Glenn Pierce, "Deterrence or Brutalization: What Is the Effect of Executions?" *Crime and Delinquency* 26 (October 1980): 453ff. The findings of Bowers and Pierce have been supported by studies comparing the murder rates in states and countries that have abolished the death penalty with those in jurisdictions that have retained it. See

But our focus is on the abolition of prisons, and not on the abolition of the death penalty. No matter the flaws of the prison system, most people would argue that at least prisons serve to protect society from murderers and other violent predators. In fact, of the people in America's jails and prisons today, less than twenty percent have been convicted of violent crimes and less than five percent have been convicted of murder. Thirty percent have been convicted of property crimes and over thirty percent have been convicted of drug offenses.[26]

I am a prison abolitionist because I believe that justice should be about peacemaking and reconciliation.[27] Justice should be about mediation and conflict resolution. Justice should lead us to determine the actual harm that a victim has suffered and to strive for restoration — insofar as possible, restoring the well-being of those who have suffered harm, and restoring the offender to community.[28] Prisons serve none of these purposes.

Indeed, when close to one-third of all prisoners are doing time for drug offenses, it is not clear that anyone has suffered harm as a result of these crimes, with the possible exception of the offenders themselves and their loved ones. Even in the cases of other crimes that result in actual harm to clearly identifiable victims, the prosecution of these cases is not depicted as the victim versus the accused defendant, but rather as the U.S. versus the

---

"Death Penalty Facts and Figures: Exploding the Myths," in *Criminal Injustice*, pp. 199-200. The idea that the trauma of the survivors of murder victims might somehow be eased by executions is renounced by members of groups like Murder Victims' Families for Reconciliation.

26. Lazare, "Stars and Bars," p. 29. It should be noted that a murder conviction in the U.S. today does not require evidence that the accused has ever killed anyone, nor even that he or she has ever wielded a weapon. When there is a killing in the commission of a crime such as robbery, all who participated in the robbery can be charged with murder, even if they were not in the vicinity of the killing and gave no consent to it.

27. Peacemaking and reconciliation belong together. If reconciliation is discounted, it is too easy to adopt the cynical view that peace is achieved when all potential adversaries have been consigned to the graveyard or the prison. When weapons are regarded as "peacemakers," which is what Samuel Colt called his revolvers, then there can be no coherent differentiation between warmaking and peacemaking. Colt's appellation for his revolvers is cited by Michael A. Bellesiles, *Arming America: The Origins of a National Gun Culture* (Brooklyn: Soft Skull Press, 2003), p. 430. During the Reagan Administration, the MX missile was also dubbed "the Peacemaker."

28. In the biblical view, God's justice is always expressed as the will to restore — to restore community and to restore the covenant between community and God. This is why, as Jacques Ellul notes, God's judgment is always followed by pardon. In pursuit of restoration, God's justice is neither distributive nor retributive but substitutive justice. Ellul, *The Theological Foundation of Law*, trans, Marguerite Wieser (New York: Seabury Press, 1969), pp. 43, 88.

accused, or the Commonwealth of Pennsylvania versus the accused. How did this develop that the state is now depicted as the victim of all crime and the people who have suffered actual harm are regarded as less relevant? The idea that the state is the victim of all crime can be traced back to some mystical, theological notions attached to the monarchy in medieval Europe, especially in England. Through some tortured theologizing that we need not trace here, the monarch's divine right to rule was grounded in a belief that the monarch actually had two bodies.[29] First, there was the commonplace, physical body of whatever mortal happened to wear the crown, but then there was a second, mystical body that was coextensive with the realm. A crime that was committed anywhere within the realm was an offense against the king or queen, and whatever debt was incurred by the offender was owed to the monarch. Later, this idea of the monarch's two bodies would have unfortunate consequences for a few kings when some discontented subjects asserted that, in defense of the realm and of the monarchy, they needed to get rid of the particular mortal who happened to be wearing the crown. At any rate, it was from this strange medieval brew of politics and theology that the idea emerged that what offenders owe is a debt to society, not a debt to individuals who have suffered actual harm.[30]

Back in 1985, I visited a Chemung County Court Judge in his chambers in Elmira, New York. The only reason I was able to secure an appointment with the man was because I was serving as Campus Minister at Elmira College at the time, and apparently the position of "minister" carried favorable

---

29. The premier commentary on the history and theology of this notion is by Ernst H. Kantorowicz, *The King's Two Bodies: A Study in Medieval Political Theology* (Princeton, N.J.: Princeton University Press, 1957).

30. In early English law, prior to the medieval developments in political theology, when notice was taken of the victim of a crime, it did not necessarily mean that the actual victim would be compensated. The rank of both the offender and the victim determined the nature of the penalty that could be imposed and the identity of the person to whom compensation was paid. Under the laws of Ethelbert, if a female slave was raped, compensation was paid, not to the woman, but to the slaveholder, with greater penalties imposed if she was the slave of a nobleman rather than a commoner. If a freeman raped the slave of a commoner, the penalty was five shillings compensation to the owner. If a slave was found guilty of a similar crime, the slave was castrated. Rank also entered into the determination of the nature of the ordeals that were imposed to arrive at a finding of innocence or guilt. For those of lesser rank, the ordeal might entail immersing one's arm in boiling water or walking across red-hot plowshares, and if there were no blisters after three days, innocence was proven. Priests, on the other hand, were simply required to swear an oath to their innocence and successfully swallow a piece of consecrated bread in order to prove that they were not guilty of the charges against them. Hibbert, *Roots of Evil*, pp. 4-7.

connotations (quite undeserved in my case, I must confess). I phoned, and the secretary said, "Oh yes, Reverend, we can get an appointment for you." So, I went in to see the Judge, who immediately inquired, "Reverend, what can we do for you?" "Well," I explained, "All I'd like you to do is to let me take the place of a prisoner over Thanksgiving. I go in to get locked up on Wednesday evening and you let the prisoner go to spend Thanksgiving and the weekend with family and friends. Sunday evening, he comes back and I go home." The Judge asked, "Oh, is *that* all." And I said, "Well, not exactly. I'd like to do it at Christmas, too." The Judge's questions (all polite, seeing as how I'm a Reverend) started with the practical. How do we pick this prisoner? Since I had been volunteering inside the jail with a literacy program, perhaps we could choose one of my students, or it could be anyone who the Judge might suggest. "And what happens if this prisoner doesn't check back into the motel on Sunday night?" Well, I explained patiently, I would be taking the place of the prisoner, so I would be kept locked up until the prisoner returned or the sentence was served, with time off for good behavior if I deserved it. The Judge objected that there was no legal precedent for him to take such an action. In fact, I noted, the U.S. system of jurisprudence is based on the English system, and in seventeenth-century England, Quakers did exactly what I was proposing. If a prisoner had special needs, a Quaker would take the place of a prisoner for days or weeks or months.[31] If prisoners are paying a debt to society, it should not matter if someone helps them to pay it, the same as it does not matter to the bank if I give my neighbor some money to help her to pay for her mortgage. Well, the good Judge got a little more testy near the end of our visit. The prisoners *he* sentenced were not going to be getting any help paying their debt to society. But thanks for stopping by, Reverend.

The phrase "paying a debt to society" is a fundamental acknowledgement that the very definition of what constitutes a crime is fully divorced from any evaluation of what (if any) harm has been caused to real people or to genuine human communities. Actions are crimes or not based on the changing whims of legislative bodies.[32] Since the Harris Act of 1914, the

31. In April 1659, 164 Friends appeared in Parliament to ask that they be allowed to take the place of other Quakers who were suffering in prison. This particular proposal for a large-scale prisoner exchange was denied. Donald F. Durnbaugh, ed., *Every Need Supplied: Mutual Aid and Christian Community in the Free Churches*, Documents in Free Church History Series (Philadelphia: Temple University Press, 1974), p. 201.

32. On the definition of poverty as a crime in nineteenth-century England, see Sabina Virgo, "The Criminalization of Poverty," in *Criminal Injustice*, pp. 47-60. It is not unusual that

U.S. federal government has been involved in policing drug trafficking based on its power to tax interstate commerce. Prior to that, drug laws were under the purview of state and local governments, and enforcement efforts would ebb and flow with perceived threats to class and race.[33] So in the late 1800s, the perceived threat in the Northwest was the opium-smoking Chinese immigrants, in the Southwest it was the peyote-addled Natives and the coca-using Hispanics (never mind how a popular cola beverage got its name), and in the South and the urban areas of the North it was the black people driven wild by cannabis. The racism and classism of the war on drugs has not changed. Drug raids are conducted in South Central L.A., not on Wall Street. Nor has there been any change in the perception that the drug threat comes from "outside." The drug lords are Colombian or Mexican or Afghan — that is, the *illegal* drug lords. The *legal* drug lords are the perfectly respectable CEOs of the alcohol, tobacco, and pharmaceutical companies that continue to feed our Prozac nation. What has changed, beginning with the Nixon Administration in the late 1960s and growing to quite hysterical proportions, is that the federal government has become the driving force in drug criminalization. If state and local governments wish to qualify for federal funds, they need to join the "war on drugs." Is it an explosion of drug use and drug-related harm that has filled the prisons, or is it an explosion of criminalization, media hype, and vastly expanded policing that has created a society of mass incarceration?

Who are these prisoners? Sixty-five percent of all prisoners do not have a high school diploma. Prior to arrest, fifty-three percent earned less than $10,000 a year, with many being totally unemployed.[34] Does this mean that poor people are less honest and more violent than people of other socioeconomic classes? Does it mean that poor people are more likely to commit crimes, or does it mean that poor people are more vulnerable to arrest, prosecution, conviction, and imprisonment than are people with greater fi-

---

crime is simply equated with what the prevailing governmental authorities regard as sin or heresy. In seventeenth-century Massachusetts, blasphemy, adultery, and failure to observe the Sabbath were identified as crimes. Quakers were outlawed because their particular expression of faith tended to undermine authority. The preferred punishment for Quakers was banishment, but in 1659 and 1661, exiled Quakers who dared to return to Massachusetts were executed. Lawrence M. Friedman, *Crime and Punishment in American History* (New York: Basic Books, 1993), pp. 32-36.

33. Parenti, *Lockdown America*, p. 9.

34. Marc Mauer and The Sentencing Project, *Race to Incarcerate* (New York: The New Press, 2001), pp. 162-63.

nancial resources? Indeed, the poor are even more vulnerable than the wealthy in the very definition of what constitutes criminality. We are told that the law applies equally to everyone. The law that says that it is illegal to sleep on a park bench does not just apply to homeless people, but it applies to President Bush and to Governor Rendell as well. But the practical impact of that law is considerably different for the poor than for the wealthy, and the same is true for a whole host of other prohibitive laws governing everything from panhandling to hitchhiking to bouncing checks.

Who are these people in prison? In the U.S. today, half of all prisoners are African-American and another twenty percent are Hispanic. If you are born black and male in America, chances are nearly one in four that you will spend time in jail or prison.[35] Indeed, the risk of being incarcerated is much greater for simply being black and male than it is for committing a crime.[36] Black people are not genetically predisposed to crime; the juridical system is institutionally predisposed to racism.[37] The illusion that America has overcome the legacy of racism is promoted by focusing on the economic and political successes of several prominent African-Americans, but it is totally contradicted by the identity of the people in

35. Davis, "Racialized Punishment and Prison Abolition," in *Davis Reader*, pp. 104-5. Due to the disenfranchisement of ex-felons, one in four black men are prohibited from voting in the states of Alabama, Florida, Iowa, Mississippi, New Mexico, Virginia, and Wyoming. Mauer and Sentencing Project, *Race to Incarcerate*, p. 186.

36. While black males face a one in four risk of incarceration, two decades ago, Kevin Wright calculated that breaking the law carried only a one in sixty-seven risk of incarceration. Wright noted that one of three jailable offenses were reported, one of five reported offenses resulted in arrest, one of two people arrested were formally charged, nine of ten people who were charged were convicted, and one of two people who were convicted were sentenced to jail or prison, all of which works out to a one in sixty-seven chance of incarceration for committing a jailable offense. Kevin Wright, *The Great American Crime Myth* (New York: Praeger, 1987), p. 115. Such statistics support the assertion by Angela Davis that what the prison system punishes is race, not crime. Davis writes, "While academics and popular discourses assume a necessary conjunction between crime and punishment, it is the conjunction of race, class, and punishment that is most consistent.... While most imprisoned young black men may have broken a law, it is the fact that they are young black men rather than the fact that they are law-breakers which brings them into contact with the criminal justice system." Davis, "Racialized Punishment and Prison Abolition," in *Davis Reader*, pp. 104-5.

37. Marc Mauer cites the results of the National Youth Survey, which tracked the self-reported behaviors of 1,725 young people over two decades beginning in 1976. The survey examined the prevalence of assault, robbery, and rape in this cohort, and, while race was a major factor in the variations in rates of *arrest*, it was only a minor factor in the variations in rates of *offense*. Mauer and Sentencing Project, *Race to Incarcerate*, pp. 163-66.

prison. I am a prison abolitionist because prisons are a major manifestation of institutionalized racism and classism.

The trauma that the prison system inflicts on poor communities and communities of color is not limited to the people who are locked up. One of my colleagues where I work is a black woman whose son has a prior conviction for possession of marijuana. A few months ago, he was stopped again by the police. (Some officers believe that "driving while black" is sufficient cause for stopping motorists.) He was arrested again for possession of cannabis and for disorderly conduct because he cussed out the cop who had stopped him. My friend was not going to let her son sit in jail, so she shelled out a thousand dollars in bail money. On his previous arrest, he had a public defender who had met with him for a grand total of two minutes to encourage him to cop a plea. Since he's already on probation, his mother wanted him to have a more attentive lawyer this time, so she shelled out another thousand dollars as a retainer for a lawyer. Her checking account was almost depleted. She had been helping another son and his family with some money toward their mortgage, and she had been contributing generously to her A.M.E. church, but now she fears that she will have to limit her giving for awhile. So the people who have been punished so far include the young man who was arrested, his mother, his brother and his brother's family, the church, and the people served by the church — and the trial hasn't even started yet. Take this single example of ripple effect in the black community, multiply it by a million black prisoners, and what you have is not an example of justice at work; it is an example of the nitty-gritty functioning of racism in America.

Of course, penologists and those who are in charge of the American prison system do not believe that they are propagating racism, classism, or totalitarianism. What they believe they are doing is either rehabilitating prisoners or deterring crime or exacting just retribution or at times combinations of all three. Rehabilitation, deterrence, and retribution are the dominant ideological justifications for the prison system today.

Of the three, rehabilitation has been in eclipse. Some proponents of law and order fret that educating, training, or counseling prisoners is equivalent to coddling them, but some penologists still maintain that the rehabilitation model offers the best hope for lowering recidivism rates among offenders. I believe that there are at least three reasons why prisons are not viable tools of rehabilitation.

(1) Most cultures have rituals designed to label, shame, and stigmatize offenders, and in modern cultures, prosecution and imprisonment serve

that ritualistic function.[38] Institutions that are designed to stigmatize and segregate offenders are ill-suited to facilitate their reintegration into community. Prisons shatter family relationships and mark prisoners with a modern-day scarlet letter that makes them much less likely to be able to form friendships and find employment after their release.[39]

(2) Very little of the preventable loss of life and wealth in our society is caused by the people sitting in prison. Over sixty percent of American corporations have been found guilty of criminal violations,[40] but you can't imprison a corporation, and it's big news indeed when a corporate CEO is unfortunate enough to darken a prison cell. Since far more lives are lost to accidents than to murder, and far more private and public wealth is lost to laziness and incompetence than to burglary, I fail to understand why prisoners need rehabilitation any more than you or I do.

(3) The idea of rehabilitation suggests that offenders have abandoned societal values and that, through remedial work, they can be taught to embrace those values once again. The idea is flawed from the outset. Many offenders are affirming societal values, not rebelling against them. Thieves and perpetrators of fraud are affirming the value of greed in a hyper-capitalist society, and they are merely using different methods to get their piece of the pie. Gangs are affirming the territoriality of a nation that builds a fence along the southern border. Perpetrators of crimes against women are affirming the culture of sexism. Drug users are embracing the self-numbing escapism that others find through TV or Internet or con-

38. The classic psychological study of rituals of stigmatization is Frank Tannenbaum, "The Dramatization of Evil," in *Deviance: The Interactionist Perspective*, ed. Earl Rubington and Martin S. Weinberg, 2nd ed. (New York: Macmillan, 1973), pp. 214-15.

39. The political leaders who preach "traditional family values" pay little heed to the manner in which 2.2 million families have been torn apart by prisons. In New York State, offenders from New York City or Long Island are often sentenced to terms in Elmira or Attica, while upstate offenders are frequently sentenced to prisons near New York City, thus making family visits more expensive and less likely. In an era of mass incarceration, the prison is a major contributor to the creation of single-parent households (or, far too often, no-parent households). Mauer and Sentencing Project, *Race to Incarcerate*, p. 185. The laudable desire to protect children from harms like sexual predation does not extend so far as to protect them from the punitive impulses of the juridical system. In some states, 13-year-old children are routinely tried as adults. As the movement toward "quality of life policing" seeks to apprehend graffiti artists and window breakers, even younger children are being labeled as "gang members." Parenti, *Lockdown America*, pp. 66, 70-72.

40. The percentage has likely increased since this statistic was first cited by L. Harold DeWolf, *Crime and Justice in America: A Paradox of Conscience* (New York: Harper & Row, 1975), p. 12.

sumerism. Most absurd of all is the notion that murderers and other violent assailants are rejecting America's supposed valuing of human life. Oh yes, when there's an Oklahoma City bombing or a Columbine or Virginia Tech shooting, politicians shove their way to the front of the camera to proclaim, "We've just got to stop this violence in America," while they're spending half a million dollars a minute bombing Iraqis. I am a prison abolitionist because I don't believe that prisoners or anyone else should be rehabilitated or habituated to the values of the American Empire.

Along with rehabilitation, a second presumed justification for the prison system lies in the ideology of deterrence. Simply stated, deterrence theory holds that punishment prevents crime. If the theory of deterrence were consistently applied, however, the harshest penalties should be meted out for crimes with the highest rates of recidivism — crimes like shoplifting — while there would be little deterrence value in punishing crimes with low rates of repeat offense — crimes like murder. While random stranger-on-stranger murders and serial killings grab all the headlines, these are very rare indeed compared to the murders of family members, neighbors, and acquaintances.[41] This more prevalent murder of "loved ones" is often an impulsive, circumstantial crime of passion and rage and is least likely to be repeated or deterred.

Does deterrence work? Look for a moment at Tyburn Hill in eighteenth-century London. Historical data indicates that Tyburn was one of the locales where the good citizens of London were most likely to be victimized by pickpockets. For the successful plying of their trade, pickpockets need crowded areas with people bumping into one another. They need spectacles that distract people, and the citizens of London gathered on Tyburn Hill for an interesting spectacle indeed — public hangings. The snapping of necks provided the perfect distraction for the lifting of wallet or purse. Since such pilfering was a capital crime in eighteenth-century England, some of those being hanged were certainly pickpockets.[42] As Karl Menninger observed two centuries later, the thing that punishment deters is not crime but getting caught.[43]

41. Wright, *Great American Crime Myth*, p. 24.

42. In 1940, Malcolm X referred to the pickpockets of Tyburn Hill when his debating team from Norfolk Correctional Facility debated the team from MIT on the proposition, "The Death Penalty is Ineffective as a Deterrent." Arguing in the affirmative, the team from Norfolk won the debate. Cited by Peter Linebaugh, *The London Hanged: Crime and Civil Society in the Eighteenth Century,* 2nd ed. (New York: Verso, 2003), p. xxii.

43. Menninger, *The Crime of Punishment* (New York: Viking Press, 1969), p. viii.

Does deterrence work? Although U.S. courts typically impose harsher penalties than their European counterparts, crime rates in the United States exceed those in Europe for almost every category of offense. In some U.S. jurisdictions, the sentence for murder might be life in prison without parole or even execution, but for each year of the past three decades, U.S. homicide rates have been between five and ten times greater than those in Europe.[44] Between 1985 and 1995, the number of drug offenders in prison grew by 605 percent, and yet in 1997, Barry McCaffrey, who was then director of the Office of National Drug Control Policy, reported that "if measured solely in terms of price and purity, cocaine, heroin, and marijuana prove to be more available than they were a decade ago."[45]

But my problem with the idea of deterrence has less to do with its lack of effectiveness than with its fundamental lack of fairness and its disregard for human dignity. There are actually two theories of deterrence, specific and general. Specific deterrence contends that the individual being punished will be dissuaded from future offense. With general deterrence, individual punishment is intended to set an example that will deter the criminality within the rest of us. Like a George Bush war, preemption is the goal of both specific and general deterrence. The punishment is not intended to fit some crime that has been committed; it must fit some potential or imaginary crime in the future. With such a rationale for punishment, we move *Through the Looking-Glass*:

> The Queen said, "Here is the King's messenger. He is in prison now being punished and the trial does not even begin until next Wednesday, and of course, the crime comes last of all."
> "But suppose he never commits the crime?" asked Alice.
> "That would be all the better, wouldn't it?" the Queen responded.
> Alice felt there was no denying that. "Of course it would be all the better," she said, "but it wouldn't be all the better his being punished."
> "You are wrong," said the Queen. "Were you ever punished?"
> "Only for faults," said Alice.
> "And you were all the better for it I know," the Queen said triumphantly.

44. Lazare, "Stars and Bars," p. 30.
45. The statistic and the McCaffrey quotation are cited by Mauer and Sentencing Project, *Race to Incarcerate*, p. 191.

"Yes, but I had done the things I was punished for," said Alice. "That makes all the difference."

"But if you hadn't done them," the Queen said, "that would have been better still, better, better and better!"[46]

With deterrence theory, people are regarded as mere means toward the achievement of the supposed higher goal of reducing crime. I am a prison abolitionist because I believe that people should never be treated as mere tools. By the standards of deterrence, the worst role model imaginable is Jesus of Nazareth. "But I say to you that listen, Love your enemies, do good to those who hate you, bless those who curse you, pray for those who abuse you" (Luke 6:27-28).

The ideology of retribution is not concerned with whether prisoners are rehabilitated or crime is deterred. The very essence of justice, say the advocates of retribution, is that people should get what they deserve. If people act in a way that deserves to be punished, withholding punishment

46. Numerous commentaries on deterrence theory quote this passage from Lewis Carroll's *Through the Looking-Glass*. See, for example, Knopp, et al., *Instead of Prisons*, p. 111.

47. Consistent advocates of retribution might contend that God acted unjustly by marking Cain for protection (Genesis 4:13-15). Indeed, the qualities of mercy and grace are obstacles to the pursuit of retributive "justice." But one of the problems with retributive theory is that there is no objective set of criteria for determining what we each deserve. How is it determined that gay people "deserve" execution in Saudi Arabia and human rights in the Netherlands? One would need to believe in a literal transmigration of souls to argue that a child born into a wealthy family somehow "deserves" a better start in life than a child born in the slums of Port-au-Prince.

Likewise, there are no objective criteria for determining what offenders deserve. Many U.S. states have enacted "three strikes, you're out" legislation allowing (or even mandating) sentences of life in prison without the possibility of parole for offenders convicted of three felonies. After California passed a "three strikes, you're out" law, Governor Pete Wilson began arguing in favor of a "two strikes, you're out" bill. Angela Davis comments, "Soon we will hear calls for 'one strike, you're out.' Following this mathematical regression, we can imagine that at some point the hardcore anticrime advocates will be arguing that to stop the crime wave, we can't wait until even one crime is committed." Davis notes that, since certain populations have already been criminalized, there can be no doubt that those who will be targeted before the first strike will be black or brown and poor. Davis, "Race and Criminalization," in *Davis Reader*, p. 66. Actually, some prominent public figures have already proposed variations of "no strikes, you're out." Dr. Arnold Hutschnecker, President Nixon's physician, proposed that psychological testing be administered to all schoolchildren at the age of six so that those with violent tendencies could be sent to special camps for treatment. Jessica Mitford, *Kind and Usual Punishment: The Prison Business* (New York: Alfred A. Knopf, 1973), p. 56.

is a denial of justice.[47] "Eye for eye, tooth for tooth" (Exodus 21:24; Leviticus 24:20; Deuteronomy 19:21). This *lex talionis* passage from the Hebrew Bible is often read as a call for revenge, but even without the radical redefinition of *lex talionis* by Jesus (Matthew 5:38-39), its function in ancient Israel was to place limits on retaliation. Neither retribution nor restitution may exceed the scale of the actual injury that was suffered in an offense. If you steal my sheep, I get my sheep back and maybe one of yours as well (Deuteronomy 22:1-13). Crime is a disruption of covenant, and the answer to crime is a restoration of fairness and covenant.

Tell me what is wrong with this scenario. You break into my house and steal a hundred dollars. As a result, I get nothing, but you get a year in jail, a thousand dollar fine, and the loss of your job and maybe your family as well. That is not an eye for an eye. That is mean-spirited vengeance, and vengeance is a downward spiral. Most prisoners will get out someday, and some will be getting out with an eye to exacting retribution for what's been done to them. "Turn the other cheek" is a way of saying that retaliation and vengeance must stop with me. The judicial system says to the offender, retaliation must stop with you. You must be of better moral character than the judicial system itself.

With retribution, all the focus is on the offenders rather than on the victims and survivors of crime. Hundreds of billions of dollars are spent on apprehending, prosecuting, and punishing offenders, while very little is spent on addressing the needs of the victims of crime. Prisons increase the suffering of offenders while doing nothing to diminish the suffering of victims. I am a prison abolitionist because I believe that any system that has the net effect of increasing suffering does not deserve the title "justice."

So what does a prison abolitionist do about crime? In a form that I admit is too brief, allow me to list some ideas:

(1) Decriminalize. If it is not an action that is causing harm to a person against his or her own will, it is not a crime. Addiction certainly clouds the question of volition, but no more so for illegal drugs than for substances that are not outlawed. Is the person who is using illegal drugs engaging in self-harm? Yes. Is it more harm than eating greasy hamburgers? It probably depends on the type of illegal drug that is being used. Is it more harm than smoking cigarettes? Probably not. Does the use of illegal drugs contribute to more accidental death or injury than the use of alcohol or prescription medications? Probably not.

(2) When people have suffered harm, criminal justice should be about peacemaking and conflict resolution. Criminal justice should employ me-

diation in an effort to restore victims to well-being and offenders to community.[48] Whenever possible, justice should strive for reconciliation.[49] Instead of being devoted to punishment, resources should be devoted to victims for property restitution and, if need be, for medical care and counseling for trauma.

(3) If criminal justice is going to be about peacemaking, then we need alternatives to SWAT teams and the domestic military. Advocates of nonviolence who are unwilling to wield guns themselves might well be un-

---

48. In Canada and the United States, the Victim Offender Reconciliation Program has been a helpful model for mediation efforts. VORP was begun by Mennonites in Kitchener, Ontario, in 1974 and in Elkhart, Indiana, in 1977. For an introduction to the history and objectives of VORP, see Howard Zehr, *Changing Lenses: A New Focus for Crime and Justice* (Scottdale, Pa.: Herald Press, 1990), pp. 158-74. In New Zealand, Maori traditions of communal mediation and Celtic traditions of restitution have contributed to the establishment of several programs that offer alternatives to retribution. While cycles of retribution tear communities apart, Maori and Celtic traditions are resonant with the Hebrew vision of *shalom* as communal restoration. See Jim Consedine, *Restorative Justice: Healing the Effects of Crime* (Lyttelton, New Zealand: Ploughshares Publications, 1995), and Jim Consedine and Helen Bowen, eds., *Restorative Justice: Contemporary Themes and Practice* (Lyttelton, New Zealand: Ploughshares Publications, 1999). There has been justifiable concern that these programs of mediation, restoration, and reconciliation will become mere "add-ons" to a punitive system rather than alternatives to it. To maintain the integrity of alternatives, Dutch criminologist Herman Bianchi has proposed reviving the biblical practice of sanctuary so that offenders and victims have space and time in which they are shielded from the judicial system in order to work toward a restorative settlement. In effect, Bianchi is proposing a dual system to address criminal offense. Unfortunately, under Bianchi's proposal, the current system remains intact, but the revival of sanctuary could be an important first step in reducing reliance on the punitive paradigm. For an introduction to Bianchi's ideas and the responses to them, see David Cayley, *The Expanding Prison: The Crisis in Crime and Punishment and the Search for Alternatives* (Toronto: Anansi Press, 1998), pp. 317-29.

49. For a good, brief summary of the distinctions among forgiveness, pardon, and reconciliation, see the poignant and insightful book by Donald B. Kraybill, Steven M. Nolt, and David L. Weaver-Zercher, *Amish Grace: How Forgiveness Transcended Tragedy* (San Francisco: Jossey-Bass, 2007), pp. 126-28. These authors look to Amish faith and tradition as well as to current psychological and sociological studies on forgiveness to understand Amish responses to the horrible shooting of ten Amish schoolgirls in Nickel Mines, Pennsylvania, in 2006. Forgiveness is the process in which the forgiving person, while not forgetting the offense, moves from feelings of anger and resentment to regard the offender with unmerited generosity. Forgiveness requires no involvement from the offender. Pardon, however, requires that the offender acknowledge guilt while the person who has suffered harm acts to free the offender from the legal consequences of wrongdoing. Reconciliation is the movement toward initiating or reestablishing a relationship of trust between the offender and the one who has suffered harm.

willing to call upon the police to wield guns on their behalf. Groups like Peace Brigades International, Witness for Peace, Voices in the Wilderness, Nonviolent Peaceforce, Christian Peacemaker Teams, and Muslim Peacemaker Teams have been creating and employing models for nonviolent intervention in the midst of wars.[50] We need similar models for nonviolent intervention in the midst of crimes.[51]

(4) We need to stop stigmatizing people. On the international front, all evil is loaded onto a caricature of "Islamic terrorists." On the home front, it is a caricature of "child molesters." Stigmatizing achieves nothing but an accumulation of public rage. It does nothing to alleviate the likelihood of harm. In fact, if you want to create a monster, the quickest way to do it is to tell someone incessantly, "You are a monster."[52] Which brings us to . . .

(5) As a society, we need to decide whether we want to differentiate between harm that is inflicted as the result of a conscious and witting decision and harm that is inflicted under the influence of psychosis, auditory

---

50. On the history and experiences of the Christian Peacemaker Teams, see Tricia Gate Brown, ed., *Getting in the Way: Stories from Christian Peacemaker Teams* (Scottdale, Pa.: Herald Press, 2005).

51. I like the early films of Peter Weir, especially for the way in which they depict the precipitous meeting of cultures and the senselessness of violence. In *Gallipoli* (1981), credulous young men from Australia are transported into the middle of war in Turkey. In *The Year of Living Dangerously*, an Australian journalist finds himself covering political upheaval in Indonesia. And in *Witness* (1985), a hardened Philadelphia policeman goes to Amish country. In *Witness*, the violence is finally brought to an end, not by guns, but by the piercing, observant eyes of the many Amish neighbors who have been called to the scene of an unfolding gunfight. This is not to suggest that nonviolent intervention is either easy or inevitably successful, but its potential for conflict resolution has been woefully neglected in favor of the military paradigm.

52. J. Peter Cordella writes, "Much of the failure of our present criminal justice system can be traced to the continued isolation of those labeled deviant. They are not trusted by society and therefore do not trust society, which is the recipe for recidivism." Cordella, "Reconciliation and the Mutualist Model of Community," in *Criminology as Peacemaking*, ed. Harold E. Pepinsky and Richard Quinney (Bloomington: Indiana University Press, 1991), p. 42. In contrast, while it is not inevitable that offenders (or, indeed, any of us) will respond to respect and trust, there are some hopeful stories. When young vandals destroyed the image of the bodhisattva Quan Yen that stood in front of a Vietnamese Buddhist temple near Boston, the Buddhists refused to press charges. Instead, the offenders were invited to a "festival of forgiveness" at which they were appointed as "guardians" of the temple. Such unexpected and undeserved embrace has apparently begun to work changes in the lives of the offenders. The story is told by Diana Eck, "The Measure of Diversity," in Bob Abernethy, William Bole, et al., *The Life of Meaning: Reflections on Faith, Doubt, and Repairing the World* (New York: Seven Stories Press, 2008), pp. 340-41.

hallucinations, delusional ideation, or other symptoms of mental illness. This question is important and complex. The vast majority of people with mental illness are no more dangerous than the rest of us, and for those who are more dangerous, it is usually to themselves. What's more, illness does not necessarily elicit compassion from the rest of us. As Susan Sontag reminded in her book, *Illness as Metaphor*, sickness elicits war; we battle heart disease, and we cut out cancers, and we conduct chemical assaults on infections. In our need to feel safe, we often blame the victims of illness: Did they smoke? Did they have unprotected sex? Did they eat Twinkies?[53] For those with mental illness, what passes for treatment can be quite abusive. In a practical sense, there may not be much difference between throwing people into prisons and locking them up against their will in psychiatric wards. The Soviet Union sent dissidents to institutions that were called "hospitals" and "reeducation camps"; elsewhere, they were simply called "prisons."[54]

Nonetheless, this is an important question for those who support imprisonment and other punitive measures. Kleptomania, pedophilia, addiction — are these illnesses or moral failings or both? If there is a man with psychotic delusions who has never been diagnosed or properly treated with medication, should we treat him as a criminal? Perhaps he had a head injury as a child, or perhaps his parents and grandparents passed on a genetic predisposition to bipolar disorder and, in a fit of manic delusion, he was totally convinced that the person he was trying to kill was the devil himself and that this single act of violence would liberate humanity. It's interesting that when some person with schizophrenia or bipolar disorder talks like that, we call it "sick." When politicians talk like that, we call it "leadership." Osama bin Laden is the devil, and if we can just kill him, we will have moved a considerable distance toward peace and freedom. The only difference is, the people with mental illness who suffer this delusion have more integrity — they really believe it.

But the question of willful victimization versus illness is also important for prison abolitionists. With models of mediation, restoration, and

53. Susan Sontag, *Illness as Metaphor* (New York: Farrar, Straus and Giroux, 1988).

54. Some of the most revealing accounts of life inside prison have been written by re-sisters and dissidents. For the Soviet Union, the premier example is Alexander Solzhenitsyn's *Gulag Archipelago*. For prison memoirs by dissidents in Australia, Britain, Canada, New Zealand, and the United States, see the excellent compilation by Peter Brock, ed., *"These Strange Criminals": An Anthology of Prison Memoirs by Conscientious Objectors from the Great War to the Cold War* (Toronto: University of Toronto Press, 2004).

reconciliation, we need to know if someone entering into mediation has an illness that prevents him or her from comprehending the harm that has been suffered. We need to know if untreated compulsions and addictions stand in the way of the potential for any meaningful reconciliation.

(6) What does a prison abolitionist do about crime? You take to the streets. You get involved in community organizing, in protesting, in volunteering with service projects. During the civil rights movement of the 1950s and '60s, crime rates plummeted in communities where the organizing was most intense.[55] Why was that? Perhaps it was because there were more people on the streets, but also because these were people who were getting to know their neighbors — people who had a sense of higher calling. The women who organize "Take back the night" rallies and marches are alert to the fact that isolation and fear are invitations to crime, while activism is a partial antidote.[56]

(7) Although this list of abolitionist responses to crime could go on, allow me to cite just one more. It must be acknowledged that, until Jesus returns, there will never be a society without some crime, some harm, some victimization.[57] The goal, then, is not to stamp out evil, a quest that

---

55. Frederic Soloman, Walter L. Walker, Garrett J. O'Connor, and Jacob R. Fishman, "Civil Rights Activity and Reduction in Crime among Negroes," *Crime and Social Justice: Issues in Criminology* 14 (Winter 1980): 27-35. With dated vocabulary but pertinent data, this article originally appeared in *Archives of General Psychiatry* in 1965.

56. From the era in which the "Take back the night" movement was started, Dorothy T. Samuel listed numerous neighborhood groups that organized participants for increased activity on the streets, not as a mode of law enforcement but as a means of building community. Samuel, *Safe Passage on City Streets* (New York: Abingdon Press, 1975), pp. 80-87. Samuel's book is also notable for its recounting of creative, nonviolent responses that averted potential assault.

57. Durkheim contended that crime is a phenomenon intrinsic to societal life, but he also argued that rates of violent crime can be altered by the ways in which a given society values human life. Emile Durkheim, "Crime as a Normal Phenomenon," in *Crime and Justice*, vol. 1: *The Criminal in Society*, ed. Leon Radzinowicz and Marvin Wolfgang (New York: Basic Books, 1971), pp. 391-95. Abolitionists have always struggled to address the question of what to do about the "dangerous few" offenders who are genuinely predisposed to commit repeated violent assaults. Is it possible to envision a form of nonviolent restraint that does not simply constitute a thinly-veiled prison? Canadian abolitionist Ruth Morris has proposed group homes that involve "humane separation," treatment, intense supervision, and responses to victims that will educate offenders to the consequences of their actions. If there is a danger that such group homes would become "mini-prisons," Morris is certainly correct in her critique of the current system: "The entire court and prison system is always defended on the ground that they are necessary for containment of the dangerous few. . . . Three impor-

quickly becomes evil in itself. The realistic goal is to shape a society in which victimization becomes less thinkable and less likely. U.S. crime rates alone tell us that prisons are not contributing toward that goal.[58] With guns readily available for "self defense" and with the highest rate of imprisonment on the planet, the U.S. also has one of the highest rates of homicide. For other models, we must look to societies with few guns, no foreign military adventures, low military spending, low rates of imprisonment, and low rates of murder.[59]

I am a prison abolitionist because, if harm reduction is the goal, it is not possible to limit the focus to the people who have broken laws. When it comes to actual harm, the largest portion of it by far has not been produced by the people sitting in prisons. Murderers would have to go on a horrible killing spree to match the death toll of the past four and a half years in Iraq, a death toll that by some estimates runs into the hundreds of thousands. Burglars would have to be very busy indeed to match the dispossession of millions of Iraqi refugees. Each year on this planet, millions of people die from malnutrition and preventable disease, yet the neglect and dispossession that cause these deaths are not regarded as criminal offenses. It cannot be called "justice" to ignore the immense but perfectly legal harm that is produced by people with political power and social respect, harm in which we are all complicit.

I must acknowledge too that I am a prison abolitionist because of the

---

tant points emerge from this. First, the prison system is NOT dealing primarily with the dangerous few, but rather with the hapless multitude. Second, far from protecting us, it makes the dangerous few more dangerous. Finally, prison itself is a violence creating environment that makes some previously nondangerous people become dangerous." Ruth Morris, *Crumbling Walls: Why Prisons Fail* (Oakville, Ontario: Mosaic Press, 1989), p. 158.

58. Some countries with rates of crime and imprisonment far lower than those of the United States are also more engaged than the U.S. in the search for alternatives to incarceration. See Mauer and Sentencing Project, *Race to Incarcerate*, p. 189. In the Netherlands, the search for alternative models is driven not only by estimations of the prison's ineffectiveness at curbing crime, but also by the fairly recent historical experience of Nazi occupation, an experience that left the Dutch keenly aware that internment camps and prisons are instruments of totalitarian control. See Zehr, *Changing Lenses*, p. 227.

59. Among several countries that could be cited, one interesting example is Costa Rica. Following a series of military coups in the middle of the twentieth century, Costa Rica found a solution to the coups and to the turmoil: eliminate the military. With no standing army, there are no coups. Although Costa Rica is by no means a utopia, it remains a largely demilitarized society with low rates of both imprisonment and crime. For more on the successes and struggles in Costa Rican society, see Richard Biesanz, Karen Zubris Biesanz, and Mavis Hiltunen Biesanz, *The Costa Ricans* (New York: Prentice-Hall, 1993).

experiences I've had as both a victim of crime and a prisoner. When I was at Jonah House in Baltimore in 1976, two men with a gun broke into the house and twenty minutes of sheer terror followed. As the violence and the robbery unfolded, I was not wishing that I could call upon the police and their firepower; I was wishing that there were fewer guns in the world, not more. In the days that followed, as I experienced my own small version of post-traumatic stress (paranoia, startled reaction to noises, depression, anxiety), the knowledge that I live in a punitive society did not leave me feeling safer. But along with being a victim of crime, I am also a criminal. As I've been sent to jail on more than a dozen occasions, I've become aware that the qualities of the people I meet on the inside are like nothing so much as the qualities of the people I meet on the outside. Both inside and out, I have met people of remarkable kindness as well as people who have succumbed to hatred and rage.

If I seem to have been touting my stance as a prison abolitionist, it is actually a confession of my own irrelevance. The abolitionist position is really quite peripheral to the contemporary debates in criminology and penology in America. No doubt, abolitionists are doing significant work with bail projects, mediation efforts, and programs that strive for restoration and reconciliation. But the prison will not collapse based on the sincerity of the work or the cogency of the arguments of contemporary abolitionists. What portends the fall of the prison is the gospel.

Biblical perspectives on prisons were persistently shaped by Israel's own experience of captivity and by its historical identification with those held in bondage.[60] This is not to deny that there were prisons in Israel, but they were few in number and were often built and used at the behest of occupying powers.[61] In the accounts of biblical witnesses, prisoners are not

60. Several scholarly works of recent vintage explore biblical perspectives on prisons. For example, biblical insights pervade the critique of American imperialism and the prison system by Mark Lewis Taylor, *The Executed God: The Way of the Cross in Lockdown America* (Minneapolis: Fortress Press, 2001).

61. The first mention of imprisonment in Scripture is that of Joseph in Egypt in Genesis 39. An example of the influence of colonizing powers on the utilization of imprisonment in Judah and Israel is provided in the account of the instructions to Ezra by Persian King Artaxerxes in Ezra 7:25-26. While Israel's unease with the prison was certainly influenced by its own history of captivity, an added factor that contributed to the paucity of prisons in Israel and Judah was the relative lack of garrisons and fortresses, which were the standard locales for prisons. There was no distinction between soldiers and police, and the standing army was a fairly late development in Israel's history. When Jeremiah was arrested, he had to be thrown into a makeshift prison in the house of Jonathan the secretary (Jeremiah 37:15). Later under Ro-

presented as dangerous criminals. With a keen awareness that the wealthy could purchase the enactment of statutes (Isaiah 10:1-2) and bribe their way to acquittal (Amos 5:12; Micah 7:3), biblical witnesses counted prisoners among the oppressed (Psalm 146:5-9; Lamentations 3:34-36). Messianic hope looked forward to the day when one would come to set the prisoners free (Isaiah 61:1-2; Zechariah 9:9-12).

The proclamation of freedom for the prisoners had roots in the Jubilee and Sabbath Year calls to forgive debts, redistribute land, and liberate slaves in remembrance of God's liberation of the Hebrew people from slavery in Egypt (Leviticus 25:1-10; Deuteronomy 15). In the social and juridical structures of ancient Israel, the kinsperson who was responsible for ransoming a relative who had been taken prisoner or driven into slavery through indebtedness was called the *"go'el."*[62] But what would happen to the slaves who were bereft of family ties or to those who were so heavily indebted that no *go'el* could possibly ransom them? The Jubilee Year proclaimed that, for those who were destitute and without any hope of ransom, God would serve as *Go'el*. God had already paid the ransom price by liberating all the Hebrew slaves from Egypt. To deny jubilary liberty to the captives was a serious affront to God because it was cheating the *Go'el* out of the ransom that had already been paid (Jeremiah 34:15-17). When Israel failed in this work of liberating slaves and prisoners, the prophet recalled the people to their role as Suffering Servant: ". . . to open the eyes that are blind, to bring out the prisoners from the dungeon, from the prison those who sit in darkness" (Isaiah 42:7).

This Hebrew Bible theme of liberty for the captives resonates throughout the New Testament. Believers are admonished to refrain from reliance on unjust courts that have no concern for reconciliation (1 Corinthians 6:1).[63] Believers are called upon to care for prisoners and to visit

---

man occupation, the prison was still a military institution. When Paul was arrested in Jerusalem (Acts 21:33-34), he was detained in the "barracks" of the Fortress Antonia. See Brian Rapske, *Paul in Roman Custody*, vol. 3 of *The Book of Acts in Its First Century Setting* (Grand Rapids: Eerdmans and Carlisle: Paternoster Press, 1994), pp. 137-40.

62. See Robert B. Sloan, Jr., *The Favorable Year of the Lord: A Study of Jubilary Theology in the Gospel of Luke* (Austin: Schola Press, 1977), pp. 6-7.

63. William F. Orr and James Arthur Walther maintain that a concern for reconciliation was one of the motivations that led Paul to admonish believers not to rely on the courts of the state. "The Christian mediator should have in view the reconciliation of the parties that they might get rightly related to the forgiving and loving God by forgiving one another." Orr and Walther, *1 Corinthians*, Anchor Bible, no. 32 (Garden City, N.Y.: Doubleday, 1976), p. 197.

them (Matthew 25:31-46). This call to "visit" (Greek, *episkeptomai*) carries a sense that is greater than just socializing. Biblical visitation is repeatedly associated with liberation and redemption (see, for example, Luke 1:68). In the book of Acts, captivity is renounced in the accounts of the miraculous deliverance from prison of Peter (12:1-11) and of Paul and Silas (16:25-34). But the boldest reassertion of the liberation theme is at the very outset of the ministry of Jesus when he proclaims liberty for the captives (Luke 4:18-19). The amnesties that are declared when kings are enthroned and prime ministers are inaugurated are cynical affairs, with prisons being emptied only to be filled again with freshly designated offenders of the new regime. In contrast, the amnesty proclaimed by Jesus has eschatological rather than mere political significance, which is to say, it applies in a final sense for all times and all people. We must learn to hear this proclamation of freedom for the prisoners as *good* news.

The biblical renunciation of the prison is not simply the rejection of an institution that has failed to achieve its stated goal. Our modern ideologies of deterrence, rehabilitation, and retribution matter not at all to the biblical depiction of the prison. In the biblical presentation of it, the prison is not an apparatus that may be managed in a more or less efficient manner. The prison is a principality that holds us in its power, and that is the power of death.[64] The biblical association of prisons with the spirit of death may have originated with the practice of holding prisoners captive in pits and cisterns (see Jeremiah 38:6). These pits are like graves, like entrances to Sheol and the underworld, and the prisoner is like one given over to death (Psalm 69:1-2, 15, 33; 107:10).[65] While Satan was once depicted as serving as a type of prosecuting attorney in the heavenly law court (Job 1:6-12; Zechariah 3:1), under the influence of apocalypticism Satan becomes the lord of the underworld of death, and he is identified as the one who casts people into prison (Luke 22:31-33; Revelation 2:10). The biblical identification of the prison with the spirit and power of death demythologizes all our contemporary theorizing about incarceration. The problem is not that the prison fails to forestall the reign of violence and chaos; the problem is that the prison is identical in spirit to the very violence that it claims to combat. Jesus' procla-

---

64. On imprisonment as a manifestation of the power of death, see Christoph Barth, *Introduction to the Psalms*, trans. R. A. Wilson (New York: Scribner's, 1966), p. 51.

65. Othmar Keel, *The Symbolism of the Biblical World: Ancient Near Eastern Iconography and the Book of Psalms*, trans. Timothy J. Hallett (New York: Seabury Press, 1978), pp. 69-73.

mation of liberty for the captives is a renunciation of death itself; it is a harbinger of resurrection.

For people of faith, all talk of prisoners must begin and end with the recognition that Christianity was born inside the prison, born as a promise of life in the midst of death. Our foremothers and forefathers were prisoners, and our sisters and brothers still are. All the apostles were jailbirds, and as Karl Barth noted, the first true Christian community was made up entirely of criminals, that is, the three criminals on the crosses at Golgotha.[66] For people of faith, all talk of prisoners must begin and end with Jesus of Nazareth, the prisoner at the center of the gospel.

66. Barth, "The Criminals with Him," in *Deliverance to the Captives* (New York: Harper, 1961), pp. 77-78. Barth is certainly correct in his forthright and rather startling identification of Jesus as a criminal. Northrop Frye writes, "Christianity is founded on a prophet who was put to death as a blasphemer and a social menace, hence any persecuting Christian is assuming that Pilate and Caiaphas were right in principle, and should merely have selected a different victim. The significance of the life of Jesus is . . . that of being the one figure in history whom no organized human society could put up with. The society that rejected him represented all societies: those responsible for his death were not the Romans or the Jews or whoever happened to be around at the time, but the whole of mankind down to ourselves and doubtless far beyond. 'It is expedient that one man die for the people,' said Caiaphas (John 18:14), and there has never been a human society that has not agreed with him." Frye, *The Great Code: The Bible and Literature* (New York: Harcourt Brace Jovanovich, 1982), pp. 132-33. It follows from this that, as Rowan Williams observes, the trial narratives of the Gospels put all of us on trial. Williams, *Christ on Trial: How the Gospel Unsettles Our Judgement* (Grand Rapids: Eerdmans and Toronto: ABC Publishing, Anglican Book Centre, 2000), p. 92.

5. Against Patriotism

When I was a student at Elizabethtown College, I participated in protests of what was, at the time, compulsory chapel, and here I am, speaking to a captive audience in what appears to be a chapel.[1] I ought to be ashamed of myself. Call it self-justification, but at least today you won't be hearing any calls to worship. You'll be hearing a call to end the worship of nation and of state. You won't be hearing me say that you have to "get religion." I'll be saying instead, along with R.E.M., that we ought to be sitting over in the corner losing our religion.[2]

Religion, spirituality, faith — I don't believe those three are all the same. In fact, one may be antithetical to another. The Hebrew prophets often said that God does not want your religion, your sacrifices, your pious observances of high holy days. But whether in the form of religion, spirituality, or faith, the yearning for transcendence has been a stubbornly persistent feature of the human experience. For the enlightened and technologically advanced folks of the twenty-first century, just as we thought that we were too sophisticated to indulge the superstitions, rituals, and mythologies of more primitive eras, we are hit by these waves of what some would call "religious fanaticism." Along with new religions (Aum Shinrikyô, Heaven's Gate, Unification Church) and restorationist movements (Branch Davidians, polygamist Mormons), we are awash with Christian fundamentalists, Hindu nationalists, and militant Islamic activists.

1. This talk was part of a lecture series that all first-year students were required to attend.
2. R.E.M., "Losing My Religion" (Bill Berry, Peter Buck, Mike Mills, Michael Stipe), produced by Scott Litt and R.E.M., copyright 1991, Night Garden Music BMI.

Leffler Chapel and Performance Center, Elizabethtown College, November 7, 2007.

The case of Islamic militancy provides an illustration of how the global spread of technology, capitalism, and secularism can itself fuel resistance in the form of religious resurgence.[3] The rise of militant Islamic activism is sometimes referred to as "Islamic fundamentalism," which is a misnomer. Born in the early twentieth century, fundamentalism is a movement within Christianity; it has nothing to do with Islam, and, depending on who you ask, little to do with traditional Christianity.[4] The recent upsurge of violence among some militant Muslims is best understood, not as a foundational return to the traditional faith of the Prophet and the Koran, but as a violent reaction against neo-colonial incursions from the West. Islam is not a "hate-filled religion," as some have called it. It is simply that, within Islam, the same as within many religious or ethnic groups, perceived threats from the outside might be met with violence and with the strengthening of the ritual boundaries that keep alien influences at bay.[5]

3. This is not an endorsement of the "clash of civilizations" model proposed by Samuel P. Huntington, *The Clash of Civilizations and the Remaking of World Order* (New York: Touchstone, 1996). In Huntington's version, the "clash" is portrayed as a conflict between the enlightened, democratic culture of the West and the entrenched, traditional cultures of the East. This model ignores the way in which the spread of hegemonic global culture has evoked resistance in the form of religious resurgence in the West as well as the East. It also ignores the fact that the communitarian, consensus styles of decision-making in some traditional cultures would put to shame the claim that Western-style elections constitute the height of democracy.

4. The term "fundamentalist" was first used in 1920 to refer to adherents of *The Fundamentals*, twelve volumes of essays financed initially by two California oil millionaires, brothers Milton and Lyman Stewart. The essays expounded a list of doctrines and beliefs (among them, the virgin birth of Jesus and a literal heaven and hell) that were held to be essential to true Christianity. George M. Marsden, *Fundamentalism and American Culture: The Shaping of Twentieth Century Evangelicalism, 1870-1925* (New York: Oxford University Press, 1980), pp. 118-19. The expansion of the use of the term "fundamentalism" to apply to movements within any and all religious faiths is owing in part to the work of Martin Marty and R. Scott Appleby, founders of the "Fundamentalism Project" of the American Academy of Arts and Sciences. Marty and Appleby are cautious in appropriating and redefining the term, a caution that is often lacking in popular, pejorative dismissals of Muslim "fundamentalists." In the careless use of the term, even some Christian evangelicals who differ with *The Fundamentals* are nonetheless labeled "fundamentalist."

5. It must be noted that the effort to defend a supposedly pristine faith against outside incursion through reliance on violence or boundary-reinforcement meets with inevitable failure. Even if influences from the outside are resisted, the faith and the faith community will have been altered by the resort to violence and by the imposition of the rigid definitions of orthodoxy that are intended to fortify the perimeters of faith.

Throughout history, the threats to Islam have been more than mere figments of the Muslim imagination. When the papacy launched crusades in the eleventh century, crusades that would span the next 300 years, of course they met with violent resistance from some Muslims.[6] When the British colonized Egypt and Sudan in the nineteenth and early twentieth centuries, certainly they encountered violent resistance from some Muslims, including those who looked for the coming of Mahdi, the Imam of the final days who would restore the dignity of the faithful.[7] British officials called them "Satan worshippers." And when Soviet troops occupied Afghanistan in the late 1970s, they met with violent resistance from the mujahideen. American political leaders called them "freedom fighters," and decided to assist them with covert aid. The CIA recruited fighters from over thirty countries, most from right next door in Pakistan, but also from Egypt, Algeria, Bosnia, Yemen, Saudi Arabia, and elsewhere. They were funded and armed, and they were trained in the tactics of insurgency, including how to attack soft civilian targets.[8] U.S. leaders loved those freedom fighters who hated that Soviet imperialism; the mistake — the delusion, really — was in thinking that they would like the American variety. And that's the only difference between the freedom fighter and the terrorist: the freedom fighter is the enemy of my enemy, while the terrorist is the enemy of me. Like Dr. Frankenstein, like Dr. Moreau, we have created our own monsters. For Americans to then describe Islam as a religion filled with hate is to smear an entire faith with the bloody consequences of our own scheming.

So yes, religion, faith, and spirituality are all alive and well in the twenty-first century, buzzing through the hard drives of our sophisti-

6. When President Bush referred to the invasion of Afghanistan as a "crusade," he was insensitive to historical allusion, an insensitivity that was matched by Taliban and Al Qaeda references to "Christian and Jewish crusaders." As the crusaders of the eleventh century set off on their mission to retake the holy land, they routinely slaughtered Jews along the way. Peter Partner, *God of Battles: Holy Wars of Christianity and Islam* (Princeton, N.J.: Princeton University Press, 1997), pp. 78-79.

7. Muslim resistance to the British was rich and varied, and some of it was nonviolent. In Egypt, Hasan al-Banna (1906-1949) founded the Society of Muslim Brothers as a movement of spiritual regeneration and charitable social action independent of British influence. On the varied responses to British occupation, see Karen Armstrong, *Islam: A Short History* (New York: Modern Library, 2000), pp. 147-56.

8. One of the most carefully documented sources on the covert U.S. involvements in Afghanistan is by John K. Cooley, *Unholy Wars: Afghanistan, America and International Terrorism* (Sterling, Va.: Pluto Press, 2000).

cated consciousness. Are we humans hardwired for religion? I don't know about that. I have no wish to deny my atheist friends the dignity of their nonbelief. But I also suspect that when people are insistent that they have hit upon the hard bedrock of human rationality, that they have purged themselves of all notions of transcendence, we ought to be on the lookout for mythology unaware. I do not use "mythology" as a synonym for "falsehood." Mythology is a struggle for truth wrapped in the language of legend, and whatever else they tell us, the fat volumes by Joseph Campbell say that humans are mythmaking creatures, and we have not evolved our way past that. The question, then, is not whether we are devoid of myths, but whether our modern mythologies have become too unexamined and plentiful, too tawdry and downright dangerous — like the consumerist quest for the Holy Grail, like the end-time battle against the axis of evil.

"Patriotism," said Samuel Johnson, "is the last refuge of a scoundrel." In a time of crisis, however, patriotism is the first refuge of many, including those who are not scoundrels. Recall the surge in patriotic fervor in the days and weeks following the horrors of September 11. "God bless America" was the slogan that was visible everywhere — on bumper stickers and billboards, on the signs in front of burger joints, "God bless America." Clearly, those who used the slogan wanted to proclaim their patriotism, but who is this "God" to whom the slogan referred? Looking to the Bible that most Americans claim as a source of inspiration, there is a presentation of "the blessing" that offers little reassurance to the most powerful nation on the planet. In Jesus' sermons on the mount and on the plain (Matthew 5–7; Luke 6:17-49), those who are deemed worthy of God's blessing are not the wealthy but the poor. The blessed are the peacemakers who turn the other cheek and return good for evil, not some superpower like the U.S. that spends more on the military than the next thirty highest-spending nations *combined*. The prayer that America might be a land worthy of God's blessing is either a masochistic prayer or a prayer offered to some altogether different god — perhaps the god of nation, power, and wealth.

When it comes to defining "religion," scholars of comparative religions don't always agree. (For those of you just starting out in college, you're going to encounter that a lot — experts who can't even agree on a common definition of what it is on which they're supposed to be experts.) Among these scholars, however, there is broad agreement about several elements or dimensions that need to be present for a collective movement to qualify as "religion" (from the Latin *religare*, "to bind fast"),[9] and lo and behold, under these criteria, patriotism qualifies as religious faith. Religion entails allegiance by a group to a transcendent version of reality, to transcendent principles like freedom, democracy, and the American way of life. The religious group has shared history that's heading somewhere, like Manifest Destiny, and that's enveloped by myth and legend, like Lincoln as great emancipator, like Washington and Jefferson as fathers of freedom, slaveholders though they were. Religions have doctrines, like those enshrined in the Constitution and the Declaration of Independence. There are ethical precepts, like obeying the law and voting and paying your taxes. As religions pass from cultic and sectarian phases to greater institutionalization, there are hierarchies and offices, like presidents and Supreme Court justices. Religions have rituals, like pledging allegiance, that involve sacred objects, like the flag. Religions have holy days, like Memorial Day and Independence Day, and there are holy sites to which the faithful might go on pilgrimage, like the Vietnam War Memorial and the Tomb of the Unknown Soldier. Oh yes, religion is alive and well in America, and it often takes the form of worshipping America itself.

Back in 1967, the sociologist Robert Bellah wrote "Civil Religion in America," an essay that is still influential.[10] In his essay, Bellah granted the point that patriotism is a manifestation of religious faith, but as such, he suggested, it is a source of our civic virtue. Didn't Martin Luther King, Jr., inspire us with appeals to the American dream? It is certainly true that, while Malcolm X spoke of the American nightmare, King was far more likely to make appeals to patriotic sentiment.[11] Of course, others who were also making appeals to the American dream were segregationists like George Wallace, Orval Faubus, and Lester Maddox. Robert Bellah

9. Scholars who list the dimensions cited in the text below include Ninian Smart, *The Religious Experience of Mankind*, 2nd ed. (New York: Charles Scribner's Sons, 1976), pp. 3-23, and Geoffrey Parrinder, ed., *World Religions from Ancient History to the Present* (New York: Facts on File, 1971), pp. 9-21. Belief in a god or gods is an element that is pervasive but not inherent to "religion." Some adherents of Theravada Buddhism or philosophical Hinduism, for example, are *both* atheist *and* Buddhist or Hindu.

10. Robert N. Bellah, "Civil Religion in America," *Daedalus* 96 (Winter 1967): 1-21, reprinted in Bellah, *Beyond Belief: Essays on Religion in a Post-Traditional World* (New York: Harper & Row, 1970), pp. 168-89.

11. An exploration of the contrast and convergence of Malcolm X and King on the topic of patriotism is provided by James H. Cone, *Martin & Malcolm & America: A Dream or a Nightmare?* (Maryknoll, N.Y.: Orbis Books, 1991).

notes that John Kennedy inspired us with those words, "Ask not what your country can do for you — ask what you can do for your country." What Bellah fails to mention is that similar pleas to put the country first were made by figures less benign, like Joseph Stalin, like Adolf Hitler.

Robert Bellah is a Christian, and since he acknowledges that patriotism functions as a religious faith, he seems anxious to build the case that it is possible to worship at more than one altar.[12] This duality of religious allegiance has proven possible for Americans because, while Christianity is burdened with specific content (Jesus, for example), American civil religion is doctrinally vapid. There are intermittent references to God, but little consideration of who God is. In fact, says Bellah, one of the few theological assertions in American civil religion is that God has a special concern for America. If this God of civil religion is assumed to share identity with the God of Jewish or Christian faiths, then it is not altogether clear why this God who forged a covenant with a group of insignificant Hebrew slaves should now have a greater concern for America than for, say, Sri Lanka or Burundi.

This idea that the Judeo-Christian God especially loves America can be traced back to a theology that was brought by the earliest European settlers on the continent. The Puritans came armed not only with weapons but also with the belief that they were on a mission from God, an errand into the wilderness to build a bright, shining city on a hill.[13] The only problem was, the hill on which they proposed to do their building did not belong to them. When there are people who are not averse to the use of violence and who are on a mission from God, the neighbors had better watch out. The U.S. War of Independence pales in comparison to the far bloodier five hundred years war that those of European ancestry have waged against the native people of the Americas, a war that continues to this day. This five hundred years war is evidence that the 1776 struggle for independence had less to do with human rights and political freedom than with economic freedom. The emerging middle and upper classes of the American colonies had a keen desire for freedom from the economic

12. Bellah's identity as a Christian is noted by J. Philip Wogaman, *Christian Perspectives on Politics*, rev. ed. (Louisville: Westminster John Knox Press, 2000), pp. 183-84.

13. See the classic work by Perry Miller, *Errand into the Wilderness* (New York: Harper & Row, 1964). The idea of a divine covenant with America is traced from the Puritan settlers through the twentieth century in the primary sources appearing in Conrad Cherry, ed., *God's New Israel: Religious Interpretations of American Destiny* (Englewood Cliffs, N.J.: Prentice-Hall, 1971).

controls of Britain, freedom to exploit slaves in extracting the resources of the land that had been stolen from natives. I am not an economic determinist or a Christian Marxist, which I think would be only slightly less absurd than being a Christian capitalist, but when people are killing one another in the name of "freedom," it's time to start sniffing around for the bucks. It doesn't take much sniffing to find in the spirit of 1776 and the spirit of the five hundred years war another, different spirit — the spirit of mammon.

The Indian philosopher Ramajit Guha wrote that history is not like some foreign country that we may visit on vacation with all the interesting spots already marked out on a tourist map. History is contested terrain, a locale of struggle that is often colonized by the powers that be in order to illustrate how contemporary power arrangements are the natural and just outcome of a long historical process.[14] When we read history through a patriotic lens, we colonize it. In contrast to the colonizers are those who visit the historical terrain searching and listening for voices heard too little: the voices of the people underneath, the losers, the hanged, the crucified; the voices of the women, the poor, the rebels; the voices of pacifists in times of war; the voices of heretics in times when palace priests claimed that they had God all nailed down. Listen to those voices, and if you listen long enough, you hear the sound of hope. Arundhati Roy wrote, "Another world is not only possible, she is on her way. On a quiet day, I can hear her breathing."[15]

Some historians are skilled at listening for voices heard too little. For biblical history, these include Norman K. Gottwald,[16] George E. Mendenhall,[17] and Richard A. Horsley.[18] For church history, there are Norman

14. Guha traces the role of Hegel in concocting a view of "World-history" that serves the purposes of statism and colonization. Common people and people who are not yet colonized are people without history. "The noise of World-history and its statist concerns has made historiography insensitive to the sighs and whispers of everyday life." Ramajit Guha, *History at the Limit of World-History* (New York: Columbia University Press, 2002), p. 73.

15. Roy, quoted in Teishan Latner, ed., *The Quotable Rebel: Political Quotations for Dangerous Times* (Monroe, Maine: Common Courage Press, 2005), p. 7.

16. His *magnum opus* is Gottwald, *The Tribes of Yahweh: A Sociology of the Religion of Liberated Israel, 1250-1050 B.C.E.* (Maryknoll, N.Y.: Orbis Books, 1979).

17. Mendenhall, *The Tenth Generation: The Origins of the Biblical Tradition* (Baltimore: Johns Hopkins Press, 1973).

18. Horsley, with John S. Hanson, *Bandits, Prophets, and Messiahs: Popular Movements at the Time of Jesus*, New Voices in Biblical Studies (New York: Harper & Row, 1985).

Cohn[19] and Rosemary Radford Ruether.[20] For English history, there are
E. P. Thompson[21] and Christopher Hill.[22] And for U.S. history, there is certainly Howard Zinn. If you have not read it yet, you'll be giving yourself a
gift if you take the time to read Howard Zinn's *A People's History of the
United States.*[23]

Patriotism is a very recent phenomenon, and so is the nation. Indeed,
when measured against the span of human existence, the state itself is a
newcomer on the scene. While anthropologists trace our bipedal ancestors back for millions of years, our species, homo sapiens, has been
around for maybe a hundred thousand years. During 94 percent of that
time, we were anarchists (and some of us still are). Throughout 94,000
years, people somehow managed to survive without kings and presidents.
While this was a prehistorical period of which we have no written records,
some anthropologists contend that these people survived quite nicely. In
his book *Stone-Age Economics,* Marshall Sahlins contends that these anarchist ancestors of ours probably lived in sharing, egalitarian communities,
and they probably had more leisure time than we do.[24]

The state is a contagious creature. Once it is established, the state pattern quickly reproduces itself among the people it encounters, not because it constitutes a superior form of social organization, but because it
provides for an efficient, hierarchical military organization. As the vora-
cious state expands out to conquer and subjugate the people at its periph-

19. Cohn, *The Pursuit of the Millennium: Revolutionary Millenarians and Mystical Anarchists of
the Middle Ages,* rev. ed. (New York: Oxford University Press, 1970).

20. Along with her many excellent studies on women in the history of the church, an
important inaugural work was Ruether, *The Radical Kingdom: The Western Experience of Messianic Hope* (New York: Harper & Row, 1970).

21. Thompson, *The Making of the English Working Class* (New York: Vintage Books, 1966).

22. Of many books, the most influential is Hill, *The World Turned Upside Down: Radical
Ideas during the English Revolution* (New York: Penguin Books, 1975).

23. Zinn, *A People's History of the United States* (New York: HarperPerennial, 1990). See
also the companion volume, Howard Zinn and Anthony Arnove, *Voices of a People's History of
the United States* (New York: Seven Stories Press, 2004).

24. Sahlins, *Stone-Age Economics* (London: Tavistock, 1974). Sahlins's contention re-
ceives support from the anthropological explorations of Pierre Clastres among Amazonian
people without a state. For people in these societies, no value is attached to the accumulation of individual wealth, and as a result communal welfare is enhanced and the emergence
of hierarchical power is obstructed. As Clastres writes, "Primitive society, the first society of
abundance, leaves no room for the desire for overabundance." Pierre Clastres, *Society against
the State: Essays in Political Anthropology,* trans. Robert Hurley with Abe Stein (New York: Zone
Books, 1989), p. 205.

ery, some of the societies at the margins devise hierarchical structures of their own in an effort to forestall conquest by the neighboring state.[25] But what would account for the rise of the pristine state? The first state may have been formed in Mesopotamia 5,300 years ago.[26] It wasn't much by today's standards. There was a central "government" precariously ruling a land bounded by frontiers instead of borders. The hierarchical power arrangement included a king and a proto-bureaucracy of a few advisors, some priests, some collectors of revenues and tributes, and an army — of course, an army.

The historian Charles Tilly writes that three factors combined to facilitate the emergence of the state: (1) cities, the earliest of which were much smaller than Elizabethtown (population 12,000), but they provided an adequate labor pool for (2) the accumulation of economic surplus, which meant that excess wealth could be used for (3) the most wasteful enterprise in all of human history, war.[27] Warriors and standing armies drain

25. It is not inevitable that societies on the periphery of an expanding state will form states of their own in self-defense. Even among those non-hierarchical societies that are not averse to the use of violence, military leaders or "warrior chiefs" might emerge in times of crisis, and then when the threat has passed, the ad hoc leaders renounce all claims to power. One prototypical example is the role of the judges in pre-monarchic Israel. The danger, of course, is that the provisional leader might seek to retain power through a variety of means, including the perpetuation of military exploits. The warrior chiefs who seek to retain their grip on power (e.g., Geronimo of the Apaches and Fousiwe of the Yanomami) meet with communal resistance, sometimes in the form of prophetic or millenarian movements. Clastres, *Society Against the State*, pp. 29-30, 208-18.

26. With debate on some specifics, archaeologists agree that there are several global sites of pristine state formation: Mesopotamia around 3300 BCE, Egypt around 3100 BCE, the Yellow River basin of northern China and the Indus Valley around 2000 BCE, and Peru and Mesoamerica around 100 CE. There is greater debate about the pristine nature of the states that formed in Crete in 2000 BCE and in the lake region of East Africa in 200 CE. This list is provided by Marvin Harris, *Cannibals and Kings: The Origins of Cultures* (New York: Vintage Books, 1978), p. 103.

27. Charles Tilly, *Coercion, Capital, and European States, AD 990-1992* (Cambridge, Mass.: Blackwell Publishers, 1992), pp. 5-28. While Tilly focuses on Europe, his observations are applicable to state formation in other times and places, including the rise of the pristine state. Tilly's contribution is to combine these three factors that had previously been treated independently by social theorists. For Lewis Mumford, urbanization is the primary factor in the emergence of the state. Economic surplus was the prominent factor in the world system/Marxist analysis of Immanuel Wallerstein. For Max Weber, war was integral to his very definition of the state as that body which manages to establish a monopoly on the permissible use of force within a given territory. Tilly argues persuasively that these three factors converge.

off a huge amount of wealth from any society, and with a large enough labor pool, the first states had the wherewithal to support them. In one way only, however, the earliest warriors did provide for their own keep; conquest meant slaves, and slaves meant more excess wealth that still more warriors could waste. Without people to be exploited, without wealth to be wasted, without warriors to be bloodied, there can be no state.

The question then arises, what would possibly motivate people to cooperate with this new power arrangement of the state? They certainly were not motivated by patriotism. The modern religion of patriotism only emerged more recently from the nationalist struggles of the Romantic Era in Europe, although a few thousand years ago, there was already a rudimentary love of fatherland — and I do mean *father*. Our word "patriotism" derives from the Latin word for "father." Horace wrote, "Lovely and honorable it is to die for one's fatherland *(patrie)*." And what were the women saying? Their voices are rarely heard, but it is telling, perhaps, that in Sophocles' play *Antigone* it is a woman who declares that she will not obey the edicts of some king. Far better to show reverence for the gods and to respect the ties of kinship than the say-so of some king. It is telling, perhaps, that at the very beginning of Exodus (1:15-22), it is two lowly midwives, Shiphrah and Puah, who defy the order of Pharaoh, the most powerful man on earth. The whole story of God's liberation begins with this simple act of subversion by these two unsung women.

So the question recurs, what motivates people to obey when some warrior chief stumbles onto the scene and says, "I'm king." As Mohandas Gandhi knew, there is a huge gap between the state's claim to have the right to rule and its ability actually to enforce that claim. In the United States, the state would utterly collapse if only five percent, or four percent, or three percent of the people were to say, "We will not cooperate in any way; we will withhold our taxes; we will barter and will not use your currency; we will block arms shipments with our bodies." The state could not survive, not even with a million-person army aiming all their guns at other Americans.

So, the question is not only for the subjects of the pristine state, but for us as well. Why do we obey? Who or what controls us? It is a question that might be worth asking often in life, and not only in relationship to the state: who or what controls you? In the classroom, when the professor says, "Do as I say and you get an A," the subject matter being taught is obedience. Is obedience learned behavior, a type of core curriculum that we are taught in a thousand different ways by family, school, workplace, and state?

Four decades ago, a psychologist named Stanley Milgram conducted a series of experiments which suggested that people have a certain procliv-ity to obey authority, especially if we are reassured that we bear no legal or moral culpability for simply following orders. They became known as the "Eichmann experiments," named after Adolf Eichmann, who had coordi-nated the nearly successful Nazi effort to kill all the Jews of Europe.[28] Years after the end of World War II, he was apprehended in South America and taken to Israel for trial. A young journalist and philosopher, Hannah Arendt, got permission for a series of interviews with him, and she later wrote her book, *Eichmann in Jerusalem*.[29] What was Eichmann's defense? He was only following orders. But what alarmed Arendt was how absolutely "normal" the man appeared. There was no hate-filled speech, no obvious pathology. He presented himself as a pleasant, moderately intelligent bu-reaucrat. Arendt coined the phrase, "the banality of evil." The greatest horrors in history are not committed by revolutionaries or wild-eyed ter-rorists, but by people who are just following orders, just doing their jobs.

How does the state elicit obedience and fill the gap between its claim to power and its ability to enforce that claim? Several prominent political theorists have maintained that the gap is filled by fear. In *The Prince*, Machiavelli wrote that, if a ruler cannot be loved, at least he should be feared. In fact, said Machiavelli, fear is preferable to love when it comes to governance. While the prince may not have the military resources for mass coercion, if he administers punishments selectively, conspicuously, and, to a degree, unpredictably, he can elicit cooperation from citizens who are eager to avoid his attention. In *Leviathan*, Thomas Hobbes agreed that fear sustains the state, but it is not our fear of the prince; it is our fear of one another. Prior to the emergence of the state, wrote Hobbes, human-ity did not dwell in some idyllic Eden but in a brutish world where people routinely preyed on one another. Hobbes hypothesized that there was a

---

28. Milgram notes that it was Gordon Allport who first used this phrase to describe his research and, writes Milgram, "The 'Eichmann experiment' is, perhaps, an apt term, but it should not lead us to mistake the import of this investigation. To focus only on the Nazis, however despicable their deeds, and to view only highly publicized atrocities as being rele-vant to these studies is to miss the point entirely. For the studies are principally concerned with the ordinary and routine destruction carried out by everyday people following or-ders." Stanley Milgram, *Obedience to Authority: An Experimental View* (New York: Harper Torchbooks, 1975), p. 178.

29. Hannah Arendt, *Eichmann in Jerusalem: A Report on the Banality of Evil*, rev. ed. (New York: Penguin Books, 1977).

moment of insight in which our ancestors forged a social contract, chose a king and obeyed him rather than continue in the condition of all at war against all.[30]

Machiavelli and Hobbes are certainly correct in observing that fear plays a role in eliciting obedience. Moreover, Machiavelli is prescient in observing that the state can manipulate these fears to its advantage. Fear is an endlessly renewable resource. If allegiance starts to waver, simply change the threat level from orange to red and tell citizens of the horrors that await them if they fail to follow onto the path charted by their leaders. But where Machiavelli and Hobbes err, perhaps, is in adopting a view of humanity that is overly simplified. If it is true that we act instinctively at times because we want to avoid pain and fear, that is not all that we want. We also want community, loyalty, and a sense of belonging. The writings of both Machiavelli and Hobbes antedate the patriotic fervor of the Romantic Era and the birth of this new "community" to which we can belong — the nation.

While the state itself has been around for over 5,000 years, the modern nation-state was born less than 300 years ago. "Community" is one of the most abused words in our language, and to call the nation a "community" contributes to cheapening the word. But the idealized vision of the founding of a nation as a communitarian venture is owing to the fact that the nation made its appearance in Europe at a time when genuine communities were in sharp decline. In eighteenth-century Europe, rural villages were losing out to urbanization. Trade guilds and workers' associations were being washed away by the capitalist concentration of wealth. The

---

30. In *Leviathan*, Hobbes acknowledged that kings and other rulers constitute the one group for whom the natural condition persists even after the social contract is formed. Since kings are not bound by social contract with one another, the violence that Hobbes posits as endemic to the state of nature continues in relationships among kings. Hobbes made little comment on the fact that these persisting, brutish wars among kings undermine the supposed benefits of the social contract for the larger population. The formation of the social contract is a device of political theory rather than an actual event, which is why Hobbes had no interest in anchoring it to a specific period of history or prehistory, nor any need to detail the legal rationale for future generations to be bound by a contract to which they had given no consent. Hobbes was a monarchist in a time of revolutionary fervor in England. He was less concerned with propounding theories of state formation than with warning the subjects of the crown of the horrors that awaited them if they yielded to the calls of brutish revolutionaries. On the historical context of Hobbes's work, see J. S. McClelland, *A History of Western Political Thought* (New York: Routledge, 1996), pp. 192-227.

parish-level church was faltering.[31] As empires faded and monarchs were toppled from their thrones, the Romantic revolutionaries of the eighteenth and nineteenth centuries proposed a new source for identity and belonging; we belong to a nation, a people united by common history and shared blood sacrifice, a people united by land, language, religion, and culture, and above all, a people united by a shared spirit — the French spirit, the German spirit, the American spirit.

Nationalist claims to solidarity notwithstanding, the nation is, in the memorable phrase of Benedict Anderson, "imagined community."[32] As nation-states have carved out their borders, there has never been a nation where all people share one history, language, religion, culture, or even "spirit," whatever that means.[33] To be sure, there have been xenophobic and ethnocentric efforts to enforce such uniformity. "Stop the dark-skinned immigrants at the Rio Grande. Speak only English. The United States is a Christian nation." To the extent that these efforts meet with any success, however, it is just one more indication that the nation is an ideol-

---

31. Ranging from Eastern Europe to South America, the communitarian visions of nationalist revolutionaries are traced by Adam Zamoyski, *Holy Madness: Romantics, Patriots, and Revolutionaries, 1776-1871* (New York: Penguin Books, 2001). Since faith communities present narratives of meaning that are different from or even antagonistic to the accumulation of political power, many scholars have discerned a relationship between the decline of these communities and the growth of the power of the nation-state. See, for examples, Martin van Creveld, *The Rise and Decline of the State* (New York: Cambridge University Press, 1999), pp. 54, 60-61, and Anthony W. Marx, *Faith in Nation: Exclusionary Origins of Nationalism* (New York: Oxford University Press, 2003), p. 37. But there is a chicken-or-egg quandary here. Did the erosion of faith lead people to look about for another reality that could be the object of their devotion, thus contributing to the rise of the nation-state, or did the emergence of the nation-state attract the devotion and allegiance that had previously been invested in faith, thus contributing to the decline of faith communities? There are possibilities in addition to these. Some historians contend that the earliest phases of the rise of nationalism in Europe coincided, not with the decline of faith, but with the establishment of new churches following the Reformation. No longer owing allegiance to ecclesiastical power in Rome, these churches were at liberty to form alliances with the fledgling powers that were shaping the nations of central and northern Europe. Surrender to power, ally with power, aspire to power: the decline of faith communities can come in multiple guises.

32. Anderson, *Imagined Communities: Reflections on the Origin and Spread of Nationalism*, rev. ed. (New York: Verso, 1991).

33. The one meaning of "spirit" that would seem to make sense in this context is the biblical assertion that "the nations" (*goyim*) are represented and substantially controlled by an assortment of fallen angels and demonic spirits. Somehow, I doubt that this is what nationalists mean by "spirit." See Walter Wink, *The Powers*, vol. 1: *Naming the Powers: The Language of Power in the New Testament* (Philadelphia: Fortress Press, 1984).

ogy and a power imposed on people rather than a naturally occurring source of unity. The nation is also "imagined community" because it is simply impossible that any of us could have communitarian contact with 300 million people. What possible reason in the world would I have to believe that I share greater commonality with a Simi Valley CEO or a Wall Street broker than with a New Zealand peace activist, a Canadian Doukhobor, or, for that matter, a gay Ethiopian farmer?

To say that the nation is imagined community is not to deny the power of nationalism or patriotism. Patriotism *is* a power, a religious power, and like fear, it can possess us. Also like fear, it can fill the gap between the state's claim to sovereignty and its ability to enforce that claim. Patriotism is the god of that gap because, in a country of 300 million or even one million people, the state becomes the nexus of patriotic fervor, the organizer of imagined community. Like fear, patriotism predisposes us to obedience. Speaking from contrasting perspectives, two leaders who testified to the potent combination of fear and patriotism were U.S. General Douglas MacArthur and Nazi leader Hermann Goering. In 1957, MacArthur said, "Our government has kept us in a perpetual state of fear — kept us in a continuous stampede of patriotic fervor — with the cry of grave national emergency. Always there has been some terrible evil at home or some monstrous foreign power that was going to gobble us up if we did not blindly rally behind it." Speaking from his Nuremberg trial, Goering said, ". . . the people can always be brought to do the bidding of the leaders. That is easy. All you have to do is to tell them they are being attacked, and denounce the pacifists for lack of patriotism and exposing the country to danger."[34]

Patriotism functions as religious faith, but does it also have an ideological role in generating hatred akin to the animosity fostered by other "isms" — racism, sexism, classism? While disdain for others is not intrinsic to love for one's own "imagined community" (no more than disregard for others is inherent to love of one's own family), patriotic fervor is often sustained through assertions of superiority and exceptionalism. In the United States, the very way we live constitutes an assertion that we have an exceptional right to a large portion of the earth's wealth. With a planet already approaching ecological collapse, it is simply impossible that all six

34. The quotations from both MacArthur and Goering are cited by David McGowan, *Derailing Democracy: The America the Media Don't Want You to See* (Monroe, Maine: Common Courage Press, 2000), p. 59.

and one-half billion people in the world can have a typical, middle-class American lifestyle. This lifestyle constitutes theft, not only from people living elsewhere, but also from future generations and from other species of animals and plants. One way to resist this exceptionalism, one way to end the theft, is to climb down the social ladder. If you are getting a college degree with the aspiration of climbing up the social ladder, please pause to challenge yourself on the direction of your climb.

U.S. military policy constitutes another form of exceptionalism. Appeals to patriotism are made to elicit support for military adventures that would provoke outrage from us if they were conducted by other nations. These patriotic appeals are often made under the rubric of "support our troops," a plea that is disingenuous to the extreme. To send young women and men off to kill and be killed is abusive, not supportive. A truly supportive action would be to shut down the Pentagon and to use the entire military budget to care for the people on this planet who are suffering the physical and emotional scars of war, including U.S. troops. No, my argument is not with the troops, who are certainly among the victims of war. Frankly, I fail to see how the person who pulls the trigger bears greater moral culpability than those of us who pay for the trigger. Oprah Winfrey (who I do not often quote) once said, "I've killed more people than the Unabomber because I've paid more taxes than he has."[35] Tax resistance is one path chosen by some people of conscience. During this week at Elizabethtown, I've been inspired by hearing students of conscience talk about the paths they plan to explore. They plan to help the college check investment portfolios for any military contractors or corporations involved in injustice. They plan to go to local military recruitment offices to share the word that joining the military is not just about getting a job and getting help with college tuition. They plan to open dialogue on nonviolence in the student newspaper, and to produce counter-recruitment spots for the campus radio station. For now, these students are keenly aware that they are few, but the hope they represent is great indeed.

Patriotism is the ultimate appeal of military recruiters as they tell young people that they will be serving their country and serving the cause of freedom. A little over forty years ago, Lyndon Johnson sent troops to the Dominican Republic. U.S. troops and Dominicans died. Can you tell me why? Can you tell me who the good guys and the bad guys were? Can you tell me how the cause of freedom was served? Can you tell me the

35. Quoted in Latner, *The Quotable Rebel*, p. 316.

names of any of those who died? Can you tell me how the cause of freedom was served twenty-five years ago when Ronald Reagan sent troops to
Lebanon, or to Grenada to overthrow the government there? How about
less than twenty years ago when George H. W. Bush sent troops to Panama to overthrow some guy who had been on the CIA payroll?[36] The way
to support the troops is not to send them anywhere, not to have them killing and dying in causes that will be forgotten in forty years or forty
months as the U.S. launches still another war on which the fate of the
planet depends.

War accomplishes any number of things, but spreading peace and
freedom is not among them. Nothing does more than war to create refugees and to spread disease and famine. Nothing does more than war to
spread contempt for life. The Pentagon would have us believe that our
modern wars are carefully laser-guided and smart-bombed to protect the
lives of civilians, but that is not true. From the battles of medieval Europe
to the senseless trench warfare of World War I, roughly 80 percent of casualties in wars were soldiers and 20 percent were noncombatants. With
expanded reliance on air attacks in World War II, the percentages of military and civilian casualties were almost equal. In the wars since then,
however, nearly 90 percent of the people killed have been noncombatants.[37] I do not believe that soldiers should be fair targets, but the idea
that we are all fair targets in times of war was not concocted by some terrorists; it was an idea propounded by the nation-state in the blitzkrieg on
London, the firebombing of Dresden, the atomic bombings of Hiroshima
and Nagasaki.[38]

The terrorists of nineteenth-century Europe were decent folks as far
as terrorists go. They wanted to kill only the politicians. Albert Camus's

36. General Manuel Noriega had been paid $300,000 by the U.S. government to dis-
close information about his own government in Panama. Later, when U.S. troops invaded
to oust Noriega, 23 Americans were killed, 324 were wounded, and the uncounted Panama-
nian dead may have numbered in the thousands. Edward S. Herman, *Beyond Hypocrisy: De-
coding the News in an Age of Propaganda* (Boston: South End Press, 1992), pp. 36, 50.

37. Carolyn Nordstrom, "The Backyard Front," in *The Paths to Domination, Resistance, and
Terror*, ed. Carolyn Nordstrom and JoAnn Martin (Berkeley: University of California Press,
1992), p. 271 n. 1.

38. Robin Morgan comments, "I think it is not coincidental that random murder of average citizens, including those in no way connected to power, emerged as a strategy of insurgent struggle *after* the random murder of average citizens had become a 'legitimate' military tactic in conventional warfare." Morgan, *The Demon Lover: On the Sexuality of Terrorism*
(New York: W. W. Norton, 1989), pp. 44-45.

play, *The Just Assassins,* is based on the true story of a plot by nineteenth-century Russian anarchists to kill Grand Duke Sergei in the strange belief that doing so would somehow end the starvation of Russian peasants.[39] They planned to throw a bomb into the carriage of the Grand Duke as he passed by, but they aborted their first attempt when they discovered that the Grand Duke's two young nephews were riding in the carriage with him. These terrorists could not bring themselves to kill children. Moving forward to twenty-first-century America, President Bush issued a directive for troops in Afghanistan and Iraq that, if they located some "high-value target" (e.g., leaders of certain militia groups), commanders in the field could order an attack that would kill the high-value target if they were reasonably assured that fewer than thirty innocent bystanders would be killed in the attack. If the number of noncombatant deaths was likely to reach thirty or more, then commanders on the ground would need to seek permission for the attack from the President or the Secretary of Defense.[40] In other words, U.S. policy has been somewhere in the range of thirty times less moral than the practices of nineteenth-century Russian terrorists.

Americans would be outraged if, in the process of getting at some high-value target, the President ordered the intentional killing of thirty U.S. soldiers. We would be appalled to think that, in the process of nabbing someone on the most-wanted list, FBI agents had approval to kill thirty innocent bystanders in Nebraska. The only difference is the patriotic exceptionalism which claims that the lives of Americans are somehow more valuable than the lives of people from Afghanistan and Iraq. I would also want to advocate for the lives of the "high-value targets," up to and including the life of Osama bin Laden, but if you cannot join in that plea, would you be able to renounce patriotic exceptionalism to the extent of saying that the life of a U.S. citizen is not one bit more or less sacred than the life of an Iraqi?

Since the end of World War II, the United States has invaded, bombed, or overthrown the governments of *dozens* of countries on five continents.[41]

39. Camus, *The Just Assassins,* in *Caligula and Three Other Plays,* trans. Stuart Gilbert (New York: Vintage Books, 1958).

40. Mark Benjamin, "When Is an Accidental Civilian Death Not an Accident?" Salon .com, July 30, 2007.

41. Although the list would be lengthier now, many of the interventions prior to the twenty-first century are enumerated by William Blum, *Killing Hope: U.S. Military and CIA Interventions since World War II* (Monroe, Maine: Common Courage Press, 1995).

Any other nation acting in a similar fashion would be viewed as a major threat to world peace. It is only blind patriotism that would leave most U.S. citizens believing that their country serves the cause of world peace.

Patriotic exceptionalism plays a stunningly dangerous role in nuclear policy. Since the end of World War II, the U.S. has maintained that these weapons are actually instruments of peace because, with mutually assured destruction, nuclear weapons deter wars. But if the deterrence argument is valid, then we ought to be busy ensuring that all sides in potential conflicts have nuclear capabilities. Israel already has nuclear weapons; give them to Syria and the Palestine Authority. China already has them; give them to Taiwan. Give them to North and South Korea, to Ethiopia and Eritrea. But if such a deterrence scenario is too absurd to consider, then the rationale for any nation to have nuclear weapons is undermined. I am not in favor of the nonproliferation of nuclear weapons. I am in favor of the eradication of these weapons. It is only by asserting its own exceptional status that the U.S. can claim the prerogative to possess these weapons while denying that prerogative to others, as if nations need to demonstrate that they are up-standing members of the world community before they will be allowed to possess this mad capacity to obliterate life on the planet. Nuclear weapons have never prevented wars; they have generated wars by proxy. And now, nuclear nonproliferation becomes the excuse for invading Iraq and for both Republicans and Democrats to rattle sabers at Iran.

Mark Twain wrote that, when all you have is a hammer, all problems start to look like nails. Armaments are the one resource — the one hammer — that the U.S. has in abundance. With the U.S. accounting for a majority of the world's arms exports, it is simply hubris to believe that these weapons will target only America's enemies. These weapons will kill others as well, including Americans, as they already have in Somalia and Panama. As political leaders express shock that America's adversaries are such thugs, the amnesia about yesterday's U.S. support for today's enemies is downright Orwellian. In 1988, the city of Halabja was destroyed with chemical weapons on orders of Saddam Hussein. In the 1980s, a bloody war had been raging between Iran and Iraq, and the U.S. was providing covert assistance to *both* sides. As Oliver North was secretly funneling weapons to Iran, Donald Rumsfeld was dashing off to Baghdad to reassure Saddam Hussein of U.S. friendship. Suddenly in 1991 and 2003, Saddam Hussein was a thug, for which the evidence was his use of chemical weapons against Iraqi Kurds. Well, when he did that in 1988, he was our thug.

Again in June 2007, all problems looked like nails as it was revealed that the U.S. was arming specific Sunni militia groups in Iraq because these particular militias were opposed to Al Qaeda. Somehow, it no longer mattered that members of these militias had also been part of the government of Saddam Hussein that the U.S. had deposed in 2003. We oppose adversaries with weapons. We support friends with weapons. We try to turn adversaries into friends with weapons. All we have is a hammer. The professed humanitarian concern that there will be a bloodbath if the U.S. military withdraws from Iraq precipitously is simply disingenuous. By spreading weapons abroad, the U.S. is creating the very conditions that make carnage inevitable in the future.

One patriotic idea that is invoked repeatedly with very little scrutiny is the notion that our troops are sent to battle in defense of freedom. In fact, war is the primary context in which freedom is undermined abroad and at home. Abroad in this current war, the U.S. has provided aid in return for military agreements with Tajikistan and Uzbekistan, both countries located near the battlefield, and both with regimes that have human rights records that barely meet the standards of Saddam Hussein. At home during World War I, conscientious objectors were routinely imprisoned, and so were Wobblies for the crime of saying that the U.S. was involved in a "rich man's war." On the west coast in World War II, Americans of Japanese ancestry were sent to prison camps, and fast on the heels of the Korean War, the House Un-American Activities Committee set to work. The Vietnam War saw the surveillance and infiltration of groups ranging from the Black Panthers to the Quakers. And today need I mention the Patriot Act and Abu Ghraib, Guantanamo and extraordinary rendition, waterboarding and secret prisons in Eastern Europe, detention without charge and free speech zones, as if zoned speech can ever be free? It was as recent as the 1930s that Herbert Hoover's Secretary of War, Henry Stimson, opposed the creation of a national intelligence agency because "Gentlemen do not read each other's mail."[42] Today, they can read and listen to whatever they please. Despite patriotic assertions to the contrary, war is the enemy of freedom, not its defender.

Elections are touted as evidence that America is "the land of the free."[43] We get to choose our leaders, often from a pool of those who have

42. Stimson, quoted by Richard J. Barnet, *Roots of War* (Baltimore: Penguin Books, 1972), p. 31. Barnet notes that it was in this same "prehistoric era" that a general vetoed plans for producing a bomber because it was immoral to plot the killing of noncombatants.

43. It should be noted that U.S. officials have not regarded elections elsewhere as

managed to garnish sufficient financial backing from corporate interests. But as the government's ability to know what we are doing and saying has increased exponentially, our ability to know what the state is doing has been in sharp decline, especially in times of war. In the name of national security, vast quantities of information are classified. "We do not torture," said President Bush, but then we are denied access to information about what it is that we actually do. So, how am I supposed to vote when I am denied the ability to know what is being done in my name? I am given the choice between Republicans who want a troop surge in Iraq and Democrats who don't like that idea, but like the idea of funding it under the rubric of "supporting the troops."

What are the criteria by which a society's claims to "freedom" can be evaluated? One relevant tool of measurement would be to count the number of people living in chains and cages. The United States has the highest per capita rate of incarceration in the world, with fully one percent of the adult population of the country imprisoned. When people talk about a free society, it matters less how many people step into voting booths; even Hitler got elected. It matters more how many people are sitting inside cages, and when we have the highest per capita number in the world, we are not free.

As noted earlier, patriotism is a power that possesses us. In cases of possession, the appropriate response is exorcism. Through prayer and repetition of Scripture and display of symbols like the cross, the exorcist enters into a struggle to move the possessed individual away from the power that is holding him or her captive and toward a new allegiance.

I'm not opposed to allegiance, but patriotic allegiance is too small, hemmed in by national borders. Each year, 40 million people on our planet die of hunger and diseases linked to malnutrition. To equal that horror, terrorists would have to be very busy indeed, crashing 320 filled-to-capacity jumbo jets each and every day, with half of the passengers being children.[44] Like you, perhaps, I love those people whose allegiance is

---

providing similar evidence of freedom. When candidates unfriendly to U.S. policy are elected in Nicaragua or Venezuela or Iran, these leaders are routinely dismissed as "dictators," even when international observers judge that they are chosen in "free and fair" elections. In recent Palestinian parliamentary elections, there was considerable U.S. financial intervention in favor of Fatah, but when Hamas won, the U.S. State Department denounced the tainted election of "terrorists."

44. Daniel Berrigan, *Lamentations: From New York to Kabul and Beyond* (Chicago: Sheed & Ward, 2002), p. 96.

written large, across all national boundaries — Oxfam, Doctors without Borders, the Christian Peacemaker Teams. Make your allegiance large — as large as peace and justice, as large as God.

No, I'm not opposed to allegiance, but patriotic allegiance is not small enough. The imagined community is no community at all. Like you, perhaps, I love those genuine communities of people who actually work together and whose allegiance is written small — as small as the park they hope to save from development, as small as the children they hope to save from homelessness. Make your allegiance small — as small as the birds of the air and the flowers of the field, as small as the crazy, hungry bag lady you encounter on the street, as small as God.

Finally, insofar as it matters, let me mention that I do not dislike all patriotic people. I even have a few in the family. Insofar as it matters, do I believe that all patriots are demonically possessed? Well, I have my demons too. Nonetheless, I do sincerely hope that all of us, patriotic or not, might share that longing for a new world of which Arundhati Roy spoke, and that on a quiet day, we too might hear her breathing. And it is my fondest hope that next time and every time some Decider steps forward to announce that, in the name of peace and freedom and all things holy, it's killing time, we can all respond that, no, it's not. It's time for life. It's time for life.

6. In Praise of Inutility

In Western culture and in the emerging global monoculture, utilitarianism has become the dominant approach to moral reasoning. By this, I do not mean to suggest that utilitarianism is necessarily the favored school of thought in philosophy departments or among scholars for whom "ethics" is an academic discipline, but rather that for most of us who are not in ivory towers, the utilitarian framing of our decisions and actions has become virtually instinctive. Whether it is governments' decisions about foreign policy or individuals' decisions about personal finance, there is diminishing reliance on any rules or guidelines that were once thought to have been handed down by the ancestors or the gods as aids in the struggle to live the good life. Deontology (from the Greek *deon*, "obligation") has been giving way to the teleological focus of utilitarianism. While deontologists insist that certain kinds of actions may be evaluated as moral or immoral without regard to goals or intentions, utilitarians contend that the morality of particular actions depends on the outcome that is sought. For better and for worse, the rules are being replaced by teleology.[1]

1. Is this claim contradicted by the significant number of Americans who are opposed to abortion? Opposition to abortion would seem to be based on a rule that is simple and straightforward: do not kill. Even though many abortion opponents allow for exceptions, the arguments that are used to justify these exceptions are not always utilitarian. When exceptions are made for the life of the mother, the rationale is still "pro-life." In cases that involve the horrors of rape and incest, some abortion opponents make exceptions based on the victims' right to self-defense, an argument which, whether cogent or not, begins to introduce elements of utilitarianism. But the clarity of the opposition to killing becomes to-

Presentation for classes taught by Dr. William Ayres and Rev. Tracy Sadd, Elizabethtown College, November 6 and 8, 2007.

But these are not the only two options.[2] In order to challenge utilitarianism, it is not necessary or desirable to regard ethical standards as mere collections of commandments, rules, and laws. Biblical perspectives on a life of faithfulness are not founded on deontology, let alone on utilitarianism, but rather on the ethics of ontology (from the Greek *ontos*, "being"). The foundational question for ethical action does not concern goals or rules but identity, not in the abstract, individualistic sense of perpetually wondering "Who am I?" but in the very concrete sense of asking, "Who has God created us to be? Who does God call us to be?" The faithful are called to live in response to the "life-giving spirit" of the last Adam (1 Corinthians 15:45) rather than being immersed in the death that came through the first Adam (1 Corinthians 15:21-22). For the faithful, action flows from being in the community of which Christ is head rather than from adherence to a catalogue of rules which are of no help in the avoid-

---

tally muddled when we consider that the vast majority of abortion opponents are not pacifists. While some Roman Catholics have espoused the "seamless" morality of renouncing abortion, the death penalty, and all wars, their numbers pale in comparison to the many abortion opponents who lend their support to "just" wars or even preemptive wars. For them, to put the matter crassly, the right to life ends at birth. To phrase the matter in terms of ethical discourse, a deontological approach to ethics holds sway in relationship to all of those who are not yet born, but in relationship to everyone else, the sanctity of life may be mitigated by utilitarian considerations. What is it about the moment of birth that provides the hinge for such a dramatic shift in ethics? Some nonpacifist opponents of abortion insist that they are not abandoning the commandment against killing at the moment of birth because it is a rule that applies only to "innocent" life. At this point, all manner of serious questions arise that are rarely broached in the abortion debate. Whatever became of the doctrine of original sin? Who determines innocence? Does it end at birth or does it persist until children acquire a consciousness of sin? What of the Pauline reminder of the unconscious grip of sin in our most righteous moments? If innocence is lost with the ability to differentiate right from wrong, then why do humans have so little regard for the sanctity of the lives of nonhuman animals who are innocent in precisely this sense of lacking consciousness of sin? Since "collateral damage" is inevitable in every war, are nonpacifist abortion opponents engaging in a utilitarian suspension of rules? Suffice it to say that, first impressions notwithstanding, widespread opposition to abortion does not necessarily indicate widespread opposition to utilitarianism, let alone widespread respect for the sanctity of life.

2. In academic circles, the polarity between utilitarianism and deontology seems stark indeed. There is a certain oxymoronic quality to the name "rule-utilitarians" for those ethicists who have sought a way out of the impasse by melding (with variable success) elements of both approaches to ethical reasoning. The development of rule-utilitarianism is traced by David Lyons, *Forms and Limits of Utilitarianism* (New York: Oxford University Press, 1965). Lyons finds resonance between the rule-utilitarian approach and John Rawls's reflections on "the duty of fair play" (pp. 182-97).

ance of sin, let alone in leading a life of righteousness (Romans 5:12-21). For the faithful, the one teleology that matters is not that of setting goals and calculating the most effective means of reaching them, but rather that of the promised return of the slaughtered Lamb (Revelation 7:16-17), a promise that already pulls believers to live in the presence of God's reign. Identity is shaped by narrative, by the story of God and the story of the people of God. God is love, and this determines who believers are called to be (1 John 4:7-16). In brief, this is what I mean by an ethics of ontology, an ethics that is alien to utilitarianism.

Jeremy Bentham is known as the father of modern utilitarianism. In an effort to free ethics from a rules orientation, Bentham argued that truly ethical actions are means toward the higher goal of producing (in his famous phrase) "the greatest happiness of the greatest number." Bentham recognized that "happiness" was a word fraught with all manner of definitional possibilities, and he sought to exclude the more hedonistic of these by arriving at an understanding of happiness as a condition of well-being that went beyond a mere emotional state.[3] A more formidable problem than the clarity about happiness, however, is the recognition that, in order to produce the greatest happiness for the greatest number, it is often necessary to produce unhappiness for some people in the short term. Along with being a philosopher, Bentham was a jurist and an architect, and he designed a model prison called Panopticon. In order to create the greater happiness of a society with less crime, Bentham was fully prepared to create unhappiness for lawbreakers by locking them up. But even for lawbreakers, Bentham insisted, the goal was not to produce unhappiness ("punishment" was a word that Bentham called "evil"), but to rehabilitate them for the sake of their own well-being along with that of society.

Putting aside the paternalism of presuming to know what will make for the greater happiness of the individual, let alone that of the greatest number, the goal orientation of utilitarianism entails a certain pretension to omniscience. It is difficult enough to evaluate whether an action is good in and of itself, but utilitarians take the additional step of claiming to know whether the result of an action will be good in the future. Indeed, utilitarians are willing to sacrifice the present for the future. We may engage in a little evil now for the sake of avoiding a future result that is really

---

3. Bentham's inclusion of security and prosperity in his understanding of "happiness" was by no means unique in the English-speaking world of the late eighteenth century. Note the reference to "the pursuit of happiness" in the U.S. Declaration of Independence.

— well, evil. The people who are made to suffer now are treated as mere means — mere tools — toward reaching a future condition that (it is somehow known) will be happier for a greater number.[4]

When it comes to supposed justifications for violence, utilitarianism amounts to little more than doing ethics by body count. In John 18:14, the high priest Caiaphas is the one who advised that it was "better to have one person die for the people." Individuals are highly expendable once the case is made that they are being sacrificed for the sake of the masses. Better to have one person die. But since the one person is being killed to spare lives that might otherwise be lost in the future, it is impossible to prove that the killing will be efficacious. Since the good goal to be achieved by killing lies in some imaginary tomorrow, it is impossible to reliably assert whether this one killing will spare the lives of ten people or a hundred or a thousand or none at all. Therefore, it is safer for utilitarians to assert with greater abstraction and greater ambiguity that the killing is for the sake of the social order or freedom or God or country. The governing authorities clearly *and accurately* perceived Jesus as a threat to the religious and political order. Jesus was killed in the name of good government. Jesus was killed in the name of all things holy.[5]

One prominent illustration of doing ethics by body count in the modern era was the rationale presented for the atomic bombings of Hiroshima and Nagasaki. The Truman Administration argued that the one hundred thousand deaths that were the immediate result of these bombings actually prevented the one million deaths that would have resulted from an Allied invasion of the Japanese mainland. This rationale employs the prognostications and pretensions to omniscience that are routine ele-

4. Philosopher William L. Reese summarizes the seven criteria of the "hedonic calculus" that Bentham used to weigh the consequences of behavior: "a) the intensity of the pleasure or pain; b) the duration of the pleasure or pain; c) the certainty or uncertainty of the pleasure or pain; d) the propinquity or remoteness of the pleasure or pain; e) the fecundity of the pleasure or pain; f) the purity of the pleasure or pain; g) the extent of the pleasure or pain, i.e., the number to whom it extends." Reese, *Dictionary of Philosophy and Religion: Eastern and Western Thought* (Atlantic Highlands, N.J.: Humanities Press and Sussex, England: Harvester Press, 1980), p. 53.

5. Satisfaction theories of the atonement claim that God demanded this death or somehow needed this death in order to proceed with the divine work of salvation. One perverse consequence of such a claim is that it places a divine stamp of approval on the state's self-appointed role as crucifier. Such theories of the atonement are challenged in the excellent essays brought together by Brad Jersak and Michael Hardin, eds., *Stricken by God? Nonviolent Identification and the Victory of Christ* (Grand Rapids: Eerdmans, 2007).

ments in the mathematical ethics of utilitarians. Why would the prognostications posit an invasion of Japan as inevitable? Since the Japanese government was already making diplomatic peace overtures to the Soviet Union, why not forecast that the war was about to end and that many lives could be spared by not using atomic weapons? Why was the temporal horizon of the prognostication so limited? In the tabulation of body counts, why did the forecasters not see that the use of atomic weapons would help to launch an arms race in which millions would die as the nuclear powers sponsored wars by proxy in Korea, Vietnam, Afghanistan, Angola, Mozambique, and elsewhere? The U.S. decision to use atomic bombs was certainly motivated in part by a desire to prevent the Soviet Union from setting the terms for an end to the war. But it was also the utilitarian ethics which determined that there were only the two options of (a) using weapons of mass destruction or (b) invading Japan, and not (c) waiting for Japan to surrender. Utilitarians do not just do nothing. Since the goal is to produce a greater happiness than that which is currently available, inaction is an obstacle to the moral life.

I must confess to sharing some of the utilitarian bias in favor of action. In a militaristic society, passivity can constitute a mere endorsement of the violent status quo. But before declaring that inaction is an obstacle to the moral life, there must be greater clarity about the nature of action and inaction, the nature of assertion and quiescence. If paying taxes for militarism is an "action" (which it surely seems to be), then the simple refusal or failure to pay is an "inaction" which certainly causes all hell to break loose. Which is action and which passivity: showing up for induction after being drafted into the military or simply staying home? But the utilitarian bias is not just in favor of action per se. The action must be oriented toward the goal of increasing the quality and quantity of happiness. From a utilitarian perspective, monasticism might be judged as morally suspect or irrelevant insofar as it is a movement of retreat from the world and, moreover, a movement that has little regard for worldly standards of happiness. From a utilitarian perspective, the carnival might be judged as morally suspect or irrelevant because it generates a frivolity that is too fleeting and that is not oriented toward a higher goal. And yet, both monasticism and carnivals have had serious social consequences that elude the goal-oriented focus of utilitarianism. Briefly, then, let us go to the monastery and the carnival.

Of what possible use is prayer?[6] Of what possible use are those monas-

6. In his profound reflections on prayer, Jacques Ellul is thoroughly critical of any ef-

tic communities that devote themselves exclusively to prayer, contemplation, and study divorced from the "real world"? Still, in the first few
centuries of Christianity, the movement of wild-eyed hermits and communitarian visionaries into the wilderness at the periphery of the settled
world carried an implicit (and often enough, explicit) renunciation of what
passed for "civilization." There in the desert, they not only battled demons
but also waited for the revelations and the sacred visitations that were never
manifest nearer the centers of power. Hermits, monks, and nuns pose a
threat to society, not because of what they are doing, but because of what
they are not doing. They are not adequately supportive of the values of
work, wealth, and power that are intrinsic to the health of any society. The
Spiritual Franciscans of medieval Europe were judged to be heretical even
though they were not organizing violent revolution or even espousing
theological doctrines that were particularly unorthodox. They were simply
rigorous in their understanding of their own vows of poverty. While other
orders of monks and nuns claimed adherence to poverty because they did
not have ownership of the comfortable monasteries and convents in which
they lived, the Spiritual Franciscans abstained from the use as well as the
possession of property that exceeded the basic requirements of suste-
nance.[7] The Waldensians, the Cathars, the beguines and beghards — it is
no mere coincidence that all these groups that were declared heretical were
movements that espoused voluntary poverty. In their very uselessness and
self-renunciation, monastics and heretics carried the germ of an idea that
threatened civilization itself. In his reflections on the life of Francis of
Assisi, Christian Bobin summarized the idea: "I will be enriched by everything that I lose. The world of the spirit is nothing different from the material world. The world of the spirit is just the material world finally
set right. In the world of the spirit, one makes one's fortune by going bank-

---

fort to understand prayer on the basis of its utility. To view prayer as being effective at altering events and circumstances is not only unbiblical, writes Ellul, but it is also refuted by the
empirical evidence. "Prayer is ridiculed because its effectiveness is entirely unpredictable,
and statistical techniques are able to show that the percentage of 'answers' to prayer corresponds exactly to the percentage of success which would have been the case had events
been allowed to take their own course, and without prayer." Ellul, *Prayer and Modern Man*,
trans. C. Edward Hopkin (New York: Seabury Press, 1970), p. 79. The only biblical foundation for prayer is obedience to the call to pray. Prayer is an act of eschatological hope, writes
Ellul, and a somewhat absurd assertion of human freedom in the face of necessity and
worldly circumstance.

7. Malcolm Lambert, *Medieval Heresy: Popular Movements from the Gregorian Reform to the
Reformation*, 2nd ed. (Cambridge, Mass.: Blackwell, 1992), pp. 189-214.

rupt."[8] Flying in the face of all earthly utility, such an idea could not be tolerated. Monastics and heretics surprise us. The more staunchly they adhere to a vision that seems otherworldly and impractical, the greater the danger they pose to the social order.

And the carnival surprises us, too. Some theorists maintain that religion was born in dance, in ecstasy, in trance and spirit-possession.[9] From the perspective of those who seek to impose hierarchical social organization, the problem with ecstatic ritual, glossolalia, and spirit-possession is that they all tend toward the anarchic defiance of structure. How can one hope to control the timing and the nature of a spirit's visit? The Romans sought to exercise control by outlawing the more extreme Dionysian rites and by seeking to channel unruly and subversive impulses into officially sanctioned festivals like Saturnalia in which, *for one day only,* slaves exchanged places with their masters and social boundaries were erased. In medieval Europe, officially sanctioned carnivals in which mere peasants played the "king of fools" served to restrain the subversive edge of joy.[10] But even these carnivals that once were authorized by princes and by bish-

8. Christian Bobin, *The Very Lowly: A Meditation on Francis of Assisi,* trans. Michael H. Kohn (Boston: New Seeds, 2006), p. 53.

9. Israeli archaeologist Yosef Garfinkel observes that, in the depictions of human interactions, dance was the only activity portrayed by the cave artists of the Neolithic and Chalcolithic eras. Not a single scene of warfare or violence among humans was depicted by these prehistoric artists. Of course, anthropologists have looked for a *functional* explanation for the prevalence of this seemingly useless activity, dancing. Perhaps dance provided for group cohesion. In hunting or in defending against predatory animals, perhaps coordinated movement created the helpful illusion that the dancers were a single large beast rather than a collection of small and vulnerable individuals (or maybe not). See Barbara Ehrenreich, *Dancing in the Streets: A History of Collective Joy* (New York: Metropolitan Books, 2007), pp. 9-10, 22-30.

10. Ehrenreich, *Dancing in the Streets,* pp. 38, 78. State efforts to establish official regulation of carnivals is not a phenomenon of Europe alone. In Taiwan, there has been a struggle of long duration over the control of the annual Universal Salvation Festival (Pudu). During Pudu, there is an effort to appease the ghosts of people who were treated with disrespect in both life and death. These are the angry ghosts of marginalized people (beggars, bandits, gamblers, prostitutes) who were often persecuted by the state while they were alive. Since Pudu is too significant a festival to outlaw, the Taiwanese government has been struggling to reinterpret the meaning of this annual event that combines an explosive mixture of celebration, unruly ghosts, and remembrance of state oppression. Robert P. Weller, "Bandits, Beggars and Ghosts: The Failure of State Control over Religious Interpretation in Taiwan," in *Across the Boundaries of Belief: Contemporary Issues in the Anthropology of Religion,* ed. Morton Klass and Maxine K. Weisgrau (Boulder, Colo.: Westview Press, 1999), pp. 271-90.

ops were eventually suppressed. Even the carefully restrained mockery of the king of fools was too derisive of power. Even the carefully limited expressions of joy always seemed in danger of flowing out of containment. So, beginning with the Reformation and continuing for centuries thereafter, all but the most staid carnivals and festivals were outlawed. As the people of Europe encountered the people of the western hemisphere and Africa and the Pacific islands, the contention that these newly encountered people were "savages" was based in part on the ecstatic nature of their celebrations and rituals.[11] A portion of the colonial mission was to teach these people to put aside their frivolity and superstitions for the sake of development. Of course, there were similar savages inside Europe. In England, the growth of capitalism required that the supposed libertinism of the Ranters should be eradicated,[12] and that the tempered festivals that were allowed to continue should be concentrated into the seasons of the year when the demand for labor was light.[13] So which is it? Is the carnival subversive or is it useless? In its very uselessness, the carnival is subversive of capitalism.

Any reflection on the meaning of inutility cannot help but cite one of the masterworks of spiritual literature, the Bhagavad Gita. The Gita totally renounces the goal orientation that would come to typify utilitarianism. From the Bhagavad Gita, 2.47-48:

On action alone be thy interest,
   Never on its fruits;
Let not the fruits of action be thy motive,
   Nor be thy attachment to inaction.

11. Ehrenreich, *Dancing in the Streets*, pp. 1-9. European explorers described the wild celebrations of native people with contempt, but it was always a fascinated contempt that betrayed a hint of longing — perhaps for something that the Europeans had repressed within themselves. In the European encounter with "the other," a bewildering confluence of repression and projection was brought to the surface. The colonizer's violence was projected onto the cannibal. The colonizer's appetite for power and control was projected onto shamans, magicians, and practitioners of Voodoo to the point that the savages were made all the more fearsome and the courage of the conqueror was magnified. See Ruth Mayer, *Artificial Africas: Colonial Images in the Time of Globalization* (Lebanon, N.H.: University Press of New England, 2002), pp. 191-92, 196.

12. Christopher Hill, *A Nation of Change and Novelty: Radical Politics, Religion and Literature in Seventeenth-Century England* (New York: Routledge, 1990), pp. 152-94.

13. E. P. Thompson, *Customs in Common: Studies in Traditional Popular Culture* (New York: The New Press, 1993), p. 51.

Abiding in discipline perform actions,
  Abandoning attachment . . . ,
Being indifferent to success or failure;
  Discipline is defined as indifference.[14]

One must act, yes, but only with a focus on the duty to perform the act it-self and not on the result that one hopes to achieve (Gita 3.19). Actions do bear fruits (Gita 14.16-17), but we must surrender the pretense of being able to know them or control them. Even and especially "religious" acts must be freed from any desire to attain a particular goal (Gita 18:5-9).

Throughout the Bhagavad Gita, the speaker who imparts wisdom is Lord Krishna, an avatar of the Hindu deity Vishnu. Krishna counsels unattachment to success or failure, but when you fail, says Krishna, then bring your failure to me (Gita 12.6-11; 18.57). For all its philosophical reflec-tions on action, in the final analysis, the Bhagavad Gita is devotional litera-ture. I am not a proponent of the claim that all spiritual traditions are basi-cally alike, but Juan Mascaró is certainly correct in discerning some points of reverberation between the words of Krishna and the epistles of Paul.[15] Gita 9.27: "Whatever you do, or eat, or give, or offer in adoration, let it be an offering to me; and whatever you suffer, suffer it for me."[16] 1 Corinthi-ans 10:31: "So, whether you eat or drink, or whatever you do, do every-thing for the glory of God." The worth of an action is determined by devo-tion and discipleship, not by success or failure. In the Pauline way of putting it, we are justified by the grace of God rather than by deed.

Of course, even very devout actions can be wrong actions. Gita and Gospels diverge most sharply, not on the refutation of attachment to goals and worldly standards of success, but on the nature of the actions that are reconcilable with who God calls the faithful to be. The Bhagavad Gita is a text that was written in a time (the sixth century BCE) when duty was fully determined by caste. The propriety of various actions depended on whether one belonged to the class of priests, or kings and warriors, or pro-fessionals engaged in commerce, or laborers, or outcastes. The narrative that provides the context for the philosophical and devotional insights of the Gita is a story that is directly focused on the duties that pertain to

14. *The Bhagavad Gītā*, trans. Franklin Edgerton (New York: Harper Torchbooks, 1964), p. 14.

15. Juan Mascaró, "Introduction," *The Bhagavad Gita*, trans. Juan Mascaró (New York: Penguin Books, 1962), p. 33.

16. Mascaró translation.

caste. Arjuna, one of the two main characters in the story, is a warrior who hesitates on the brink of battle when he discovers that relatives and friends are members of the army that is arrayed against him. At this point of hesitation, it is revealed that Arjuna's charioteer is none other than Krishna, who urges Arjuna forward into battle. Do the duty that is given to you in life. Even if death is a consequence of your action, death itself is illusory in the great cycle of rebirth and the transmigration of souls (Gita 2.16-38). In contrast to the nonviolence of the gospel, it is caste alone that permits — no, requires — the violence of Arjuna. Indeed, the Gita struggles to hold in tandem the virtue of harmlessness (Gita 16.2) and the duty that is required of Arjuna. While the Gospels relentlessly associate Jesus with the lowly, with the manger, with the cross, the author of the Gita conveys respect for the upper classes by portraying Krishna as possessing qualities of wealth, majesty, beauty, and power (Gita 10.19-42).

It was one of the great contributions of Mohandas Gandhi that his commentary on the Bhagavad Gita served to liberate its spiritual insights from the battlefield setting and from sympathy with the caste system. Gandhi was consistently opposed to distinctions based on caste; he called the untouchables *harijan*, meaning "children of God." He readily acknowledged that the Gita was not a pacifist treatise, but that did nothing to diminish the relevance of its meaning for the *satyagrahi*, the one who is engaged in the struggle for nonviolence and truth. Just as Krishna urged Arjuna to act out of duty rather than out of attachment to the goal, so too, those who are called to nonviolence must act without attachment to effectiveness.[17]

If there is an action, a virtue, a way of being that is good in and of itself, then why must we establish that it is of utility toward the achievement of some higher goal? Take honesty, for example. Does honesty work? Is it effective? These are nonsensical questions — questions that might make sense if we asked them about computer software. Does it do what it is intended to do? But what is honesty intended to do? I suppose honesty is part of what Plato and Aristotle would call "the good life" because to be honest is to respect the dignity of others by avoiding intentional manipulation and deceit. To go much beyond that, we would need to arrive at detailed definitions of honesty and truthfulness. We would need to ask whether honesty can ever be wielded in a way that is disrespectful of others, as perhaps indicated by the phrase "brutal honesty." We would need to

17. Mohandas Gandhi, "The Gita and Satyagraha," in *Gandhi: Selected Writings*, ed. Ronald Duncan (New York: Harper Colophon, 1972), p. 40.

respond somehow to the memorable and eerily postmodern question posed by Pontius Pilate, "What is truth?" (John 18:38).[18] We would need to delve into downright existential and epistemological questions. Honest according to what? According to the facts? According to my feelings? How do I know if I am being honest about my feelings when they change from day to day or even moment to moment? Even without devoting the next ten years to a study of honesty and truthfulness, however, many could still agree that it is good to refrain from intentionally telling lies, and that the virtue of honesty is not dependent on utility or any higher goal.

This detour into honesty as virtue is directly related to Gandhi's perspective on nonviolence. In his commentary on the Gita, Gandhi cited two actions that are never good in and of themselves — violence and lying.[19] To be regarded as justifiable, both violence and lying must be understood as means toward the achievement of some goal that is (in theory) good. The goodness of the goal to be achieved then slops back over the violence or the lying to render them, if not good, at least justifiable or understandable.

Or necessary. In the just war theory, necessity is introduced as the justification for acts of violence that, we are assured, would ordinarily be regarded as reprehensible.[20] Jacques Ellul notes that there is a type of ethical

---

18. In contrast to the presentations of Jesus in the Synoptic Gospels, John's Jesus is bold in revealing the nature of his mission. John 18:37 says that Jesus came into the world ". . . to testify to the truth." Pilate's comment in the very next verse is less a sincere question than an indication that he wants none of whatever truth Jesus has to offer. Governors have no need to get their truth from common criminals.

Christian Bobin reflects on what the story of Balaam's ass (Numbers 22) reveals about the nature of truth. Balaam had been summoned by the King of Moab to assist him with his plans to attack the Israelites. As Balaam was traveling in response to the call of the Moabites, the ass on which he was riding saw angels repeatedly blocking the path in front of her. Balaam could not see the angels, and when he whipped her for refusing to go forward, the ass spoke to explain that they were in the presence of angels. Bobin notes that this story tells us two things. First, asses see angels, and it should not surprise us that angels are drawn to such lowly beasts of burden. Second, the truth can be spoken by an ass, and this too should not surprise us. Bobin writes, ". . . the truth is never so great as in the humiliation of the one who proclaims it." Bobin, *The Very Lowly*, p. 75. Yet, this very humiliation means that there is little about the truth that the world will find to be of utility. Pilate could find no possible use for the truth to which Jesus testified.

19. Gandhi, "Anasakti Yoga, or the Gospel of Selfless Action, an Extract from Gandhi's Commentary on the Bhagavad Gita," in *Gandhi: Selected Writings*, p. 37.

20. Chris Hedges has written insightfully on the ravages of war. Those who suffer in war are the helpless and the innocent. War is madness fueled by nationalism, writes Hedges. War is more addictive than any other drug. War is a god (Mars) who uses us despite our illu-

sleight of hand that occurs with humanity's "attempt to control necessity by submitting to it — by making a virtue out of it." The effort to equate the necessary with the good is universal, writes Ellul. "In one way or another, on different planes of activity, in all systems of morality, necessity ends up as a value, and then displays its extraordinary efficacy for allowing man to declare himself just."[21] The moment we acknowledge that necessity is what determines our actions, however, we have surrendered all possibility of freedom in moral choice. When violence is declared to be necessary,

---

sions that we are using him. Hedges writes, "And yet, despite all this, I am not a pacifist. I respect and admire the qualities of professional soldiers. . . . Force is and I suspect always will be part of the human condition. There are times when the force wielded by one immoral faction must be countered by a faction that, while never moral, is perhaps less immoral." Chris Hedges, *War Is a Force That Gives Us Meaning* (New York: Anchor Books, 2003), p. 16.

For Hedges, insofar as force is "part of the human condition," necessity is the basis for his rejection of pacifism. There is ambiguity for Hedges on the question of whether force is "wielded" (as in the quote above) or whether we are wielded by it (as suggested by his identification of war as an addiction and as a god). There is also lack of clarity about what distinguishes the "less immoral" from the simply "immoral." Hedges seems to indicate that the ready resort to violence is what characterizes the actions of the simply "immoral" in settings ranging from Kosovo to Rwanda. But would that not mean that when the "less immoral" resort to violence, they become even less distinguishable from the simply "immoral"? Jacques Ellul notes that *all* sides *always* seek to justify their resort to violence on grounds of necessity and by arguments that try to differentiate their particular type of violence from that of their adversaries. All violence is the same, writes Ellul, and arguments of utility notwithstanding, all violence gives birth to nothing but more violence. "That violence is so generally condoned today shows that Hitler won his war after all: his enemies imitate him." Ellul, *Violence: Reflections from a Christian Perspective*, trans. Cecelia Gaul Kings (New York: Seabury Press, 1969), p. 29.

Chris Hedges writes (p. 17), "The only antidote to ward off self-destruction and indiscriminate use of force is humility and, ultimately, compassion. Reinhold Niebuhr aptly reminded us that we must all act and then ask for forgiveness. This book is not a call for inaction. It is a call for repentance." Pacifism is not a call for inaction either. If the act that Niebuhr and Hedges contend we "must" do entails the use of force that is supposedly discriminate, then these references to "forgiveness" and "repentance" are antithetical to the biblical sense of those words. "Repentance" *(metanoia)* means turning around and setting out on a new path rather than being prepared to express post facto regret for setting out still again on a path that we already know to be nefarious and deadly. We are called to deeds that are consistent with repentance (Acts 26:20). In Luke 17:10, the call is for us to ask forgiveness and proclaim ourselves to be unfaithful servants *after* we have loved the enemy, turned the other cheek, and returned good for evil, not after we have intentionally bludgeoned the enemy.

21. Ellul, *To Will and To Do*, trans. C. Edward Hopkin (Philadelphia: Pilgrim Press, 1969), pp. 66, 69.

then the choice of nonviolence is not "wrong" so much as it is delusional, and the choice of violence is not "right" so much as it is predetermined. Predetermined by what? This supposed necessity of violence is certainly not a matter of DNA or intrinsic nature. By nature, cats are predisposed to catch mice, but there is no evidence that humans are genetically predisposed to attack one another. In the evolutionary scheme of things, humans would not have survived with such a predisposition.[22] So if it is not something inside ourselves, what is it that makes the choice of violence necessary? Political leaders usually eschew the argument that violence is intrinsic to human nature (an argument that deprives violence of nobility) and argue instead that there are circumstances in which violence is necessary to our survival as a nation and perhaps as a species. In this argument, violence is not related to DNA; it is more like the food and water that we must ingest if we hope to be alive a month from now. In early 2003, National Security Advisor Condoleezza Rice declared that, if the United States did not launch a preemptive war against Iraq, the consequence could be mushroom clouds over America. From this perspective, if we wished to avoid the nuclear annihilation of life on the planet, then it was necessary not to avert war but to embrace it.

Increasingly, however, people who insist that violence is necessary are not contending that it is inherent to our nature, nor even that our survival depends on it, but rather that violence provides the most effective and efficient means of attaining a goal. In earlier eras of human history, efficiency was just one of multiple factors that were considered in deciding on a course of action, but, in the technological society of the modern era, efficiency trumps all other considerations.[23] The efficacious and efficient action is the necessary action. This argument is made not only by those who favor preemptive wars, but also by the advocates of so-called "humanitar-

22. Dutch primatologist Frans de Waal observes that humans are genetically equidistant (and not too distant at that) from two species of apes — the chimpanzee, who tends to be aggressive, territorial, and hierarchical, and the bonobo, who tends to be gentle, cooperative, and "altruistic," even toward vulnerable members of other species like injured birds. It is noteworthy that, more than the ethicists who contend that our actions are governed by necessity, primatologists contend that our DNA sets us free! We are free to choose between our genetic capacity for aggression or altruism. Frans de Waal, *Our Inner Ape: A Leading Primatologist Explores Why We Are Who We Are* (New York: Riverhead Books, 2005).

23. Ellul writes that "the multiplicity of means is reduced to one: the most efficient." Jacques Ellul, *The Technological Society*, trans. John Wilkinson (New York: Vintage Books, 1964), p. 21.

ian" military intervention.[24] The argument for NATO bombing of the former Yugoslavia was that NATO military action would bring an end to ethnic cleansing. In essence, this entailed the clairvoyant assertion that any killing that resulted from NATO actions would avert a greater quantity of killing in the future. And yet, the claim that violent intervention is most effective at preserving life is not self-evident. In both Rwanda and Darfur, international intervention was horribly meager and late, not only because of a general apathy about Africa, but also because political leaders seemed incapable of conceiving of any type of intervention other than violence, as if the only options available were war or negligence. Instead of waiting to see if the public response to atrocities would become so outraged that military action would eventually be regarded as "necessary," many lives might have been spared in both Rwanda and Darfur by early, creative, and vigorous nonviolent intervention that could have included negotiating, imposing appropriate sanctions, flooding the areas with food and medical supplies, airlifting people out of danger zones, and "invading" the areas with unarmed people trained to interpose themselves in settings of potential violence. Is such a proposal naïve or unrealistic? Perhaps less so than the assumption that war saves lives or leads to peace.

I am not averse to arguing that nonviolence can be effective, but I am opposed to the notion that efficiency and effectiveness ought to be the primary or the sole criteria by which we decide to act. To trust these criteria as determinative not only lends support to the technological ethos of our age, but it is also inevitably supportive of statism.[25] Since the state has control over resources and power that are virtually inexhaustible, citizens guided by a yearning for effectiveness alone seek to enlist the state in their endeavors. This has the simultaneous impact of increasing state power and diminishing the significance of actions by any individuals or commu-

---

24. When effectiveness and efficiency are given sway, then even a book on "just peacemaking" can include a chapter on just warmaking. The case for multilateral, humanitarian military action is presented by Michael Joseph Smith, "Strengthen the United Nations and International Efforts for Cooperation and Human Rights," in *Just Peacemaking: Ten Practices for Abolishing War*, ed. Glen Stassen (Cleveland: Pilgrim Press, 1998), pp. 146-55. The essays in this volume (including Smith's) are thought-provoking, and the contributors note (p. 26) that they are not in full agreement on affirming humanitarian warfare.

25. G. W. F. Hegel is the premier modern philosopher of statism. Ramajit Guha observes that, for Hegel, if "goodness" is to become an effective force in the world, then the state must come to "constitute ethical life" in its entirety. Guha, *History at the Limit of World-History* (New York: Columbia University Press, 2002), p. 4.

nities. If true change is effected by the state alone, then the only citizen lethargy that is egregious is that which occurs on election day. Peter Maurin, one of the founders of the *Catholic Worker*, often encountered people whose social consciousness was absorbed by speculations on "What *they* ought to do," that is, what the people holding political offices should do to make change happen. Maurin countered, "Be what you want the other fellow to be. . . . Don't criticize what is not being done. Find the work you can perform, fit yourself to perform it, and then do it."[26] Catholic Worker communities have clearly followed Maurin's admonition. Rather than waiting for the state to feed the hungry and house the homeless, Worker communities have been providing food and shelter.

The popular depiction of the state as servant notwithstanding, the state has often shown itself to be ineffective in responding to human needs. In the wake of Hurricane Katrina in New Orleans, community organizations and self-help groups were more successful than the federal government in delivering aid to victims.[27] A change of government policy or even a change of government itself rarely heralds a change in conditions of oppression. In the last ten years of the apartheid regime in South Africa, 700,000 poor people in the townships were evicted from their homes; in the ten years after apartheid ended, with the introduction of economic liberalization and privatization, over 900,000 poor people were evicted from their homes.[28] What the state giveth, the state can take away. When what passes for justice is founded on legislation and court decisions, it can just as easily be undone.[29]

26. Peter Maurin, quoted by William D. Miller, *Dorothy Day: A Biography* (New York: Harper & Row, 1982), p. 244. In conversation, Elizabeth McAlister told me that she was briefly enamored with electoral politics during the McGovern campaign of 1972. While McGovern certainly had his liabilities, electing him seemed like it would be a simple and effective route toward ending the war in Vietnam. McAlister visited Dorothy Day and asked her to "just this once" abandon her anarchist antipathy to electoral politics. Day responded that, since she didn't want a commander-in-chief, she didn't see why she should go to the polls to choose one.

27. Rebecca Solnit, "The Lower Ninth Battles Back," *The Nation* 285, no. 7 (September 10-17, 2007): 13-17.

28. Statistics cited by John Pilger on "Democracy Now" with Amy Goodman, Link TV, June 7, 2007. It hardly needs saying that Pilger is not an advocate of apartheid. With the end of apartheid, multifarious forms of brutality were brought to a halt, but those who assumed that a new government portended the arrival of justice were sadly deluded.

29. Civil rights decisions by the U.S. Supreme Court from the middle of the last century are being gradually overturned by Court decisions in the early twenty-first century. Several

Totally divorced from principles, estimations of effectiveness account for shifts to and fro in political opinion. Soon after the invasion of Iraq in 2003, opposition to the war virtually evaporated in U.S. public opinion when it seemed that the Iraqi government had been toppled expeditiously. Similar to changes in public opinion on the war in Vietnam, opposition to the war in Iraq only started to rise again when it seemed as if the war was becoming a quagmire. Public opinion will support actions of questionable morality and of high cost in terms of lives and wealth, but not actions that are ineffective.

Across the political spectrum, activists perceive the acquisition of power as a sure path to effectiveness in realizing goals. Gene Sharp writes that advocates of nonviolent action "see that it is necessary to wield power in order to control the power of threatening political groups or regimes. That assumption they share with advocates of violence, although they part company with them on many other points."[30] If I wield power, there is no reason to fear what I will do with it. I will use it only for the good. But the question that is seldom asked is what *it* does to me. In order to have been effective at acquiring the power, I will have already been thoroughly imbued with pragmatic calculations about how to win people over and how to win over people.

Some of the biblical perspectives that renounce the value of power and of effectiveness have been quietly ignored by modern proponents of realism and utilitarianism. In Revelation 13, John of Patmos writes that the beast "was allowed to make war on the saints and to conquer them. It was given authority over every tribe and people and language and nation . . ." (13:7-8). In his visionary mode, John clearly saw that the ultimate victory belonged to the "slaughtered Lamb" (Revelation 21–22), yet he was living in the penultimate time of the defeat of the saints, and so are we.[31] The

---

examples are cited by David L. Kirp, "Racists & Robber Barons," *The Nation* 285, no. 4 (July 30-August 6, 2007): 4-5. Gene Sharp argues that nonviolent actions are effective, but he also warns that reliance on government decisions suffers the vulnerability of being subject to abrupt reversal. Sharp, *Social Power and Political Freedom* (Boston: Porter Sargent, 1980), p. 315.

30. Gene Sharp, *The Politics of Nonviolent Action*, part 1: *Power and Struggle* (Boston: Porter Sargent, 1973), p. 7. It should be noted that, when Sharp refers to wielding "power" and "control," he is not necessarily referring to the acquisition of authority over the governing apparatus of the state. For Sharp, "power" can also mean building a movement of noncooperation that will cause the functioning of the state to grind to a halt. Nonetheless, he clearly values the effectiveness associated with power.

31. See William Stringfellow, "A Homily on the Significance of the Defeat of the

reign of the Lamb is already fully authoritative for the community of believers, but that community is called to faithfulness in a time when the world is submitting to the reign of the empire and not of the Lamb. This does not mean that the saints will court defeat or that failure will become the one sure sign of faithfulness, but it does mean that believers will be guided by motivations other than utility and success. The point is illustrated by a single phrase in the story of Shadrach, Meshach, and Abednego. King Nebuchadnezzar ordered the three men to fall down and worship a statue that he had built, and if they refused to do so, he would have them thrown into a furnace. Who would rescue them then?

> Shadrach, Meshach and Abednego replied to King Nebuchadnezzar, "Your question hardly requires an answer: if our God, the one we serve, is able to save us from the burning fiery furnace and from your power, O king, he will save us; and even if he does not, then you must know, O king, that we will not serve your god or worship the statue you have erected." (Daniel 3:16-18, *Jerusalem Bible*)

Rowan Williams points to the surprising and pertinent phrase: "'Even if he does not' — the act does not depend on the outcome, it is simply what has to be done."[32] The passage includes the surprising suggestion that God may not be able to thwart the persecutions of Nebuchadnezzar (or of Antiochus IV Epiphanes, the despotic ruler during whose reign the book of Daniel was written). The faithful cannot count on miraculous intervention. Short of parousia, believers cannot depend on God's effectiveness, but only on God's faithfulness. If we seek evidence of God in rescue from fiery furnaces, then, Daniel notwithstanding, the evidence is scant indeed.

In the last century, Karl Barth was the leading critic of natural theology, which is the effort to find evidence for the action of God or the existence of God in the phenomena of the world around us rather than in the word of God. In the writings of Barth, Jesus is the living content of that revelatory word. Yet, in the twenty-first century, natural theology is as prominent as ever, including in the writings of some authors whom I like. René Girard has made important contributions to our understanding of mi-

---

Saints," in Stringfellow, *Conscience and Obedience: The Politics of Romans 13 and Revelation 13 in Light of the Second Coming* (Waco, Tex.: Word Books, 1978), pp. 109-12.

32. Rowan Williams, *Christ on Trial: How the Gospel Unsettles Our Judgement* (Grand Rapids: Eerdmans and Toronto: ABC Publishing, Anglican Book Centre, 2003), p. 10.

metic violence and the scapegoating phenomenon, but when Girard attempts to prove that the gospel has effectively transformed the world,[33] his reading of history becomes outlandishly progressive and optimistic. In Girard's evolutionary view, all "archaic" religions prior to Judaism and Christianity sacralized the scapegoating phenomenon.[34] This is certainly accurate regarding the imperial religions of Rome, Greece, Mesopotamia, and the Andes, but it is not valid for many of the "archaic" religious practices of the primitive, anarchistic communities of pre-colonial Africa and South America. For Girard to support his claim that concern for victims did not emerge prior to Christianity or outside Christian influence, he would have to explain away a vast number of historical examples and religious texts, including Buddhism's teachings on compassion. Indeed, Gautama's insights regarding desire as the root of suffering antedate Girard's reflections on mimetic desire by some 2500 years. In addition, Girard would need to explain why Christendom itself was so easily seduced into scapegoating pagans, heretics, Jews, Muslims, women, gays, and others. Evolutionary views of history detract from the disjunctive, radically eschatological hope of the gospel. If all history is moving toward some Teilhardian "Omega Point," globalism is easy to celebrate and the loss of local place and human diversity need not be mourned.[35] Finally, while Girard acknowledges that the powers are all "tributaries" of Satan, he nonetheless proclaims that they are "indispensable to the maintenance of order."[36] Yet, is it not fair to say that the powers effectively maintain their version of order only by scapegoating all those who are potential threats to it?[37]

33. Girard writes, "The triumph of the Cross reflects and corresponds to a tangible reality that can be rationally apprehended. The Cross has indeed transformed the world, and we can interpret its power in a way that does not have to appeal to religious faith." René Girard, *I See Satan Fall Like Lightning*, trans. James G. Williams (Maryknoll, N.Y.: Orbis Books, 2001), p. 141.

34. Girard, *I See Satan Fall*, pp. 161-69.

35. In extolling the emergence of the concept of human rights, Girard writes, "The cultures that were still autonomous cultivated all sorts of solidarity — familial, tribal, national — but they did not recognize the victim as such. . . . Prior to this discovery there was no humanity in the full sense except within a fixed territory. Today all of these local, regional, and national identities are disappearing: 'Ecce homo.'" Girard, *I See Satan Fall*, p. 167.

36. Girard, *I See Satan Fall*, pp. 96, 98.

37. My questions for Girard do not end here. He contends that Western culture carries a consciousness of the crucified Jesus embedded within it like a virus, and that this in turn nurtures concern for human rights and victims. This seems to be Girard's version of H. Richard Niebuhr's "Christ transforming culture." Yet, would Girard be willing to admit

The anxiety of theologians to prove that Jesus has effectively changed the world is notably absent from the Gospel depictions of Jesus himself. The temptations in the wilderness (Matthew 4:1-11; Luke 4:1-13) offered the perfect moment for Jesus to wrest control of the kingdoms of the world from the hands of the devil. Certainly Satan had the authority to grant such control; otherwise the call to worship him would not have been tempting in the least. Dostoyevsky's Grand Inquisitor was correct: "Hadst Thou taken the world and Caesar's purple, Thou wouldst have founded the universal state and have given universal peace."[38] In our utilitarian moments, we long for a god like that — one who will take on the purple, not one who is crucified. The crucifixion is a scandal for which there is scant compensation in the elusive utility of resurrection.

In the time of the historical Jesus, there were multiple options for potentially effective political action. One option was that of messianic revolution, a path that would eventually be chosen by the Zealots.[39] Get rid of the Roman oppressors, and oppression will end, at least until new oppressors take their place. A second option was that of Essene withdrawal into the desert. Even if this path offered little hope of changing the Romans, at least it could be effective in preventing the Romans from changing the Essenes. A third path was that chosen by the majority of Sadducees who cooperated with the Roman occupiers. By becoming part of the system, by acquiring positions of leadership on the Sanhedrin and in the Temple, by showing themselves to be loyal subjects of Caesar, the Sadducees were

---

that the Western self-confidence about its own virtuous viruses has been an incentive to imperialism? I also question whether repetitive references to "victims" are more generative of compassion or paternalism. People who are recovering from violent assaults like rape prefer to call themselves "survivors" rather than "victims." To remain embroiled in victimhood is to grant ongoing power to the assailant. Is the moment of transformation the one in which Western culture finally becomes conscious of victims? Or is it instead the moment in which oppressed people are called by the God of liberation? What becomes of the white emancipator when Harriet Tubman hears the word from God and liberates herself? What happens to Western compassion for the victims when oppressed people refuse to play the role of victims anymore?

38. Fyodor Dostoyevsky, *The Brothers Karamazov* (New York: Airmont Publishing, 1966), p. 233.

39. While Jewish messianic expectation was prominent in the early years of the first century CE, the organized party that became known as the Zealots did not appear until 67-68 CE. Prior to that time, "zealots" probably referred to loosely-knit groups of bandits and agitators opposed to the Roman occupation. See Richard A. Horsley, with John S. Hanson, *Bandits, Prophets, and Messiahs: Popular Movements at the Time of Jesus*, New Voices in Biblical Studies (New York: Harper & Row, 1985).

trying to mitigate effectively the worst of Roman abuses and maintain a narrow field in which they could preserve religious rituals and institutions. In relationship to empire today, most of us are either Sadducees or Romans.

Jesus chose none of these options. Instead of gaining access to power, he befriends the powerless. Instead of waiting for the new humanity that will blossom once the revolution has been won, he is that new humanity. Instead of withdrawing into a separatist community with the hope of maintaining purity, he shapes a new community in the very midst of old power arrangements. In this new community, the poor are blessed, the sword is put away, the last are first — and all without a single piece of legislation or a single nod from Caesar. And yet by utilitarian standards this new community is meaningless — no, even more, immoral — unless it is effective at producing greater happiness for greater numbers. The community of disciples is not called to effectiveness or happiness. The call is only to take up the cross and to follow Jesus away from the center of power and out of the holy city toward Golgotha.

Of what use is God? Like believers of other spiritual traditions, Christians often yearn for a God who is of use, a God who is like a raging river that can be harnessed to generate power. Wasn't that the way God used to be? God put in a full six days of serious work before resting, and now, where is God?[40] Like deists, we seem to be left with only the watch and not the maker. But by utilitarian standards, perhaps it is the creation itself that bears witness to the usefulness of God. At least the creation is something that we can use. We have been using it to death.

The utilitarian views humanity, not as a part of creation, but as the beneficiary of it. Creation is viewed as a giant resource that humanity may use to further the pursuit of happiness, and since happiness itself is so elusive, the rate of extraction is always accelerating. In such a way, creation is of use to people. And of what use is it to God? For some theologians, there has been an effort to tie creation to some utility within the divine personhood. God "needed" to be loved, praised, and glorified, so why not make a world that could perform those functions? We end up with a

---

40. In a very somber book, Jacques Ellul writes, "It is my belief that we have entered upon the age of abandonment, that God has turned away from us and is leaving us to our fate." Ellul, *Hope in Time of Abandonment*, trans. C. Edward Hopkin (New York: Seabury Press, 1973), p. 71. In a time when faith is no longer sustained by revelation and doctrinal certitude, it can only be sustained by hope. If faith was once the mother of hope, now it is only hope that can lead to faith.

dreary view of a creation that is tediously praising the Creator, and an un-flattering view of a deity who is soaking it all in.

Perhaps it is not like that at all. There is an extravagance in creation that defies utilitarian comprehension. There is life that teems on raindrops and specks of dust.[41] Why does the proponent of natural theology look to creation and discover order rather than astonishing wildness and crazy chaos? This creation could be suggestive of a *Deus Ludens* (a God of play) as much as a *Deus Faber* (a God of work).[42] Or perhaps a God of love, a God whose love of life could not be contained by order or utilitarian design.

If we dare to ask of what use God is, we may certainly press the in-quiry further to ask about the utility of that love with which God is identi-fied. What use do we have for love? Of course, it has become common-place to speak of various "types" of love, and some types can seem very useful indeed. In the modern era, Anders Nygren was the most prominent proponent of differentiating types of love based on Greek vocabulary.[43] *Epithymia* and *libido* refer to desire for sexual union. *Eros* refers to desire for the beloved. *Philia* refers to the love of sisters, brothers, and friends. *Agape* refers to the love that is total giving of self without any expectation of re-turn. The first three of these *can* be tied to utility, but by definition, *agape* renounces any higher goal beyond the giving of love itself. The typology is flawed and, I believe, it falls apart.[44] But let us consider further this word

41. The seventeenth-century Dutch pioneer of microscopic exploration, Antony van Leeuwenhoek, led a life punctuated by astonishment and wonder. See Guy Murchie, *The Seven Mysteries of Life: An Exploration of Science and Philosophy* (New York: Mariner Books, 1999), pp. 80-85. In the quest for happiness, the true utilitarian places little value on astonishment. Since the effective path to joy has already been plotted, surprises and miracles are unwel-come intrusions.

42. The trends and styles in theology are as changeable as those in the clothing indus-try. During the countercultural movements of the 1960s and '70s, after theologians made forays into demythologizing and secularizing and proclaiming the death of God, there was a brief moment in the sun for a school of thought called "theology of play." Of course, even fleeting trends can give expression to valid insights, and for the theology of play, some of these appear in a book by the one-time proponent of secularism, Harvey Cox, *The Feast of Fools: A Theological Essay on Festivity and Fantasy* (New York: Harper Colophon, 1970).

43. Nygren, *Agape and Eros*, trans. Philip S. Watson (London: SPCK, 1957). A similar typology appears in C. S. Lewis, *The Four Loves* (New York: Harcourt Brace Jovanovich, 1960).

44. James B. Nelson argues that the typology deprives us of any sense of the unity of love and that it engenders a dualism of body and spirit. The love of God for Israel is imma-nent and passionate. Nelson, *Embodiment: An Approach to Sexuality and Christian Theology* (Minneapolis: Augsburg, 1978), pp. 109-14. It must also be noted that, in all probability, Jesus of Nazareth did not speak Greek. He was likely fluent in Aramaic and Hebrew, and the same

agape, this love that is identified as God's love, this love that expects . . . nothing.

It makes a considerable difference when John (1 John 4:7-16) insists that God *is* love rather than that God *uses* love. *Agape* is never a tactic to be used in the pursuit of other goals.[45] Like people, love is not a means but an end in itself. Rather than an effort to maintain control, *agape* is a surrender of control, and indeed, a surrender of self — even for God.[46]

God's own surrender of self is called *kenosis* in Greek — "emptying" — and it is presented in an amazing passage (a poem, really) in Paul's letter to the Philippians 2:5-8:

> Let the mind be in you that was in Christ Jesus,
>> who, though he was in the form of God,
>>> did not regard equality with God
>>> as something to be exploited,
>> but emptied himself,
>>> taking the form of a slave,
>>> being born in human likeness.
>> And being found in human form,
>>> he humbled himself
>>> and became obedient to the point of death —
>>> even death on a cross.

And yet, this passage contains a dialectical revelation. It is in God's surrender of self that God's true self is revealed. In her commentary on this pas-

---

Hebrew root for "love" *(aheb)* is used for the love of the faithful for God (Psalm 31:23), the love of God for the faithful (Exodus 20:6), the love of neighbor (Leviticus 19:18), the love of the sexual partner (Song of Solomon 3:4), and the love of raisin cakes (Hosea 3:1).

45. Incumbent upon his reading of the Gita, Gandhi wrote that the belief that one could use "soul force" to attain political objectives was "dangerous in the extreme." There is a paradox here: unattached to the goal of ushering the British out of India, Gandhian "soul force" did precisely that. M. K. Gandhi, *Hind Swaraj and Other Writings*, ed. Anthony J. Parel (New York: Cambridge University Press, 1997), p. 141.

46. Even if only in passing (and it certainly deserves much more), it is important to note that to refer to love as "surrender of self" is *not* to propose that abused and oppressed people should simply surrender to the bidding of their tormentors. In the Gospel accounts of the trials and torture of Jesus, he nonviolently confronted his tormentors, at times with silence and at times with words (e.g., Luke 22:52-53; John 18:19-24). Total passivity is no more loving than violent retaliation. Passivity dehumanizes the abused person but also the assailant by allowing him to identify himself as a simple tool of raw brutality.

sage, Morna Hooker writes, "Christ did not cease to be 'in the form of God' when he took the form of a slave, any more than he ceased to be the 'Son of God' when he was sent into the world. On the contrary, it is *in his self-emptying and his humiliation that he reveals what God is like*, and it is through his taking the form of a slave that we see 'the form of God.'"[47]

From manger to cross, this is what God is like — a God who chooses foolishness and weakness (1 Corinthians 1:18-31). "Let the one who boasts, boast in the Lord."

---

47. Morna D. Hooker, "Letter to the Philippians," in *The New Interpreter's Bible*, vol. XI (Nashville: Abingdon Press, 2000), p. 508, with emphasis in the original. Karl Barth makes a similar point that *kenosis* was not a shedding but a revelation of divine nature. "From now on he is equal with God in the obscurity of the form of a servant. He is *in humility* the highest." Barth, *Epistle to the Philippians*, trans. James W. Leitch, 40th Anniversary Edition (Louisville: Westminster John Knox Press, 2002), p. 62, with emphasis in the original.

7. Arguing with God

In upstate New York, I work with a nonprofit, nongovernmental community mental health program for people who have been diagnosed with severe and persistent mental illness. For some of these sisters and brothers who have been diagnosed with schizophrenia, bipolar disorder, or major depression, their minds are plagued by thoughts of suicide. Some hear voices from long ago, voices that tell them, "You are worthless. You cannot do anything right. You are evil." I meet with people in individual sessions and listen to their stories, and I facilitate some groups. One is a group for survivors of trauma, including the trauma of childhood abuse, of rape, of war — more and more, the trauma of war.

I trust that God will forgive me when I feel a little surge of anger each time I see the car magnets that say, "Support our troops." That is a cruel joke. To send people into a setting where their very job is to perpetrate and suffer violence is not support; it is abuse. When as many as one-quarter of all homeless people in America are veterans, one way to support the troops would be to convert the Pentagon into a homeless shelter.

Survivors of trauma need to tell their stories.[1] I have met one man who has never told. Forty years ago outside of Nha Trang, Vietnam, he stepped into a field, and he has never told what happened there. When he talks, he takes us to the edge of the field but not one step farther. No matter how long we sit and listen in silence, he does not enter the field. It is as if he wants to protect the rest of us from the horror that lies ahead.

1. In order to assure confidentiality, I have not used names and I have altered some details in the accounts that follow.

Young Center for Anabaptist and Pietist Studies, Elizabethtown College, November 8, 2007.

Another man has talked after years of being visited by ghosts. In the Persian Gulf following Desert Storm, he is on a battle cruiser when a small boat with four people on board comes too close. Suicide bombers? Fisher folks? He and his shipmates take aim and fire. In slow motion, bodies fall. Boat is tipped. Blood is in the water. And one arm — one arm, he tells us — unattached, rises out of the water and stays suspended. Is it in midair? Is it on the surface of the water? He cannot say. One arm. The ghosts who come to visit him always come at night. Is he awake? Is he asleep? At times, he does not know. They always come with severed body parts — a leg, a head, an arm — and he works feverishly to reattach them, always without success. It is a recurrent effort at literal re-membering.

What good does it do him to tell this story? There is no happy ending or instant healing. Though their visits are less frequent, the ghosts still come. He tells us his story, but we are not his victims. We are not the people on that boat and we cannot forgive him in their stead. We are not them and we are not God. All that we can do is to let him know that, even though he pulled the trigger, even with his diagnosis and his ghosts, he can still be loved. Is that enough? For now, it must be.

The stories that can hurt you are not the ones you tell but the ones you do not tell. But stories are not just about the teller, not just about some purging of the psyche. The value of a story is not only in the telling of it but also in the listening. The stories that can hurt you are not the ones you hear but the ones you do not hear. We are impoverished when we do not hear the stories of gay men and lesbians, of wild-eyed heretics, of homeless people living in cardboard boxes by the freeway, of black men sitting in prison cages, of brown families scaling border fences, and of all the rest of undocumented humanity and humanity documented too much. Like threatened habitats and endangered species, marginalized stories die in a culture that insists on the tedious and noisy repetition of hegemonic narratives.

It is not only the prodigious flow of blood that leaves me disliking films such as *Rambo* and *Green Beret* and *Terminator 2* and *Lethal Weapon 3* and *Death Wish* ad infinitum. I dislike them because I have heard that story so many times before, and here it is again, without change or nuance. I will tell it to you in ten seconds. Spoiler alert! Here's the story: the weapons are in the wrong hands; concentrate the firepower in the right hands and you will have a happy ending. It's the lethal weapon story preached from bully pulpits about Vietnam, Iraq, Iran, or other enemy *du jour*, and it's echoed by stenographers to power on CNN and Fox, and our bellies are so full of it that we cannot ingest the other stories.

We need to hear other stories with plot lines like this: it's not the person who pulls the trigger; it's the trigger that pulls the person.[2] When the power of death falls into the right hands, they become the wrong hands. Daddy, which side won the war? The legions won. Whose legions? The legions of hell. Fade screen. Roll credits. Co-produced by imperial America and the so-called terrorists who need one another so badly.

There is no war on terror. There's a terror love-fest, an orgy of terror in which the violence of one side commingles with that of the other until you can't tell whose is whose. The ending, if it comes at all, will not be happy. As the brutality of both sides escalates, the identity of the victor becomes less relevant.

So, the lethal weapon story is one we've heard too often, as if we're being proselytized, as if some crazed revivalist has been cut loose in the White House briefing room, in Hollywood, on the aluminum-tubed front pages of *The New York Times*.[3] No, I don't want to censor the lethal weapon story. I don't want to censor anything. I want to listen for stories that I have not heard before or, just as good, stories that, even though I've heard them many times, offer something new with each retelling — a change in sound or mood, a word that I never noticed there before, a different light, a fresh revelation. These stories that are new with each retelling are not just about spinning a good yarn. At their best, they elicit nothing less than freedom — the freedom to hear in new ways and to be knocked out of ruts of mind and spirit that have been traveled for too long, the freedom to respond in ways that have no *a priori* prescription.

Now, I know that "freedom" is a prominent word in the American lexicon, prominent to the point of being cheapened: as if freedom could be won once and for all in 1776 and then institutionalized and nailed down;

2. The notion that guns are simply tools that people may choose to use or not is called into question by researchers cited by Michael Kramer, "Why Guns Share the Blame," *Time*, May 8, 1995, p. 48. In research with high school students, psychology professor Ann Frodi found that merely placing a weapon within the students' field of vision increased aggressive behavior. She concluded that the mere presence of guns escalates the potential for violence. Leonard Berkowitz, former professor of psychology at the University of Wisconsin, studied the "weapons effect" for forty years. In response to the claim that "Guns don't kill people, people kill people," Berkowitz said, "The finger pulls the trigger. But the trigger may also pull the finger."

3. Prior to the 2003 invasion of Iraq, *The New York Times* published several inaccurate reports that served to bolster the case for invasion. One of these was an article reporting inaccurately that aluminum tubes imported by Iraq were being used for uranium enrichment as part of a nuclear weapons program.

as if freedom had to do with sporadic trips to voting booths and with pulling levers and pushing touch screens; as if freedom were the product of a capitalist system that frees autocratic CEOs to forge multinational trade agreements with the dictators of their choice, and frees you and me to sell our time, bodies, and souls for consumer "goods"; as if freedom were transmitted through the military invasions that could happen only because we were first invaded in our heads and in our guts by the Ministry of Fear and Loathing. The hegemonic story in modern America, the lethal weapon story, is not about freedom. Our response is prescribed by the story itself. We're told that we have to get more power. We're told that we have to get some guns. That's not freedom. That's captivity. Genuine freedom is like conversion, like being born again. It does not happen at only one point in time, and you cannot institutionalize it. It must happen every day, and perhaps more often than that.

There are some stories that I love precisely because, upon occasion, they are new in the retelling. They are wild and unpredictable, and therefore they elicit a response of freedom. Sometimes the Bible is like that for me. With the pervasive narrative structure noted by theologians and biblical scholars, it is a fair characterization to call the Bible a story, or a compilation of stories. From creation to new creation, from exodus out of Egypt to exodus out of Babylon and Rome, from Adam to new Adam, it is story. Of course, there are other literary forms in the Bible as well, like Proverbs (which I don't pretend to understand), and Psalms, and the theologizing from Paul and the deutero-Paulines, but even the hymnody and the theology must refer back to the story. The worst thing we can do with such a story is to try to nail it down, to try to prescribe the one, true, holy response, to try to hold it captive in "the fundamentals," to try to keep it safe in some structure of power, some mean institution that will tell you what it means.

In his work on Brethren theology, Dale Brown notes that the blessings of both Anabaptist and Pietist traditions include a healthy skepticism toward doctrinal pronouncements and a reluctance to use dogmatic certitude to mug and batter the heterodox.[4] Of course, reticence to impose those doctrines brings risks. You can end up with some Church of the Brethren kids who join the military. You can end up with a Brethren general. (Dwight Eisenhower should have listened to his River Brethren

4. Dale W. Brown, *Another Way of Believing: A Brethren Theology* (Elgin, Ill.: Brethren Press, 2005).

the gatekeeper will be. Some say Peter. I like to think it might be the thief on the cross. Hold on to your wallets!) While we're waiting in line for our entrance through the gates, we discover that a certain friend is missing. We discover that this friend has been sent to the nether world, to Sheol, to the pit. I have an idea. Let's form a picket line and let's picket the gates of heaven until God agrees to let our friend come in. What do you say? Let's form that heavenly picket line. Will you do it?

The response from our spirituality group comes in fast, furious, and unanimously negative, often with comments like, "Are you crazy? I thought we were supposed to be the crazy ones." I ask, "Why is that such a crazy idea?" Because, they answer, you do not argue with God. God is omnipotent and omniscient, and who are we to argue with that? Now, there's no doubt that our spirituality group is in the mainstream of Western theology in pointing to omnipotence and omniscience as central attributes of divinity. What's more, these two qualities are inextricably linked. In Calvinist predestinarianism, God's foreknowledge is barely distinguishable from God's foreordination. God knows that it will be so because God makes it to be so. Put aside, for now, the question of what this theological proposal does to any notion of freedom in the human adventure. Perhaps a greater quandary is what it does to God. How can God retain an everlasting concern for so obvious a tautology?[5]

But what is of interest now is this link between omniscience and omnipotence, between knowledge and power. For people of faith, a great service was rendered by those two notorious atheists, Ludwig Feuerbach and Karl Marx, when they alerted us to the dangers of projection inherent to religiosity. Said Feuerbach, followed by Marx, in the religious enterprise we take those human qualities and potentialities that we value most highly and project them onto the heavens, thus creating God in the image

---

5. With these comments, I do not wish to reject the theological concept of predestination. Indeed, I believe a compelling presentation of "double predestination" is offered by Karl Barth in *Church Dogmatics*, vol. 4, pt. 3, second half: *The Doctrine of Reconciliation*, trans. G. W. Bromiley (Edinburgh: T. & T. Clark, 1962). Barth contends that God's "no" of divine judgment is fully in the service of God's ultimate "yes" to reconciliation and redemption. In a version of predestination that is candidly universalist, Barth contends that all women and men are called (even compelled) to encounter both this "no" and this "yes." God's grace is experienced, not as a circumvention of God's judgment, but as a true encounter with it. Barth's theology persistently emphasizes "the freedom of God," and his rendering of double predestination is more successful than the traditional Calvinist version in affirming both divine and human freedom.

of humanity rather than vice versa. Even if we do not wish to follow these atheist brothers in their assertion that God is a human concoction, nonetheless, they pose urgent questions for people of faith about the degree to which our theology has become contaminated by mere religion. Are omniscience and omnipotence so prominent in the history of theology because these are precisely the attributes that are central to the biblical portrayal of God's story, or is their theological elevation owing to the fact that knowledge and power are the things we love? What's more, these two are treated as interdependent and coextensive. Knowledge is power and power is knowledge. From medieval alchemists to twenty-first-century nuclear physicists, many are those who have believed that knowledge is valuable in direct proportion to its economic or technical utility — its potential for enhancing domination.[6] The motto "Educate for Service"[7] urges us to disentangle academic pursuits from the pursuit of power, but in the competitive marketplace of American educational institutions, prospective students must be reassured that academic achievement carries a guarantee of greater access to money and prestige. We have become a people of careers rather than callings, with education cheapened the more it is linked to the increasing size of the paycheck.

In his book, To Know As We Are Known, Parker Palmer cites a survey of American college students conducted over two decades ago by the Carnegie Institute.[8] The students were asked first whether they were optimistic or pessimistic about their own future, and by a large margin, the students responded that they were optimistic. With graduation pending, with the job market holding steady, with the economy looking good, they were optimistic about their prospects. Then these same students were asked whether they were optimistic or pessimistic about the future of the planet, and by the same large margin, the students responded that they were pessimistic. Given nuclear proliferation, persistent wars, and the threat of environmental collapse, these students were pessimistic about the future of the planet.

6. This characterization does not apply to all alchemists or physicists, some of whom have renounced enslavement to utility. The most interesting of these have been of mystical inclination, such as the alchemists who have yearned for self-transformation more than for the magical conversion of common metals into gold, and the physicists who have not recoiled from wild flights into the realms of string theory and parallel universes.

7. This is the motto of Elizabethtown College.

8. Palmer, To Know As We Are Known: A Spirituality of Education (New York: Harper & Row, 1983), p. 4.

Now I ask you, what is happening when students believe that, even if the planet disintegrates, they will still be doing all right? What explains this startling illusion that one's personal fate is somehow divorced from the fate of the earth and its inhabitants? Parker Palmer argues convincingly that the illusion originates in part with a pedagogical style which assumes that the way we really learn, the way we really come to know the world, is to hold it at a distance, to objectify it and examine it, to run some tests on it and dissect it, and then when we have established sufficient objectivity and control, knowledge comes to us.[9] Power facilitates the acquisition of knowledge, which facilitates the acquisition of power.

There are hints about a totally different approach to learning in the Hebrew Bible euphemism "to know," which is a delicate phrase for sexual intercourse.[10] Within this euphemism, there is the rich suggestion that the way we really learn is to let go of distance, control, and pretense to objectivity. Knowledge comes with intimacy, not distance, with the embrace, not the dissection. Knowledge is possible without power. It is impossible without love.

Of course, it is not only college students who believe that they will be doing all right even if the world blows up. Back in nineteenth-century Britain, John Nelson Darby was busy devising a theology of the rapture. Based on a narrowly unpoetic and (one must say) mean-spirited reading of the book of Revelation and a single verse from Paul's first letter to the Thessalonians (4:17), Darby contended that the return of Jesus will be a most unhappy day for the greater chunk of humanity and for the earth itself. The world will in fact "blow up," but in slow motion, by means of a fire that will prolong the torture and agony of many. But, if you are a Christian of sufficient orthodoxy and righteousness, you are going to be all right because you will be taken up into the clouds with Jesus and provided with a front row seat to watch the torment down below. Darby wrote during the heyday of the British Empire, and his theology was perfectly attuned to the belief that those who are properly situated should not have to suffer the indignities visited upon the rest of the world. Hal Lindsey of *The Late, Great Planet Earth* fame is a modern-day Darbyite who was once asked

9. Palmer observes that the Latin root for the word "objective" means "to put against, to oppose." Thus, in objectivist epistemology, the knower and the known are not interdependent but antagonistic. Palmer, *To Know As We Are Known,* pp. 23-32.

10. On the use of "to know" as euphemism, see G. J. Botterweck, "*yāḏaʿ*," in *Theological Dictionary of the Old Testament,* vol. 5, ed. G. Johannes Botterweck and Helmer Ringgren, trans. David E. Green (Grand Rapids: Eerdmans, 1986), p. 464.

if he thought the world would end in a nuclear holocaust. With a breezy self-confidence, Lindsey replied that he did not worry about that because, "I ain't gonna be there."[11]

It is not only the Darbyites and the college students surveyed by the Carnegie Institute who cultivate a sense of detachment from the fate of the rest of the planet. It is also many of the leaders and citizens of the contemporary American Empire who assert this right to be safe and sound even if the world blows up. We shouldn't have to be there. That was part of the palpable rage following September 11. Oh, certainly we knew that there were parts of the globe routinely suffering terror and violence, but we shouldn't have to be there. Is that not what President Bush meant when he said that we must fight "the terrorists" over there or else they will follow us back to the homeland? We shouldn't have to be there. Oh yes, there is grinding poverty elsewhere in the world, but we will build the fence along the southern border because we shouldn't have to be there. But the Oklahoma City bombers and the Columbine shooters did not come from over there. The economically bombed-out shells of New Orleans and South Central L.A. did not come from over there. The homeless people sleeping on the heating grates did not come from over there. As empire stays vigilant on the borders, the so-called "homeland" is rotting from within.

Nonetheless, omniscience and omnipotence are perceived as the keys to staying safe in a world that is blowing apart. But Darby set his sights too low. There is no need to await the return of Jesus to be lifted above a planet in torment. The empire is already up there, not in the clouds but above them, with satellites criss-crossing space and looking down on a tortured planet, watching for unrighteous behavior and listening for unorthodox words. Faith is being undermined today, but it is not at the hands of the usual suspects. Faith is most threatened today, not by the offspring of Charles Darwin, nor by the queer folks waiting out in the narthex to get in, but by this notion that the attributes of God and empire coincide — omnipotence and omniscience.

My friend Stanley Hauerwas is among those theologians who have written about the end of the Constantinian era. Christendom is a thing of

---

11. Lindsey, quoted by Garry Wills, *Under God: Religion and American Politics* (New York: Simon & Schuster, 1990), p. 147. Drawing on biblical perspectives, an insightful critique of Darby and his successors is offered by Barbara R. Rossing, *The Rapture Exposed* (New York: Basic Books, 2005).

the past. Faith communities are in such sharp numerical decline and they are already so thoroughly co-opted that the state no longer needs to worry much about reaching accommodation with them. Does this mark the liberation of the political from the ecclesiastical realm? Does this mean that faith communities are now freed from state intrusion? No, what happens in a time such as this is that the empire ratchets up its efforts, not only to control the church, but to become the very manifestation of God.[12]

During the 2004 election campaign, President Bush came to Lancaster County to speak to Amish farmers. And by the way, what was that all about? I can understand hospitality. If the guy is hungry, give him a good, home-cooked, Pennsylvania Dutch meal. But the President was not here for hospitality. He was here for that most worldly of all pursuits, a campaign rally, and the reason for his enthusiastic reception by a group of very traditional Anabaptists eludes me. I should add, I would have been similarly baffled by an Amish campaign rally for John Kerry. At any rate, Kevin Phillips quotes the President in his talk to Amish farmers as having said, "God speaks through me."[13] Now, it is possible that President Bush was misquoted, or it is possible that the President misspoke (as if *that* ever happens), because you see, in the Bible, God does not speak *through* the king. God speaks *to* the king, but God speaks *through* the prophets, and often, when the prophets tell the king what God has to say, the king is not very happy. The king will quickly gather the palace priests and the false prophets to tell him precisely what the king thinks God ought to be telling him.[14]

---

12. I am in no way advocating a return to Christendom, the demise of which is to be celebrated as providing openings for people of faith to reacquaint themselves with the countercultural edge of the gospel. The passing of Christendom, however, does not herald a desacralization of the state or other institutions of power. As Hauerwas notes, "Secular people too often assume that once Christianity is rendered irrelevant, the world will be free of the gods. The truth is exactly the reverse, as we see in our own time how the defeat of Christianity occasions, not the death, but the rebirth of the gods. The problem with the secular, in other words, is that it has such a difficult time remaining secular." Stanley M. Hauerwas, *Wilderness Wanderings: Probing Twentieth-Century Theology and Philosophy* (Boulder, Colo.: Westview Press, 1997), p. 122 n. 4.

13. Kevin Phillips, "Theocons and Theocrats," *The Nation* 282, no. 17 (May 1, 2006): 20.

14. For examples of the plentiful prophetic renunciations of alliance between king and prophet, see Micah 3 and Isaiah 28:7-8, 14-18. Jeremiah (2:26; ch. 23) and the authors associated with him (Lamentations 4:7-13) are scathing in their critiques of the royal prophets. On the biblical resistance to the conflation of the roles of king, priest, and prophet, see Abraham J. Heschel, *The Prophets*, vol. 2 (New York: Harper Torchbooks, 1975), pp. 254-62.

In our post-Constantinian era, the empire seeks to usurp, not only the role of church and prophet, but the role of God as well. Are you longing for security, for well-being, for daily bread? The empire hears your prayers and much else as well. Omniscience and omnipotence are the qualities for which the empire yearns, but are these same qualities dominant in the biblical presentation of the story of God?

I believe that there is a biblical tradition of arguing *with* God (and we will consider some of those arguments in a bit), but alongside these arguments *with* God and sometimes part and parcel of them is another tradition, equally biblical, of arguing *about* God — about who God is. Modern believers too easily fall into the assumption that this argument *about* God only takes place in a post-biblical theological context, as if in the Bible there is the one true, unidimensional revelation of who God is, and then later we get to arguing about it. But in her book, *Models of God*, Sallie McFague presents a convincing case that this argument *about* God is already taking place within the biblical narrative itself.[15] We are not presented with a single witness. We are presented with biblical witnesses who ally with one another and vie with one another as they seek to convince each other and us that they have heard the very word of God.[16]

Among these biblical witnesses, there are certainly some for whom power and knowledge are at the forefront of what they want to tell us about God. O mighty God without equal (Psalm 89:6-13). O God from whom nothing is hidden (Psalm 139). There are other witnesses, however, who pay little heed to these attributes of omnipotence and omniscience, and others still for whom a focus on divine power would be totally anti-

---

15. McFague, *Models of God: Theology for an Ecological, Nuclear Age* (Philadelphia: Fortress Press, 1987).

16. The contemporary Hebrew Bible scholar who is most attuned to the dialogical variance and outright clashes within the biblical text is Walter Brueggemann, *Theology of the Old Testament: Testimony, Dispute, Advocacy* (Minneapolis: Fortress Press, 1997). Brueggemann writes (p. 106), "Conventional systematic theology cannot tolerate the unsettled, polyphonic character of the text. . . . Thus, for example, if theology, in its metaphysical propensity, holds to an affirmation of God's omnipotence, an interpreter must disregard texts to the contrary. . . . If it is claimed that God is morally perfect, the rather devious ways of the God of the Old Testament must either be disregarded or explained away. In truth, some of the most interesting and most poignant aspects of the Old Testament do not conform to or are not easily subsumed under church theology." In his preface (pp. xv-xvi), Brueggemann notes that the polyphony of the text is silenced whenever hegemonic authority is granted to only one version of faith affirmation, only one method of biblical interpretation, or only one community of interpreters.

thetical to the revelation that they have received from God. So, at the very core of the biblical narrative is this argument about God. Who is God? God is the Creator; in only six days, out of nothing (*ex nihilo*), God creates. And in Genesis 3:21, an oddly moving verse, God is the Seamstress who needs to stitch together clothing from animal hides after Adam and Eve had discovered that they were naked. God has all the answers (Psalm 138:3). God has only questions. Adam, where are you? (Genesis 3:9) Cain, where is your brother Abel? (Genesis 4:9)[17] An angry God demands repentance (Ezekiel 14:6-8). A weeping, rainbow God repents (Genesis 9:8-13; Exodus 32:14). God is the solid Rock on whom you may rely (Psalm 62). God is a Gambler; just ask Job (Job 1:6-12). God is the fearsome Lion who mangles and devours the prey (Hosea 13:7-11). God is the Mother Hen with outstretched wings (Matthew 23:37; Luke 13:34). God is the Father who knows everything (John 6:41-47). God is the Woman searching for the lost coin (Luke 15:8-10). God is mighty and victorious (1 Chronicles 29:10-13). And in an amazing story from 1 Samuel 4–7, God is defeated and taken captive.

It is called "the narrative of the ark," this story about the defeat of God. I was first alerted to the implications of these chapters in 1 Samuel while reading Walter Brueggemann's commentary, *Ichabod toward Home: The Journey of God's Glory.*[18] Ichabod is an anglicized name from the Hebrew *kābôd*, which refers to weight, heaviness, presence.[19] In pre-monarchic Israel, before the temple was built, the presence of God was associated with the ark of the covenant. In 1 Samuel, the tribes of Israel carry the ark with them as they go into battle against the Philistines. Israel is defeated, the ark is captured and carried off to the camp of the Philistines. There's more to

17. If one is searching for answers, the Bible is not the best place to look. In the Gospels, Jesus rarely answers direct questions, but he poses over a hundred of them. For a review of these questions and an insightful presentation of faith as a source of questions rather than answers, see John Dear, *The Questions of Jesus: Challenging Ourselves to Discover Life's Great Answers* (New York: Image Books, 2004).

18. Brueggemann, *Ichabod toward Home: The Journey of God's Glory* (Grand Rapids: Eerdmans, 2002). The story of the capture of the ark may be the referent in Psalm 78:61 and other texts. For an overview of these texts describing "divine humiliation," see Terence E. Fretheim, *The Suffering of God: An Old Testament Perspective* (Philadelphia: Fortress Press, 1984), pp. 144-48.

19. On the Hebrew association of weight with glory and honor, see M. Weinfeld, "*kābôd*," in *Theological Dictionary of the Old Testament*, vol. 7, ed. G. Johannes Botterweck, Helmer Ringgren, and Heinz-Josef Fabry, trans. David E. Green (Grand Rapids: Eerdmans, 1995), pp. 22-38.

come in the story, but Brueggemann lingers here, with God defeated, with God held captive. His lingering on moments such as this is one of Brueggemann's great contributions to the study of the Hebrew Bible. We need not wait for the New Testament to meet the God who suffers, the God who is crucified. Already in the Hebrew Bible we meet this God who is not the omnipotent autocrat defending the homeland of the righteous, but a God who is vulnerable. Says Brueggemann, some sources of God's vulnerability are the covenants forged with Noah and Abraham, with David and Israel, with humanity. Just as we are changed when we enter into covenant, God is changed as well.[20] If in some theoretical, primordial mist there was a God of unlimited power, we have no way of knowing. We know only this God, restrained and freed by covenant, made vulnerable and freed by love.

The Philistines held the ark of the covenant. They held God defeated. It was only later, after the scale of Israel's humiliation was plain for all to see, that the ark stirs itself. Tottering, limping perhaps, the ark moves itself back toward the camp of the Israelites, back to the humbled and defeated people loved by God.

Now, some of the differing biblical revelations of God are not necessarily in tension with one another, even if they present us with certain dialectical perspectives. God has a way of knowing humanity even as God questions humanity; indeed, the questions often emerge from prior knowledge. The wrath of God does not cancel the love of God; indeed, God's anger may be in the service of God's love. At times, however, the biblical witnesses are clearly arguing with one another. One way in which the argument proceeds is for one witness to take an image of God proposed by another, an image or portrait that may not be considered helpful, and then to rework that image until it stands in sharp contrast to what was originally intended.[21]

20. In his essay on "Covenant as a Subversive Paradigm," Brueggemann points to the changes that take place as God comes out of heaven and takes up the cause of slaves who are deemed unworthy of the attention of other gods. Walter Brueggemann, *A Social Reading of the Old Testament: Prophetic Approaches to Israel's Communal Life*, ed. Patrick D. Miller (Minneapolis: Fortress Press, 1994), pp. 43-53.

21. Even when it is simply used to indicate a depiction or characterization of the revelations of God, the phrase "image of God" must be treated with caution. Other than the accounts of humanity created in the image of God (Genesis 1:26; 9:6) and of Jesus as the true image of God (2 Corinthians 4:4; Colossians 1:13-15), biblical references to the "image" appear most often in the context of its prohibition. There is insistence on divine formlessness

Take, for example, the image of God as Warrior (e.g., Exodus 15:1-3; Psalm 24:8). This portrayal of God came to the fore during Israel's monarchic period and was derived in part from the depictions of deities among other Near Eastern cultures. This is an image that is sprinkled throughout the long Hebrew Bible narrative known as the deuteronomistic history (for example, Deuteronomy 20:1-4; Judges 20:27-28; 1 Samuel 15:1-3). God is a Warrior. Assemble your armies because God is on our side. God will fight with us. But this image of God as Warrior was already being tweaked within the deuteronomistic history, a history that was not the work of one author and was redacted over a period of centuries.[22] The modifications went like this: let's make the armies of Israel smaller, with fewer weapons and fewer fighters, so that it is clear whose victory this is (Joshua 6:1-5; Judges 7:1-23). This is not a victory of armies but of God the Warrior. These modifications then influenced the full-blown prophetic critique of the tradition in which the image of God as Warrior is not discarded but used instead to subvert completely any theological rationale for human participation in bloodshed.[23] As Millard Lind, John Howard Yoder, and others have

---

(Deuteronomy 4:12-24). There are to be no graven images (Exodus 20:4; Leviticus 26:1). Is there not a risk, however, that the depictions of God presented by the biblical witnesses themselves might solidify into precisely such "graven images"? The danger is averted in part as the witnesses argue and contend with one another over who God is. Of course, in the Eastern Orthodox tradition, the concept of the image of God is less fraught with peril. John of Damascus (676-749) advised that, since God is incarnate in Jesus, "Therefore, paint on wood and present for contemplation him who desired to become visible." Cited by Jim Forest, *Praying with Icons* (Maryknoll, N.Y.: Orbis Books, 1997), p. 8.

22. The deuteronomistic history runs from Deuteronomy through 2 Kings (excluding the book of Ruth). The theory that this is a unified composition was first proposed by Martin Noth in 1943. While Noth argued in favor of a single editor, he acknowledged that this editor drew from assorted traditions and that the history as a whole was subject to later redaction. In a later revision of Noth's hypothesis, Frank Moore Cross proposed that there had been two editions of the deuteronomistic history. Russell Fuller, "Deuteronomic History," *The Oxford Companion to the Bible*, ed. Bruce M. Metzger and Michael D. Coogan (New York: Oxford University Press, 1993), pp. 163-64.

23. For examples of the plentiful prophetic renunciations of reliance on weapons rather than God, see Isaiah 31:1; Ezekiel 33:26; Hosea 10:13; Amos 3:10; 6:12-13. These judgments against Judah and Israel are extended to Babylon, with its arrogant reliance on military might (Jeremiah 50:24-25, 31-32; 51:53). Since Babylon was not a party to the covenant, this judgment was not based on any assertion that Babylon's militarism was a departure from covenantal trust in God, but rather that might is Babylon's god (Habakkuk 1:11). Worse than useless, weapons are self-injurious when God the Warrior decides to fight against Jerusalem itself (Jeremiah 21:3-5, a passage with more than a hint of treason).

observed, the prophetic tradition takes this image of God as Warrior and pushes it to its conclusion.[24] If God is a Warrior, then what you must do is *not* assemble your armies. You must disband your armies. God does not fight *with* us. God fights *for* us, *instead* of us. If you really believe in this portrait of God as Warrior, then the form that your faith must take is for you to get out of your chariot, put away your sword, and get rid of your guns. If you rely on violence, then in that very act you are repudiating faith in God.

That is a powerful reformulation of the image of God as Warrior, but it is not complete, because all that has been done to this point in the biblical witness is that, as human violence is renounced, it is projected onto God. Human violence may be bad, but whatever bludgeoning God chooses to do must be good. There is one additional step that is taken as the biblical witnesses work at, not discarding, but reformulating and inverting and using this revelation of God as Warrior. That step is most evident in the Pauline and deutero-Pauline epistles and in the book of Revelation. In Ephesians 6, as the author explains that the struggle is not against flesh and blood but against principalities and powers and the demonic spirit of this age, the faithful are told to get ready for battle. Put on the sword belt . . . of truth. Put on the armor . . . of righteousness. Put on the helmet . . . of salvation. Take up the sword . . . "of the Spirit, which is the word of God" (6:17). And then in Revelation, John of Patmos tells of the vision in which it is this sword that is the weapon in the arsenal of Christ returning. John's favored image for Jesus the Messiah is the slaughtered Lamb, and the only weapons in the arsenal of the Lamb are "the sword of the mouth" and the blood of the martyrs who have already been slain by the empire. The fall of Babylon approaches as the empire becomes intoxicated on the blood of its own victims. That is not a pretty image, but it is important to recognize who shed the blood. The blood is shed by empire, not by the Warrior God.[25] God the Warrior is

---

24. Lind notes that Moses set the pattern for the messages of later prophets on how to confront Israel's enemies. Moses was armed only with the word of God as he confronted Pharaoh. Millard C. Lind, *Yahweh Is a Warrior: The Theology of Warfare in Ancient Israel* (Scottdale, Pa.: Herald Press, 1980), p. 63. See the chapter titled "God Will Fight for Us" in John Howard Yoder, *The Politics of Jesus* (Grand Rapids: Eerdmans, 1972), pp. 78-89.

25. The familiar "Battle Hymn of the Republic" has doubtless contributed to the false impression that the copious blood flowing from the winepress in Revelation 14:14-20 was shed due to the wrath of God. Yet the text itself is clear that the blood is not *shed* by God but *mixed* with God's anger (14:19). John's terms for "harvest" (*therismos, therizō*) are consistently used in the Septuagint and in the New Testament to refer to the ingathering of the faithful to the kingdom of God (e.g., Matthew 9:37; Mark 4:29; John 4:35-38). This, combined with the "call for the endurance of the saints" (14:12) and the blessing on those who "die in the Lord"

victorious through the slaughtered Lamb and the sword of the mouth. John of Patmos persistently includes these modifiers — of the mouth, of truth — in all his references to the sword of the Lamb (e.g., 1:16; 2:16; 19:15). In biblical literature, the sword of the mouth is always presented as the word of God. In Isaiah 49, the Servant himself becomes God's sharp sword, God's polished arrow. So, for John of Patmos, the Warrior God does not disappear. Rather, in John's vision, there is a new heaven and a new earth, and the victory of God the Warrior is dependent only on the word of the slaughtered Lamb.[26]

Such is the biblical conversation and the argument among the witnesses over this one image, God as Warrior. But in my presentation of it, there is an implication that I wish to renounce. I do not subscribe to views of biblical evolution which suggest that in the oldest sections of Scripture we have a primitive view of God that is somehow trumped by later, more enlightened witnesses. Indeed, in some of the oldest passages of Scripture (which likely appear in sections of Exodus and Judges, not in Genesis), there is already a portrait of the God of the lowly, the God who liberates, the God who takes the side of the slaves rather than the mighty.[27] Likewise, I do not subscribe to supersessionism, the belief that so-called Christian Scripture trumps Jewish Scripture. Of course, as one who seeks to be a follower of Jesus, I regard the Sermon on the Mount as having greater import than, say, the cultic laws of Leviticus. But part of the reason I say

---

(14:13), makes it clear that what flows from the winepress is the blood of martyrs (16:6; 17:6). For the faithful, the blood of the Lamb is purifying (7:14), but when the blood of the empire's victims is mixed with the wrath of God and poured out onto the empire (16:1, 19; 17:2, 6; 18:3, 6), it produces the final intoxication that marks the fall of Babylon. While the empire had assumed that it could attain security and glory through bloodshed, the blood itself comes back in mighty torrents. Jacques Ellul noted that, "There is an auto-destruction of political forces at the interior of history. That which makes them live, that which gives them authority, that upon which they are based, is the very spirit that finally repudiates them. . . ." Ellul, *Apocalypse: The Book of Revelation* (New York: Seabury Press, 1977), p. 193.

26. Similarly, John does not discard but reinterprets the portrayal of God as omnipotent. G. B. Caird writes, "John . . . is fond of a resonant title for God, 'the Omnipotent,' which he uses nine times. But he repeatedly makes it clear that in using it he is recasting the concept of omnipotence, which he understands not as unlimited coercion but as unlimited persuasion." Caird, *The Language and Imagery of the Bible* (Philadelphia: Westminster Press, 1980), pp. 51-52.

27. On the insurgent context of some of the earliest writings of the Hebrew Bible, see George E. Mendenhall, *Ancient Israel's Faith and History: An Introduction to the Bible in Context*, ed. Gary A. Herion (Louisville: Westminster John Knox Press, 2001).

that Christian Scripture does not eclipse Jewish Scripture is that there is no Christian Scripture, if by that we mean Scripture written by Christians. Oh certainly, the canonical writings of the New Testament were penned by members of the Jesus sect of Judaism, but they were Jews. The decisive split between church and synagogue did not occur until the second wave of the Roman wars against the Jews after 130 CE. Tensions increased following the first war against the Jews in 70 CE, but even after that point, the assembly of the followers of Jesus was still an assembly of Jews, as Paul had wanted it to be, with Gentiles invited. So from start to finish, the New Testament is a Jewish book.[28] As Franklin Littell noted, Jesus, Peter, and Paul would have all perished at Auschwitz,[29] and the same can be said of all the witnesses from Matthew through to John of Patmos.

So, within the Hebrew Bible and within the New Testament and across that old and new dividing line, witnesses converse with one another and argue with one another about who God is. We have looked at the remarkable inversion that took place with the image of God as Warrior. Let me cite just one more example, the image of God as King, which is another portrait suggestive of omnipotence. The image of God as King played a pivotal role in an early dispute among the Hebrew people, a dispute described in 1 Samuel 8 over whether Israel should have a monarch. Up to that point, there had been no central governmental authority in Israel. Judges would sometimes emerge as leaders during times of crisis, but with no ongoing center of power the tribes of Israel were held together as a makeshift confederacy, a fairly anarchic arrangement. A monarchist party arose with the unfortunate slogan that Israel ought to be "like other nations" (8:5, 20). As described in 1 Samuel 8, it was not the monarchist party but the anarchist party that emphasized the portrayal of God as King. The choice of any other king would constitute a rejection of the guidance already provided by God (8:7). Despite the warnings from Samuel and God (8:9-18), the anarchists lost and Israel got its monarch.

But the argument in the Bible continued. As Jacques Ellul observed, the portrayal of monarchy in the books of 1 and 2 Kings was so unflattering as to constitute a veritable judgment on political power itself. All the kings who were successful politically and militarily were idolaters who

28. On the Jewish character of the New Testament, see Mark D. Nanos, *The Mystery of Romans: The Jewish Context of Paul's Letter* (Minneapolis: Fortress Press, 1996), p. 4.

29. Franklin H. Littell, *The Crucifixion of the Jews: The Failure of Christians to Understand the Jewish Experience* (New York: Harper & Row, 1975), p. 24.

abandoned the covenant with God, while all the kings who were faithful to the covenant were disastrous politically and militarily.[30] There were other biblical witnesses, however, who were apologists for the monarchy, royal propagandists who argued that the glory of God the King was somehow reflected in the glory of the kings of Israel. Of course, Israel and Judah were never more than bit players in a region dominated by neighboring empires, and the recent archaeological work of Israel Finkelstein and Neil Asher Silberman casts doubt on whether the courts of Israel's greatest kings were all that glorious, even by the standards of the tenth century BCE.[31] Nonetheless, several of the Psalms (e.g., 2, 72, 89, 110) indicate that the time of the enthronement of a king in Israel was also a time to reflect upon the enthronement of God as the omnipotent and omniscient King. As the biblical witnesses continued their argument over this portrayal of God as King, the most startling reinterpretation of the kingship tradition appears in the Gospels. The palace in which your King is born is an animal shed. The courtiers and nobility who surround your King are lepers, whores, and thieves, the unfed and the unwashed. Your King triumphantly enters the capital city riding, not on a warhorse, but on a donkey. Behold your King on the cross, bleeding, barely breathing. You want glory? There it is.

So, there are plentiful biblical arguments about who God is. Many of these do not rely on images of power and omniscience, and those that do are eventually inverted in what Donald Kraybill calls "the upside-down kingdom."[32] But the theme of this talk is supposed to be arguing *with* God, not arguing *about* God. Two decades ago, Anton Laytner wrote a book titled *Arguing with God: A Jewish Tradition,* and as I read that book it became clear to me that the argument *with* God is predicated upon an argument *about* God.[33] In biblical literature, the argument with God is often pat-

30. Ellul, *The Politics of God and the Politics of Man,* trans. and ed. Geoffrey W. Bromiley (Grand Rapids: Eerdmans, 1972). See also the book by Daniel Berrigan, *The Kings and Their Gods: The Pathology of Power* (Grand Rapids: Eerdmans, 2008).

31. Finkelstein and Silberman write that "it is highly unlikely that David ever conquered territories of peoples more than a day or two's march from the heartland of Judah," and that "Solomon's Jerusalem was neither extensive nor impressive, but rather the rough hilltop stronghold of a local dynasty of rustic tribal chiefs." Israel Finkelstein and Neil Asher Silberman, *David and Solomon: In Search of the Bible's Sacred Kings and the Roots of the Western Tradition* (New York: Free Press, 2006), p. 22.

32. Donald B. Kraybill, *The Upside-Down Kingdom* (Scottdale, Pa.: Herald Press, 1978).

33. Laytner, *Arguing with God: A Jewish Tradition* (Northvale, N.J.: Jason Aronson, 1990).

terned on a heavenly law court setting in which, as C. S. Lewis said, God is in the dock.[34] God is interrogated based on nothing less than the word, the revelation of God: God, you said this, and now you act like that; you promised this, and now that happens. As Laytner observes, for Jews, the most intense post-biblical argument with God was provoked by the Holocaust. God, after such horror, what possible sense can be made of your assurance that the Jews are chosen people? Chosen for what? Chosen to bear the brunt of atrocity and genocide? God, if Dachau, Treblinka, and Auschwitz are not your will, why are you so silent?[35]

Biblical arguments with God are also based on perceptions of who God is or ought to be, whether it is Jeremiah (20:7) protesting that any decent God would not expose him to such ridicule, or the saints beneath the altar (Revelation 6:9-10) suggesting that God's timing is askew: How long, O Lord? But in the Hebrew Bible, two of the most interesting arguments with God are those of Jonah and of Abraham — interesting because both arguments are over the fates of cities (Nineveh in the case of Jonah and Sodom and Gomorrah in the case of Abraham) and because these arguments are based on contrary perceptions of who God ought to be.

Jonah, his protests to the contrary notwithstanding (4:2), insists that God ought to be omnipotent and angry, omniscient and unchanging, especially in relationship to Nineveh.[36] You know the story. God sends Jonah to pronounce doom on Nineveh. Knowing that he would not be welcome in Nineveh and seeing no reason to give forewarning in any event, Jonah flees. Storm at sea. Great fish. All right, I'll go. "Forty days more, and Nineveh shall be overthrown!" (3:4) But now the real story begins. Getting swallowed by a great fish is really quite mundane in comparison to what follows. There are changes for the three main characters in the story: Nineveh changes, God changes, and Jonah starts to mope. What sent Jonah into his blue funk? God did not destroy Nineveh (3:10–4:1). Jonah had been sent out

34. Lewis, *God in the Dock: Essays on Theology and Ethics,* ed. Walter Hooper (Grand Rapids: Eerdmans, 1970).

35. Laytner traces the struggles with theodicy in the period following the Holocaust in *Arguing with God,* pp. 196-229. Jewish responses to these struggles have ranged from the death of God theology of Richard Rubenstein to the tentative, agonized faith of Elie Wiesel.

36. As the capital of the Assyrian Empire, Nineveh was an archetypal foe of Israel. A pronouncement of doom on the city was fully congruent with biblical tradition (e.g., Nahum 3:7; Zephaniah 2:13). As Daniel Berrigan observes, "Jonah, it must be said, knows his scripture." Berrigan, *Minor Prophets, Major Themes* (Marion, S.D.: Fortkamp Publishing/Rose Hill Books, 1995), p. 179.

by an omniscient God who knew that Nineveh had broken all the rules, by an omnipotent God whose destructive power was fueled by righteous indignation. Jonah had been sent with the very word of God, an unchanging word on which Jonah had depended — and now it changed.[37] I love that sulking, blue-funk Jonah. I love that quirky, unpredictable God whose rules are trumped by mercy. That God gets no argument from me.

And then there is the much different story of Abraham arguing with God, literally dickering (from the Latin *decuria*, "a division of ten") over the fate of Sodom (Genesis 18:16-33). Abraham's argument was also based on his experience of who God is. Abraham had already encountered God's mercy and love through the covenant (Genesis 15), through the birth of Ishmael (Genesis 16), and through the promised birth of Isaac (17:15-22). And he would experience that mercy again, there on the mountain, where he would take Isaac to slit his throat and burn him as a sacrifice to God (22:1-14). Why did he not argue with God then? Did he care more for the fate of the sinners in Sodom than for the life of his own son?

My hearing of the story of the non-sacrifice of Isaac has changed over a lifetime. As a child, of course, this story makes one wary of all fathers, biological or divine. But today, I like this story, not for what Abraham did or did not do, but for how God used this setting to forswear the sacrifice of human life to cult or religion, no matter how holy. Historians and anthropologists regard the ban on human sacrifice as an achievement of primitive religion, with the practice of sacrificing people to the gods largely coming to an end in the Near East 2500 years ago and among the Aztecs and the Incas 500 years ago. I beg to differ. Human sacrifice has never ended. In fact, the pace of it has accelerated. It's just that the identity of the gods has changed. We are not so primitive as to offer up our children to Kali and Baal. They are sacrificed instead to Holy Father State. We are not so primitive as to slit their throats for crop fertility. They are dispatched efficiently for "freedom" and for "peace."[38] My favorite commentary on the

---

37. Berrigan writes that "the heart of God turns and turns about," which is an aspect of divine revelation that is scandalous to practitioners of "conventional religion," including Jonah. "God and prophet have become a scandal one to the other." Berrigan, *Minor Prophets*, p. 175.

38. On the *religious* nature of the contemporary sacrificial system of nationalism, patriotism, and militarism, see Carolyn Marvin and David W. Ingle, *Blood Sacrifice and the Nation: Totem Rituals and the American Flag* (New York: Cambridge University Press, 1999). Marvin and Ingle (p. 25) contend that "the flag is the god of nationalism, and its mission is to organize death."

story of Abraham and Isaac is by the Canadian poet, Leonard Cohen. In part, his poem is addressed to "You who build these altars now/to sacrifice the children. . . ."[39]

But it was not there on the mountain that Abraham argued with God. The argument came in Genesis 18 over the fate of Sodom.[40] As the argument proceeds, it is clear that Abraham's perception of who God is and ought to be stands in contrast with the views of Jonah. While Jonah was miffed because God's fury was not unleashed, Abraham is asking God to put aside omnipotence, to put aside the destructive power of righteous indignation for the sake of mercy and compassion. What's more, Abraham is bold enough to suggest that perhaps God is not omniscient. Perhaps God has overlooked something. What if there are fifty righteous people in the city? Will you destroy the city if it means taking the lives of fifty righ-

---

39. Leonard Cohen, "Story of Isaac," *Stranger Music: Selected Poems and Songs* (New York: Vintage Books, 1994), pp. 139-40.

40. At least by way of footnote, comment must be made on the pervasive, post-biblical association of the sin of Sodom with gay folks. In Genesis 19 there is an attempted rape by an out-of-control mob, and that doesn't typify the behavior of any of the gay people I've known. If there are those who insist that this story is a sexual morality tale, however, then it is only fair that we should search the surrounding texts for the traditional family values of heterosexuals. In Genesis 19, the righteous man Lot proposes to hand over his daughters to the mob, and then later in the same chapter the daughters have children by their father Lot, while in Genesis 16, at the urging of his wife Sarah, Abraham fathers a child with the servant Hagar, and in Genesis 20, in order to secure his own safety in Gerar, Abraham gives his wife Sarah to King Abimelech and says, "Take her, she's my sister." These stories are over 2500 years old, and that surely makes them "traditional." With the fathers and the daughters and the wife and the sister, we're surely talking about "family." It's only the "values" about which we're left to wonder. Based on these stories, heterosexuals calling gay folks immoral is like sheep calling the snowman white.

From within a biblical rather than post-biblical perspective, the story of Sodom is not a sexual morality tale. Deuteronomy 29 charges Sodom and Gomorrah with abandoning the covenant and worshiping other gods. Isaiah 1 charges that Sodom and Gomorrah are stained with blood and guilty of injustice. Ezekiel 16 charges that the sins of Sodom are pride and neglect of the poor.

This is not to deny that the post-biblical association of the sin of Sodom with homosexuality emerged early and vehemently. The sexual mores of both rabbinic Judaism and the primitive church were formulated in the context of what Daniel Boyarin calls "colonized culture." Boyarin, *Carnal Israel: Reading Sex in Talmudic Culture* (Berkeley: University of California Press, 1995), pp. 16-18. In this context, harsh renunciations of what would come to be called "sodomy" served to sharpen differentiations between these faith communities and the pagan colonizers. Peter Brown, *The Body and Society: Men, Women, and Sexual Renunciation in Early Christianity* (New York: Columbia University Press, 1988), p. 40.

teous people? Amazingly, God yields; show me fifty righteous people and I will not destroy the city. And just as amazingly, Abraham does not yield. He presses the point, and as he does so, it is evident in the text of Genesis 18 that Abraham knows that he is also pressing his luck. He turns obsequious. "Let me take it upon myself to speak to the Lord, I who am but dust and ashes" (18:27). How about forty-five righteous? How about forty? What a daring high wire act for Abraham! God gave an inch and Abraham treats it like that's just the first down. Abraham needs lower numbers because he knows that, in that city, there isn't much that's lovable. How about thirty? Press on, brother Abraham. You go. How about twenty? You be obsequious. You be whoever you need to be because, even if the city is not righteous, your cause is. Press on, good brother, because the fact is — praise God — whenever you're loving the unlovable, whenever you're loving people who don't even deserve it, God will yield. How about ten?

I love what the Hasidic Jews have done with this story from Genesis. In their legend of "the just," God allows the world to continue for one more day because of the presence of a small number of just people. We don't know who they are. Perhaps one of the just is in this room tonight, or perhaps one is a bag lady in downtown Philadelphia, or a prisoner, or a stranger who comes knocking at your door. Be kind. The fate of the world depends on it.[41]

But even though I love the legend of the just and the narrative from Genesis 18, I need to argue a little with these stories. My argument with them has less to do with the nature of God than with the nature of us. From these stories, one could be left with the misleading impression that separating the righteous from the wicked is a simple feat, like counting noses, or a simplistic feat, like designating an axis of evil. Brother Abraham notwithstanding, I don't believe that we can draw a line down the center of the room and arrange all the righteous people on one side and the wicked on the other. That line is going to go right through me, right through my very soul. I am not righteous, but maybe there is a part of me that is not wicked. Maybe I'm fifty-fifty, and maybe I'm ninety-ten, and I won't tell you which part is ninety and which part ten because maybe I don't even know.[42]

41. This legend inspires the title and many of the themes in one of the most moving works of fiction on the Holocaust, Andre Schwarz-Bart, *The Last of the Just*, trans. Stephen Becker (London: Reprint Society, 1962).

42. It must be noted that these individualistic ruminations would be anachronistic to the biblical setting. There is little biblical focus on the individual as moral agent, let alone on any effort to partition the individual psyche into regions of greater or lesser moral culpabil-

There is this perennial question about, not divine nature, but human nature. Are people basically violent or nonviolent, selfish or selfless? Among others, Martin Luther King, Jr., responded that the answer is neither. Instead, we are all created in the image of God, with great potential for acts of loving kindness and beauty, and we are all radically fallen, with potential for acts of horrendous brutality. Our task, then, becomes one of seeking to appeal to the potential for good that is never fully obliterated from any human being.[43]

This entails a different sort of argument with God, and with Abraham too, I suppose. God, do not do this to yourself because, in the city, buried underneath all the pompous pretense to greatness, underneath all the dirt and grime — in the city, resides your very image.[44] As that line is drawn down each of us, this image may not shine forth fifty percent of the time, or ten, or even one, but it is there and it is holy. Why? Because people are good? No, because God stuck that image there like some grain of sand in an oyster shell, and it is holy.

---

ity. In the exodus narrative, Pharaoh is clearly cast in an unfavorable light, but whether he was a "good or bad person" is a question that is foreign to the text. Any notion that Pharaoh's own moral predisposition determined the course of events is negated by the repeated refrain that the Lord "hardened the heart of Pharaoh" (e.g., Exodus 7:13; 8:19; 9:12; 10:20; 11:10; 14:4). Many historians claim that the focus on the moral agency of the individual did not become dominant in the West until a much later era, perhaps as late as the Renaissance in Europe. The case for an earlier emergence of individualism in the theology of Peter Abelard is made by Colin Morris, The Discovery of the Individual, 1050-1200 (Toronto: University of Toronto Press, 1987).

Abraham's argument with God is fully consonant with the Hebrew Bible's emphasis on corporate responsibility. As Gerhard von Rad observes, however, there is a "revolutionary" element to Abraham's argument. If corporate guilt-transference influences God's judgment of the whole city of Sodom, was it also possible that the presence of a small measure of righteousness could serve in a substitutionary fashion to evoke God's mercy in relationship to the whole city? The collective need for the scapegoat would be obviated by such substitutionary righteousness. Von Rad, Genesis: A Commentary, trans. John Marks, The Old Testament Library (Philadelphia: Westminster Press, 1961), pp. 206-10.

43. King's views on human nature and the antecedents to them are presented by John J. Ansbro, Martin Luther King, Jr.: The Making of a Mind (Maryknoll, N.Y.: Orbis Books, 1982), pp. 87-90.

44. Of course, the image of God is not only misshapen by a primordial fall but also by the city itself. As Jacques Ellul notes, while the city is certainly a sociological phenomenon, it is also a spiritual power. The person who is swallowed by the city is divested of all meaning except for her utility to money and the state. "The man who disappears into the city becomes merchandise." Ellul, The Meaning of the City, trans. Dennis Pardee (Grand Rapids: Eerdmans, 1970), p. 55.

God knows, there is too little love in the world, and will you destroy the city if there are ten people there who have done even one genuine act of kindness in their lives? Or maybe even not so genuine? In the *Hadith*, a collection of sayings attributed to the Prophet Mohammed, there is a story about an ornery old man who had never done a good deed in his life. He was traveling through the wilderness when he came upon a patch of thorny brambles that blocked his path. He took out his knife and cleared the thorns so he could proceed on his way. Thus, without even intending to do so, he cleared the path for future travelers, and for that one act alone, God granted his entry to Paradise.[45] Righteousness is like that, is it not? It's not the stuff we're doing when we're feeling pious. At times, we stumble into it despite ourselves.

Christians are not more righteous than other people, and don't let anyone tell you otherwise. Especially, don't let Christians tell you otherwise. Ideally, Christians are simply more aware of our own proclivities toward unrighteousness. It is a healthy tendency in the history of theology that there has been a persistent wariness of Pelagianism, of what is called "works righteousness." Rather than relying on any righteousness that we would presume to generate ourselves, look to the righteousness of Jesus. That gives another interesting twist to Abraham's argument with God. God, will you destroy the city if Jesus is there? And he is certainly there among the least of these (Matthew 25:31-46), including the least righteous.

Of course, Abraham was fighting a lost cause, which is part of the reason I want to be on his side. Could it have turned out differently? Perhaps the outcome would have been different if Abraham had not fallen into this trap of dividing up the righteous from the wicked. Perhaps the outcome would have been different if Abraham and Lot and their families had gone into Sodom and Gomorrah and said to God, "Here we stand. Let loose with your divine fury if you must. Give it your best shot. And if you do not, we will wait here until your anger passes, until there is redemption. Until Messiah comes, here we stand." But who am I to second-guess brother Abraham, who was second-guessing an omnipotent God? We can only hope that, as with the flood (Genesis 8:21), God repented of this horrible destruction. Sodom and Gomorrah are gone now.

But the argument must continue. Today, the argument is not with an omnipotent and omniscient God but with the principalities and powers

45. Cited by Peter Occhiogrosso, *Through the Labyrinth: Stories of the Search for Spiritual Transformation in Everyday Life* (New York: Viking, 1991), p. 295.

that claim omniscience. The cities in question are not Sodom and Gomorrah, but Mosul and Fallujah, Baghdad and Tikrit. Unlike brother Abraham
and God, the powers are on a search, not for righteousness, but for evil. In
the early days of the wars in Afghanistan and Iraq, the President of the
United States issued a directive that, when U.S. commanders in the field
identified a "high value target," they could launch an immediate attack if,
in their best estimation, fewer than thirty civilian bystanders would be
killed in the attack. If the number of innocent bystanders to be killed was
likely to be thirty or more, then the order for the attack would have to be
given by the Secretary of Defense or by the President himself.[46] In the legend of the just, when there are a few righteous people, the world itself is
spared. In the ideology of the powers, the presence of one person who
does evil renders the rest of the world vulnerable to attack.

Lot's wife was warned, do not look back toward evil (Genesis 19:17,
26). She turned to look back and turned into a pillar of salt. In its search for
evil, as it swoops down on whatever cities it chooses, American power has
become that hardened pillar without thought or feeling. It is power totally
fixated and controlled by the evil it claims to combat.

One of the crudest forms of contemporary blasphemy is the view
that, if God is omnipotent and omniscient, then whatever happens to happen in the world must be the will of God. Granted, the *intent* behind such a
view may not be blasphemous. Those who assert that all events in the
world are underwritten by the will of God may have the pious intent of
magnifying and glorifying God's power, or the compassionate intent of
reassuring the survivors of brutality that a providential God "has the
whole world in his hands," or the orthodox intent of avoiding ethical dualism. One need not embrace dualism, however, to recognize the influence
in the world of actors other than God, including fallen humanity, rebellious principalities and powers, and kingdoms that are still governed by
someone other than God (Matthew 4:8-10; Luke 4:5-8).

In his Saturday radio address of April 19, 2003, as President Bush was
mourning the loss of American lives in the invasion of Afghanistan and
the recently launched invasion of Iraq, the President referred to God by
saying, "His purposes are not always clear to us." The President may have
had the benign intent of reassuring family members of dead soldiers that
their sacrifice was in the service of a higher cause, but the suggestion that

46. Mark Benjamin, "When Is an Accidental Civilian Death Not an Accident?" Sa-
lon.com, July 30, 2007.

these invasions and these deaths were the result of some occult, divine "purposes" is incredibly exculpatory of principalities, of power brokers (including Bush himself), and of compliant and cooperative American citizens. The governance by the fallen principalities and powers is in the service of death, and that governance is strengthened by any suggestion that it is in alignment with the clear or unclear purposes of God.[47]

Early Anabaptism totally rejected the notion that the purposes of God were made manifest through the quarrels and the clashes of the powers that be. In 1527, Felix Mantz wrote, "The genuine love of Christ will scatter the enemy."[48] But clearly, Mantz had no confidence that the governing powers would be the instruments of that love. Mantz was writing from prison, and he was writing only a few months shy of his own execution. Where, then, did he look for his hope? Where did he look to discern the purposes of God? For Mantz and other Anabaptists, God's purposes in the world could be discerned by looking back to the biblical witnesses in the past, by looking to the movement of the Spirit among

47. William Stringfellow provides some of the most lucid commentary on the reign of death in the governance of the principalities and powers. See especially Stringfellow, *An Ethic for Christians and Other Aliens in a Strange Land* (Waco, Tex.: Word Books, 1973). A more recent compilation of some of Stringfellow's writings is provided by Bill Wylie Kellermann, ed., *A Keeper of the Word: Selected Writings of William Stringfellow* (Grand Rapids: Eerdmans, 1994).

It must be noted that American leaders in addition to Bush have engaged in this self-exculpatory practice of asserting that divine purpose is responsible for the initiation, the duration, and the body count of America's wars. In Abraham Lincoln's Second Inaugural Address, which may be the most eloquent presidential oration from one of America's best-loved leaders, Lincoln said, "The Almighty has His own purposes. . . . Fondly do we hope — fervently do we pray — that this mighty scourge of war may speedily pass away. Yet, if God wills that it continue, until all the wealth piled by the bondman's two hundred and fifty years of unrequited toil shall be sunk, and until every drop of blood drawn with the lash, shall be paid by another drawn with the sword, as it was said three thousand years ago, so still it must be said 'the judgments of the Lord are true and righteous altogether.'" Lincoln, as cited by Cushing Strout, *The New Heavens and New Earth: Political Religion in America* (New York: Harper & Row, 1975), p. 199. In fact, Lincoln had already decided that the war would only end with unconditional surrender. It must be granted that, despite their elevated office, presidents are more the acolytes than the directors of the powers and the historical forces that swirl around them. Nonetheless, there is something disturbingly disingenuous about the references to divine purpose by Lincoln and by Bush.

48. Felix Mantz, "Letter from Prison," in *Early Anabaptist Spirituality: Selected Writings*, trans. and ed. Daniel Liechty, The Classics of Western Spirituality (New York: Paulist Press, 1994), p. 19.

the gathered community of believers in the present, and by looking to the promised return of the Lamb in the future.

For Anabaptists, the purposes of God could be discerned by looking back to the testimony of the witnesses who had gone before, especially the testimony of the primitive church.[49] The gospel faith itself had been buried beneath layers of ecclesiastical hierarchy and had been warped by alliances between bishops and princes.[50] The fallen powers were seeking not to unveil the purposes of God but to obfuscate them and ultimately to reject them.

For Anabaptists, the purposes of God could be discerned by looking to the current movement of the Spirit among the gathered community of believers. By focusing on the living communion of saints, theology is relational rather than creedal, and discipleship is constantly nurtured by the *corpus Christi* rather than simply notarized by the *corpus christianum*.[51] As Dale Brown writes of the Brethren, "Basic convictions are derived from lived theology."[52]

49. Donald F. Durnbaugh comments on "the normative appeal of primitive Christianity for the Anabaptists of the Radical Reformation," an appeal that was also evident earlier among the Waldensians of France and later among the Quakers of Puritan England. Durnbaugh, *The Believers' Church: The History and Character of Radical Protestantism* (New York: Macmillan Company, 1968), p. 19.

50. George H. Williams writes, "It is useful to observe that the established and protected churches, both Protestant and Catholic, were, so to speak, churches of the exigent *present*, and therefore disposed to compromise and accommodation out of a basically conservative social concern to prevent any radical dissociation of citizenship (in civil society) and membership (in the church of the masses). The proponents of the Radical Reformation, having been inspired by the Protestant Reformers to look back to the church of the apostolic past, yearned to restore it unambiguously in their midst. Accordingly, most of them early abandoned any hope of a fully Christian society coterminous with political boundaries, except it be the Church of the End Time coterminous with the frontiers of the Kingdom established on earth." Williams, "Introduction," *Spiritual and Anabaptist Writers*, ed. George H. Williams and Angel M. Mergal, Library of Christian Classics (Philadelphia: Westminster Press, 1957), p. 22.

51. The Anabaptist perception of the body of Christ as irreconcilable with Christendom is noted by Williams, "Introduction," *Spiritual and Anabaptist Writers*, p. 25.

52. Brown, *Another Way of Believing*, p. xi. Dale Brown's book is an excellent exploration of relational theology, with relevance not limited to the Church of the Brethren. Brown's emphasis on "lived theology" calls to mind the admonition from the early Anabaptist leader, Hans Denck: "No one may truly know Christ, except he follow him in life." This call to lived theology is deeply resonant with Latin American liberation theology's focus on "orthopraxis" rather than orthodoxy. For guidance in discipleship, liberation theology looks to the "base community" rather than the ecclesiastical hierarchy, and to the oppressed

For Anabaptists, the purposes of God could be discerned by looking to the future and the approaching reign of God. The principalities and powers will not have the final word. Menno Simons wrote, "Let them vex, boast and rave, persecute and murder all they want. Your word will be triumphant and the Lamb will have the victory."[53] Guided by the biblical witnesses of the past, the community of discipleship seeks to live in the presence of the future reign of God. For this community, the one persistent argument with God is the question from the saints beneath the altar, "Sovereign Lord, holy and true, how long will it be . . . ?" (Revelation 6:10).

The story of God is not complete, and so the faithful demand, "Your kingdom come" (Matthew 6:10), "Your kingdom come" (Luke 11:2). In making this demand, the faithful are not arguing for a display of divine omnipotence. They are arguing for a return of the slaughtered Lamb (Revelation 22:17, 20). This argument must persist to the point of *parousia*. A new heaven and new earth are not produced by acquiring power. The acquisition of power is the same old story, the lethal weapon story, and peace will never come from it. Peace is the way and the gift of the slaughtered Lamb. Let this, then, be our argument with God: Come, Lord Jesus.

So, let me end where we began, with this question that I ask my friends with mental illness. If we get to the gates of heaven, you and I, and we discover that even a single sister or brother has been consigned to hell, will you join the picket line? Let's do it. Let's do it with zeal! Bring your black markers and poster boards. We'll make some signs that say, "No more hell" — banners that say, "To hell with hell." Get ready to chant and raise some hell. Wear comfortable shoes, because we're in this for the long haul. Let's do it.

But, before you agree, we should probably discuss the possibility that there just might be a consequence to our actions, a price to be paid. As my friends involved in civil disobedience are fond of saying, "If you can't do the time, don't do the crime." But I'm not referring to the consequence of divine retribution — the possibility that God might swoop down on our little picket line and say, "All right, then, if you are so fond of those people in hell, go join them." All that I know is what I can glean from the biblical

---

and marginalized rather than the powerful. On the convergence (and divergence) of Anabaptism and liberation theology, see Daniel S. Schipani, ed., *Freedom and Discipleship: Liberation Theology in Anabaptist Perspective* (Maryknoll, N.Y.: Orbis Books, 1989).

53. Menno Simons, "A Meditation on the Twenty-fifth Psalm," in *Early Anabaptist Spirituality*, p. 267.

text, the cloud of witnesses, and the living Word of God, all of which suggest that God is already arrayed against the forces of hell, that Jesus has already been there, preaching to and loving the captives (1 Peter 3:18-20; 4:6).[54] So, perhaps there won't even be a need for our protest. When it comes to accounting for those who are lost, the important questions flow from God to humanity, not the other way around. "Cain, where is your brother Abel?" But in case our protest must proceed outside the pearly gates, I have also gleaned a hint that God loves a good argument, and that the mind of God can change.

No, the consequence of which I speak is not the risk of divine retribution. It is more imminent than that. The consequence is this: if we would protest there and then, then we must protest here and now. We must protest the fate of all those who have already been consigned to hell in this time. We must protest against all the would-be gods of omnipotence and omniscience. We must end our complicity with these principalities bent on the destruction of cities. We must not listen anymore to the stories of these powers who search out evil instead of righteousness, who demonically chase after all that is demonic. We must protest. Protest how? Tax resistance? Take to the streets? Fill the jails? Love and serve the victims of empire? Yes, all that and more. Be conspiratorial with the movement of the Spirit. Be subversive in praying for the coming of that great subversion promised by God. And wear comfortable shoes.

54. Drawing on the works of Origen, Hans Denck wrote, "For the Lord can even free from hell. Damnation has no impenetrable roof on it!" Denck, "Divine Order," in *Early Anabaptist Spirituality*, p. 125.

Index of Authors

Ackerman, Peter, 28, 29
Anderson, Benedict, 89
Ansbro, John J., 146
Archer, Dane, 55, 56
Arendt, Hannah, 87
Armstrong, Karen, 79
Arnove, Anthony, 84

Baez, Joan, 24
Barnet, Richard J., 95
Barth, Christoph, 75
Barth, Karl, 28, 76, 121, 129
Barton, John, 2
Bellah, Robert N., 81
Bellesiles, Michael A., 57
Benjamin, Mark, 93, 148
Berrigan, Daniel, 42, 96, 141, 142, 143
Biesanz, Richard, 72
Blum, William, 93
Bobin, Christian, 105, 109
Boswell, John, 3
Botterweck, G. Johannes, 131
Bowen, Helen, 68
Bowers, William, 56
Boyarin, Daniel, 144
Bromlow, Robert W., 23, 43
Brock, Peter, 70
Brown, Dale W., 6, 25, 126, 150

Brown, Peter, 144
Brown, Tricia Gate, 69
Brueggemann, Walter, 2, 134, 135, 136
Burns, Thomas S., x

Caird, G. B., 139
Camus, Albert, 93
Carroll, Lewis, 66
Cassidy, Richard J., xi
Cayley, David, 68
Chaulk, Frank, 28
Cherry, Conrad, 82
Clastres, Pierre, 84, 85
Cloward, Richard A., 54
Cochrane, Arthur C., 28
Cohen, Leonard, 144
Cohn, Norman, 84
Cone, James H., 35, 81
Consedine, Jim, 68
Conway, J. S., 29
Cooley, John K., 79
Cordella, J. Peter, 69
Cox, Harvey, 119
Crossan, John Dominic, xi

Davis, Angela, 52, 55, 61, 66
Davis, Mike, 55
Dear, John, 135

Index of Names and Subjects

Index of Scripture References